SUPPORTIVE CLINICAL SUPERVISION

Enhancing Well-being and Reducing Burnout through Restorative Leadership

Derek L. Milne and
Robert P. Reiser

Supportive Clinical Supervision
Enhancing well-being and reducing burnout through restorative leadership

© Pavilion Publishing & Media

The authors have asserted their rights in accordance with the Copyright, Designs and Patents Act (1988) to be identified as the authors of this work.

Published by:

Pavilion Publishing and Media Ltd
Blue Sky Offices, 25 Cecil Pashley Way
Shoreham by Sea, West Sussex
BN43 5FF

Tel: 01273 434 943
Email: info@pavpub.com
Web: www.pavpub.com

Published 2020

A catalogue record for this book is available from the British Library.

ISBN: 978-1-913414-54-2

Pavilion Publishing and Media is a leading publisher of books, training materials and digital content in mental health, social care and allied fields. Pavilion and its imprints offer must-have knowledge and innovative learning solutions underpinned by sound research and professional values.

Authors: Derek Milne and Robert Reiser
Copy Editor: Jo Hathaway
Cover design: Emma Dawe, Pavilion Publishing and Media Ltd
Page layout and typesetting: Emma Dawe, Pavilion Publishing and Media Ltd
Printing: CPI Anthony Rowe

Contents

Acknowledgements

We owe a debt of gratitude to many friends, family members, and colleagues for their support and guidance with this book, drafted during 2018–2020. For inviting us to write this book in the first place, we thank Darren Reed (Editor), who also guided us and supported us when needed during the book's preparation. For their tireless and priceless emotional support we thank our partners, Jan Little (Derek Milne) and Susan Reiser. We greatly appreciated the informational support that came from Wendy Ducat, Craig Gonsalvez, Jan Little, Priya Martin, Ed Watkins, and Ted White. Practical support was provided through the case study material ('vignettes' and 'episodes') by: Mairi Albiston, Sean Harper, Louise Leach, Jan Little, Carol MacDonald, Vicki Montesano, and Valentina Short. We also valued the encouragement and ideas that we received throughout this project from staff and workshop participants associated with National Education Scotland, especially: Mairi Albiston, Sandra Ferguson, Sean Harper, Carol MacDonald, Joy Nisbit, and Nathan O'Neill. The Figures within the book were beautifully crafted by graphic artist Angela Butler. Jan Little ensured that our presentation was as clear as possible, as well as contributing wisdom from her extensive experience as an Occupational Health Advisor. However, the material within the book is all our responsibility, but we thank all these people for helping us to write such an important book.

Derek L. Milne and Robert P. Reiser

About the Authors

Derek Milne Ph.D. is a retired clinical psychologist, and has been a vigorous and constructive contributor to the development of clinical supervision since 1979, authoring several books and numerous scientific papers as part of a rare programmatic approach to the topic. Most recently, he published the second edition of his book, *Evidence-based Clinical Supervision: Principles and practice* (2018), which summarized this programme of research, and co-authored with Robert Reiser '*A Manual for Evidence-based Clinical Supervision*' (2017; both published by Wiley). In addition to researching and reviewing supervision, he has been a regular clinical supervisor within the UK's National Health Service and was for 10 years a clinical tutor on behalf of Newcastle University, where he became degree programme director for the Doctorate in Clinical Psychology before retiring in 2011. He continues to write about and teach clinical supervision.

Robert Reiser Ph.D. is a clinical psychologist with extensive experience in supervision. He is a Beck Institute-trained cognitive behavioural therapist (CBT) and a member of the Adjunct Faculty at the Beck Institute, Philadelphia. In addition to 10 years as a clinical supervisor and Clinic Director (for an American Psychological Association-approved doctoral programme), his grant-funded clinical research projects have involved supervising, training, and piloting clinical interventions for individuals with serious mental illnesses, in close collaboration with community mental health professionals. He served over several years as a consulting supervisor to Veterans Administration clinicians within a national training programme. Currently, he provides ongoing consultation and training for clinicians and case managers in supervision, and provides consultation and training to 3rd year psychiatrists at a major psychiatric residency training program. Since 2008 working with Derek Milne, he has co-authored a supervisor training manual and several scientific papers on supervision. Both authors have extensive experience as CBT therapists, working clinically with individuals suffering from burnout and related forms of personal distress.

Preface

Much has already been written about burnout and psychological well-being in the workplace, and the challenges are growing:

> *"There is an urgent need to develop interventions that address the high levels of stress, burnout, and dissatisfaction (among healthcare workers)"*
> (Scottish Executive, 2006, p57).

This need has been underlined with increasing concern by the World Health Organization (2019), which is now committed to developing evidence-based guidelines on mental well-being in the workplace. Welcome as these policy statements are, they have not yet been matched by organizational developments or by progress in professional practice (Department of Health, 2016). An exception is clinical supervision, one aspect of professional practice that is evidence-based and particularly well-suited as an intervention to counter burnout, or to foster well-being (Milne & Reiser, 2017). But we need a suitably restorative or supportive version of evidence-based clinical supervision to guide these developments. This is our reason for contributing this book to the large literature on burnout.

In this book, we tackle this need for a vision of supportive supervision (a kind of restorative leadership) by following our tried and tested formula, developed through our experience of researching 'evidence-based clinical supervision' (Milne, 2018; Milne & Reiser, 2017). This formula includes evidence-based practical guidance; detailing representative studies and relevant theory; providing case studies to illustrate the material; drawing out the action implications; and listing our key references drawn from the scientific, applied, and professional literature. We also present practical strategies for applying supervision to empower healthcare professionals; and we aim to guide managers and other leaders towards the creation of healthy and effective workplaces. In addition, our approach is scholarly in that we will scrutinize published material to judge its merit as evidence, rather than simply accepting what authors or other reviewers say about the significance or quality of their work. Together, we believe that these features allow us to illuminate and reformulate restorative supervision. We trust that this book will help readers to better understand the complexities of fostering well-being in the healthcare workplace, guiding them in the interventions that are most likely to succeed (for a summary, see Chapter 9, Figure 9.1).

When we undertook to write this book, we rather naively reckoned that we were simply giving some long-overdue attention to a minor and neglected aspect of clinical supervision. The task seemed straightforward and nicely focused, since so little had been written on supportive supervision. How wrong we were! As we soon discovered, supportive supervision properly belonged at the heart of some of the major issues in the workplace: occupational stress, burnout, quality of patient care, accidents, and staff sickness/absence and turnover. These all carried huge financial implications, and featured regularly in the headlines. Scores of books and countless tales of human suffering helped to make burnout a major international concern. What was less obvious were the kinds of solutions required in modern healthcare; what are the most effective, evidence-based ways to improve matters? We set about reviewing the best available literature, scanning research studies for promising results, linking these findings to the most relevant theories in order to formulate well-being at work, and to summarize the best interventions. To ensure that our understanding was sound, we also considered expert guidelines and consensus statements, and drew on our extensive experience as clinical psychologists who provided therapy to those suffering from burnout and similar kinds of personal distress. To reflect such intimate personal accounts of burnout, we have included case studies and illustrative vignettes.

Although the task dwarfed our initial expectations of this book, the result was a deeply satisfying immersion in what was known about burnout and well-being in the workplace (especially the healthcare environment). First, we had to build a decent theoretical foundation, including an empirical definition of supportive supervision, and a suitably systemic model. Then we pieced together the other key factors, including the important individual differences among staff members. This helped us to understand some perplexing phenomena in the workplace, such as why job satisfaction fluctuates so much, or why some people struggle with a task on which their colleagues thrive. But an understanding of the staff members is not enough; workplaces also have their own important characteristics. Of course, people and their workplaces then interact in all manner of complex ways. We therefore developed our 'support model' to capture the complex, systemic nature of these factors – a theoretical foundation that represents the first half of this book.

Befitting the complexity of the workplace, the second half of this book considers a wide range of evidence-based ways to improve matters individually and systemically. Our central focus is on the clinical supervisors who we believe can provide the single most effective form of support to staff. Supervision has exceptional potency because it alone straddles the relevant workplace and personal domains, and the widest range of available interventions. Also, it does so in a relatively neutral way, while offering the supervisee (healthcare staff member) a distinctively empowering, collaborative alliance. A further advantage of supervision is that supervisors can use their professional expertise in supporting and guiding patients, especially their ways of making sense of distress and well-being, and expertise in providing helpful interventions. Not least, because supervision should be an enduring feature of a supportive workplace, supervisors are able to offer their help over the long haul, monitoring and adjusting interventions as necessary.

But this book is more than just a guide to helping staff members in distress. We also regard supervisors as social agents with a responsibility to protect supervisees from harmful stressors. They can play a valuable role in preventing or reducing such stressors, as in helping to improve team-working, communication, or leadership. Supervisors may also contribute to the rehabilitation of staff who have been overwhelmed by workplace stressors. Given this broad, systemic perspective, we also consider the valuable roles played by other important individuals. These are the supervisees (the clinicians and trainees who provide care to patients), and the organizational leaders (e.g. managers, administrators, chief executives) – although we will also make some points that are addressed to researchers, professional bodies, educators and other interested groups.

In conclusion, we invite you to read this original and constructive guide to preventing burnout and promoting well-being at work, which we believe offers the most complete, practical, and scholarly account yet of how supportive supervision can contribute to better healthcare workplaces. Indeed, this book is highly relevant to improving other workplaces through restorative leadership, although the details regarding a supportive arrangement such as supervision will of course differ.

Foreword

It is with great pleasure that I write this foreword to *Supportive Clinical Supervision: Enhancing Well-being and Reducing Burnout through Restorative Leadership*. This volume makes a uniquely valuable contribution to supervision practice through a comprehensive review and discussion of evidence-based supportive supervision and restorative leadership. It brings to the forefront an insufficiently addressed and often unrecognized imperative for clinical supervision and healthy organizations – the practice of supportive supervision. The authors construct a practical blueprint for supportive supervision and restorative leadership around a superbly organized collection of evidence provided by international studies.

The volume will focus attention on exposure to diffuse trauma and stress, isolation, anxiety, burnout, and their psychological and physiological sequelae, which are harsh realities in mental health provision and supervision. It presents a unique vision of system infusion and change, providing highly articulated and evidence-supported processes. Accentuating the need for a transformation of organizational and workplace environments, the authors address multiple levels of leadership and top-down influence as well as the pragmatics of supporting well-being in competence-driven supervision practice.

There is a growing international recognition of the extent of trauma exposure, harmful supervision and deficits of supportive work generally in clinical practice and addressed in supervision. Accompanying that recognition is a growing acknowledgment that such practices are unsustainable unless there is top-down, significant leadership buy-in and support.

This volume provides direct guidance to the generally unrecognized promise of supervision to enhance well-being and to function as a buffer against client trauma disclosures and general pressures, ultimately promoting a healthy organizational culture. It addresses supervisees, supervisors, leaders, and systems, and provides direct strategies to support systematic, strength-based relational coping. Through alliance, reflective practice, contemplation, experiential learning, and supportive supervision, empowerment enhances, in tandem, both the supervisee and the supervisor's own personal resilience.

This volume builds on the authors' *Manual for Evidence-based CBT Supervision*, and provides strategies to enhance supervision and the cultural milieu. With creative, instructive, and transformational guidance, it lays the groundwork for substantive innovation in both organizational and clinical supervision practice, implicitly enhancing the value attached to clinical supervision.

Carol Falender, Ph.D.
Adjunct Professor, Pepperdine University Graduate School of Education and Psychology
Clinical Professor, University of California, Los Angeles, Department of Psychology

Chapter 1: Making the Case for Supportive Supervision

1. Overview of the book

Work defines the lives of most adults. This is because Western society sets supreme store by the kind of job that we do and the nature of our employment and salary, which is reflected in the way we introduce ourselves at social gatherings. In this sense, our job is central to our identity. But work also dominates most of us. Our job may even debilitate us, overwhelming our coping efforts because of toxic workplaces, excessively challenging job demands, or harmful relationships with colleagues. Combinations of these factors can weigh down even the most competent and confident workers, leading to personal distress, harm to patients, and organizational dysfunction. Common examples of personal distress attributable to work are depression, anxiety, and burnout. Furthermore, in relation to healthcare professionals there is a double burden of occupational distress, in that burnout can also have an adverse effect on patients. In the USA, the Patient Safety Network (Lyndon, 2016) concluded that burnout is prevalent across health care settings, with the result that it may impair clinicians' ability to maintain safe practices, or to detect emerging safety threats. One survey of early-career physicians in the US (Dyrbye *et al,* 2014, p447) concluded that "some syndromes, including burnout, symptoms of depression, and high fatigue, occurred at alarmingly high rates (i.e. 40%–50%) among [these] physicians, at a time when they are dealing with the challenges inherent to launching a career and starting a new practice".

Hyrkas (2005) found that 57% of a sample of 569 mental health nurses in Finland indicated high or average emotional exhaustion, 39% depersonalization, and that only 16% felt satisfied with their personal accomplishments at work. She concluded that burnout was a 'significant problem'. Similarly, a survey by Steel *et al* (2015) indicated that the majority of the 116 British therapist respondents experienced anxiety and emotional exhaustion. The comparable findings reported by Edwards *et al* (2006) are detailed in our 'burnout example' section below. Surveys of physicians also indicate similarly alarming levels of burnout. In a recent example, Bourne *et al* (2019) surveyed over 3,000 obstetricians and gynaecologists in the UK, reporting that 36% met the conventional criteria for burnout (a score of at least 50% on the emotional exhaustion scale, and 30% on the depersonalization scale of the Maslach Burnout Inventory).

Similar prevalence rates were reported from a survey of 3,896 physicians working for a large healthcare organization in the US (Shanafelt *et al*, 2015). These researchers found that 40% of this sample reported symptoms of burnout, but that the prevalence of burnout rates among physicians was strongly correlated with the leadership qualities of their physician supervisors. Eleven percent of the variance in burnout (and 47% of the variance in job satisfaction) was due to the supervisors' leadership style. Informing, engaging, inspiring, coaching and providing feedback characterised the most effective supervision. This finding lies at the heart of this book; we plan to explore just how supervisors can help their supervisees to move away from burnout, and towards well-being.

One study shed light on the causes of burnout, and why it may be on the increase. Mental health workers within England's Improving Access to Psychological Therapies (IAPT) programme determined that "almost 30% of IAPT staff reached criteria for minor psychiatric morbidity. Identified stressors included high-volume and target-orientated work, constant change, resource issues, team dynamics, demands of high-stakes in-service training, managing and holding distress and risk, and home-work conflict" (Walklet and Percy, 2014, p15). Although based on a small size sample, this figure was comparable to larger scale surveys of NHS staff where 38% of respondents reported work-related stress (Care Quality Commission, 2012). At the same time, the IAPT programme, due to its impressive scope (training an estimated 10,500 therapists by 2021, and treating over 560,000 patients per year (Clark, 2018), provides an incredibly important advance in terms of access to evidence-based therapies. This has the potential to improve healthcare on a large national scale. Such alarming rates of burnout make it an extremely timely and critically important time to develop solutions.

There is another reason to improve our interventions: burnout also has multiple adverse consequences for others. The most common cause of long-term sickness and absence from the workplace is depression, often due to exhaustion and burnout (Begat & Sverinsson, 2006). This spells problems for healthcare organizations. In turn, such poor psychological health is likely to affect patients, because both the quantity and quality of patient care may be diminished (Michie & Williams, 2003). For instance, burnout directly affects the rate of medical errors in healthcare organizations (Dewa *et al*, 2017; Salyers *et al*, 2017; Shanafelt *et al*, 2010). A recent systematic review concluded that "burnout may jeopardize patient care; reversal of this risk has to be viewed as a fundamental health care policy goal across the globe" (Panagioti *et al*, 2018, p1).

Therefore, given the alarming impact of burnout, this book will provide an overview of evidence-based approaches to the development of restorative leadership, specifically the supportive clinical supervision strategies that can help healthcare workers to deal with workplace stressors more effectively. These can also enhance organizational effectiveness, optimizing the delivery of high-quality patient care. As a result of supportive clinical supervision, staff members can replace burnout with well-being, experiencing deeply satisfying personal and professional growth (e.g. enhanced resilience and resourcefulness). But supervision needs to be viewed through a system-wide lens, as it entails a sustained organizational effort to turn these kinds of vicious cycles into virtuous ones (personal and systemic). At an organizational level, such virtuous cycles can have profound effects in terms of remoralizing staff, helping them find meaning and value in their work, and improving the overall quality of patient care. For example, Clark (2018, p13) noted extreme variability in care outcomes by IAPT site ("The lowest recorded recovery rate for the year was 21%, and the highest was 63%"), which he attributed to the nature of the respective clinical management and support for staff. In the sites with the best clinical results:

> "...the clinical leaders had a strong focus on patients achieving recovery, and reliable improvement. They helped create an innovation environment in which the staff were interested in the service's outcome data, primarily because it gave them clues about how to further improve their clinical work. The leaders supported staff in this enterprise by enabling them to attend multiple continued professional development events. Staff also received personal feedback on the outcomes that they achieved with their patients, benchmarked against the service's average" (Clark, 2018, p16).

In short, to succeed we need to place supportive supervision in the context of the supervisees' workplaces. This book adopts this broad and systemic perspective.

2. Is this book for you?

This book will be of interest to all who are concerned about leadership and well-being in the workplace, with a particular emphasis on healthcare workers. Among these staff, we place the clinical supervisors centre stage, as they are the primary providers of supportive or restorative clinical supervision (we use these terms interchangeably, and regard the supervisor as a restorative type of leader; by 'supportive supervision' we mean supportive clinical supervision). But consistent with our systemic perspective, we also give attention to the associated supervisees, managers, institutional leaders, administrators and others with an interest in supervision and its outcomes. This includes organizations involved in the provision of healthcare, university training programmes for health service staff, and the related professional organizations concerned with the initial and continuing professional development (CPD) of their members (e.g. British Psychological Society; British Association for Behavioural & Cognitive Psychotherapy; American Psychological Association; Psychology Board of Australia). Those engaged in private practice (self-employed) will also see direct relevance in the material in this book. Other professionals should also find much of direct relevance and value, such as social services professionals and others who liaise with healthcare staff, or who deal with similar issues within supervision (or similar interventions, such as mentoring, coaching, or preceptorship). For example, Human Resources and Occupational Health staff, who play a central organizational role in helping healthcare workers suffering from burnout and other forms of workplace distress, will also be interested in this book. We will identify the implications for these stakeholders by describing how employing organizations should train and support clinical supervisors and their supervisees (we append a detailed workshop plan for training supportive supervisors). Of course, our own experiences will influence what we judge to be illuminating and empowering, and as authors we would emphasise that we employ a scholarly perspective which values rigorous research and pursues a critical engagement with the academic and professional knowledge bases. Allied to this scholarly perspective, we are widely experienced clinicians and supervisors, so recognize the importance of practical, user-friendly approaches. Between us, we have worked in higher education and in large healthcare organizations (including the National Health Service: NHS), in addition to the private sector, collaborating closely with social service departments and voluntary sector organizations. We have many years of experience as supervisees, clinical supervisors, supervisor trainers and supporters, as well as occupying key roles such as clinical tutor and director of a professional training programme. These influences and experiences are best captured by terms such as 'scientist-practitioner' and 'practitioner-scholar', terms that embrace science and practice as inseparable and complementary foundations for the modern, evidence-based healthcare professional.

Although our background is primarily in professional education and the mental health field (especially clinical psychology and clinical supervision), we will give equal weight to other healthcare fields, and indeed to all disciplines that appear within the literature we describe (e.g. general nursing; medicine; occupational therapy; physiotherapy). Although our focus is on supervision, when the differences are purely semantic, then like others we embrace similar roles and terms such as 'mentoring' or 'preceptorship' (Lee *et al*, 2019), as is common within the wider field of leadership development (Lacerenza *et al*, 2017). This means that our emphasis will be relevant to the full multi-disciplinary team (the allied health practitioners), and to the collaborative working between health, social care, and the voluntary sector services. Befitting this inclusive approach, we will offer an international perspective, though based on the literature that is presented in the

English language and which concerns modern healthcare. For instance, the British NHS will be given considerable attention, partly as it is a suitably representative organization and partly because much of the most valuable research has been conducted or implemented by this healthcare organization (e.g. the innovative IAPT programme, as just mentioned). We believe that this broad approach enriches our material and affords the reader a more complete account of supportive supervision. Our core discipline and inspiration is applied psychology with an evidence-based ethos (e.g. supervision that is primarily based on and appropriate for Cognitive-Behavioural Therapy: CBT). We regard clinical supervision as a psychosocial activity, an intervention that is based on social and psychological processes, within a highly influential organizational context.

As we will describe in Chapter 2, clinical supervision has three main functions: 'formative' (educational), 'normative' (administrative), and 'restorative' (supportive). It is the supportive function that is the focus of this book. Such supervision includes providing social support to supervisees, facilitating their work-related learning so as to reduce distress, and encouraging adaptive personal coping within employing organizations ('stress-management').

3. Setting the stage

Clinical supervision is a key method for enhancing personal and professional coping strategies among healthcare staff, in addition to maximizing social support processes, and minimizing workplace stressors. Although clinical supervision in general has a long history, dating in its earliest manifestation from the beginnings of social work in the 18th century (White & Winstanley, 2014), only recently has it been recognized internationally as an essential part of modern healthcare systems, and as a core competence within professional practice (e.g. Department of Health, 2004; American Psychological Association, 2015). For instance, clinical supervision is now recognized by most experts as essential for the competent, career-long provision of evidence-based therapy (Beidas & Kendall, 2010), a key professional practice arrangement for enhancing clinical effectiveness (IAPT Supervision Guidance, 2011), and as a method for minimizing harm (Department of Health, 2016). We review the related research evidence in Chapter 3.

The role of supportive or restorative supervision for addressing burnout and healthcare worker distress also enjoys widespread acknowledgement in the literature, but it is rarely defined precisely and usually overlooked. We define supportive supervision as follows:

"Supportive clinical supervision addresses supervisees' emotional experience of their workplace, and their personal functioning in that healthcare context. It is a formal, case-focused, and intensive relational process, conducted with due authority by a trained, suitably experienced, and appropriate supervisor. Specific supervision techniques include problem formulation, coping strategy enhancement, facilitating peer support, empathic debriefing, and efforts to prevent or manage workplace stressors. The primary mechanisms within supervision that enable these outcomes to be achieved are experiential learning, the supervision alliance, personal coping strategies, and social support. The main intended outcomes for supervisees are reductions in personal distress and enhanced well-being."

We provide the full empirical definition in Chapter 2.

Within the research literature and systematic reviews, this type of supervision has been identified as a strategy to help professionals feel supported and protect them from burnout, which in turn is widely acknowledged as the basis for enhancing patient care (e.g. Snowdon *et al*, 2016). However, it has only recently gained formal endorsement nationally, at least in the UK and Australia, and recognition in the USA appears to be lagging behind. For example, the UK's Health and Social Care Secretary announced on his appointment in 2018 that his priority was a healthy workforce (Hancock, 2018). Specifically, he recognized that the nation's health was determined by the health of the workforce. To improve staff health, he promised to counter the pressures of the health and social care workplace, by improving funding, addressing high workloads and managerial leadership, and by providing the best possible training and support. Such measures would allow staff to achieve their full potential, providing safe, high-quality care. This follows similar policy directives for specific professional groups. For instance, supervision has played a minimal role within the nursing profession in the UK historically, but has thankfully gained momentum with a recommendation that it should be part of the working life of every nurse (Scottish Government, 2009). In these and other statements, supervision includes the supportive aspect: "There is an urgent need to develop interventions that address the high levels of stress, burnout, and dissatisfaction among mental health nurses" (Scottish Executive, 2006, p57). Welcome as these policy statements are, they have not yet been matched by organizational or professional practice (Department of Health, 2016; Novoa-Gomez *et al*, 2019). Among the possible explanations for this are inadequate training in supportive supervision, and the lack of a sound evidence base, a state of affairs that provides part of the impetus for this book. We are also encouraged by growing evidence that supportive supervision works by reducing burnout while improving clinical skills and professional efficiency (e.g. Dugani *et al*, 2018).

4. How bad is workplace distress?

What is burnout?

Burnout differs from anxiety or depression. According to the most popular instrument for measuring burnout, the Maslach Burnout Inventory (MBI), it consists of perceived emotional exhaustion, depersonalization, and low personal accomplishment (Maslach *et al*, 1996). Subsequently, Maslach and Leiter (1997) refined their conception of burnout, defining it more as an erosion of engagement with work, in the sense that work that was once perceived by the employee as important, meaningful, and challenging becomes the opposite – unpleasant, unfulfilling, and meaningless. In burnout (sometimes referred to as 'stress'), previously high energy levels are replaced by exhaustion, initial involvement turns into cynicism, and a prior sense of accomplishment turns into a sense of ineffectiveness. High scores on the MBI are associated with low self-confidence, poor sleep, impaired thinking, reduced work effectiveness and a heightened risk for developing cardiovascular diseases (Naczenski, 2017).

The cost of burnout

The financial costs of burnout are staggering. In England, the NHS estimates that staff sickness/absence alone equates to 10 million working days being lost in the NHS annually, at a cost of nearly £1.7 billion (Boorman, 2009). In turn, according to the same source 80% of NHS staff regard sickness/absence as lowering the quality of patient care. According to Naczenski (2017), the financial cost of burnout has been estimated at 136 billion dollars per year in the US, and 200 billion euros in Europe. There are other cost implications of sickness/absence. As reviewed within Bourne *et al* (2019), physicians experiencing burnout symptoms are twice as likely to comprise patient safety incidents, and to deliver a lower quality of patient care. Costs also occur in the form of complaints and litigation, with obstetric claim settlements costing the NHS over £500 million annually. This 'complaints culture' may in turn exacerbate burnout an increased cost to clinicians in terms of their anxiety or depression (including suicidal ideation, strongly associated with actual suicide attempts and death). According to the research summary in Bourne *et al* (2019), a related problem is increased 'defensive practice', representing a highly significant strain on healthcare resources (e.g. estimated to cost $46 billion annually in the USA (Mello *et al*, 2010). Defensive practice can be regarded as an avoidant personal coping strategy that is adopted by distressed clinicians, defined as sub-standard practice in response to complaints or criticism, which risks harming patients (e.g. clinicians avoiding difficult cases or over-prescribing). Burnout may also undermine professional standards (e.g. clinicians cheating and falsifying clinical exam findings (Wood, 2016). In short, quite aside from anything else, there is a strong business case for tackling burnout (Bourne *et al*, 2019).

Consistent with this, the National Institute of Occupational Safety and Health (NIOSH, 2014) estimated that 40% of American workers reported their job was very or extremely stressful, and that 25% viewed their jobs as the number one stressor in their lives and a major occupational health risk, ranking above physical inactivity and obesity, and associated with productivity losses from missed work that annually cost employers $1,685 per employee. Similarly, in his report for the NHS, Boorman (2009) predicted that productivity improvements, equating to £555 million per annum in direct savings, could be achieved if well-being interventions were able to reduce staff sickness absence by a third in the UK. Such a reduction would also enable the NHS to gain 3.4 million working days per year (equating to 14,900 extra staff), with a reduction in indirect costs for temporary staff, reduced staff turnover (recruitment costs for new members of staff were estimated at £4,500 per person), and reduced ill-health retirement costs (currently estimated at £150 million per annum). The burnout problem is even more alarming when one considers the knock-on effects, which contribute significantly to sickness/absence among staff, lost organizational productivity, and harm to patients (Panagioti *et al*, 2018). In turn, the cascade of costs for society of these successive, adverse consequences within healthcare is enormous (Naczenski, 2017). Furthermore, families and loved ones may also suffer the effects of burnout (Thoits, 2010).

A growing problem

To make matters worse, there are indications that burnout is a growing problem. The situation has become so bad that the World Health Organization (WHO) has for the first time included burnout in its list of 'factors influencing health status or contact with health services', although it is not yet classified as a disease. Furthermore, for the first time WHO is now committed to developing evidence-based guidelines on mental well-being in the workplace (WHO, 2019, https://www.who.int/mental_health/evidence/burn-out/en/). We should also note that the problem of burnout is not limited to first-world industrial countries, and has broad international scope in terms of affecting the quality of services provided by physicians, healthcare staff, and support workers. In a systematic review, Dewa and co-authors (2014) concluded that "countries all over the world are beginning to recognize the potential impact of physician burnout on productivity" (p4), and consequently physician educators are now giving far more attention to well-being (Wood, 2016).

Even among psychological therapists, a group one might expect to be well-placed to cope with workplace stressors, burnout is on the increase. A questionnaire survey of 1,300 psychological staff in the NHS indicated that 46% reported experiencing depression, and that the great majority (70%) were finding their work stressful, an increase of 12% from the same survey conducted in the previous year (New Savoy Partnership, 2016). Stressors included growing pressure to meet performance targets, and a loss of interest in work. Of these 1,300 psychological staff, 28% said that they did not have enough time to participate in supervision. When asked about suggestions for improving their well-being, respondents most often referred to the need for greater support at work (from peers or managers), and a more compassionate work culture (including more listening, offering recognition, and having assistants or support workers). Overall, the authors interpreted these findings as indicative of high levels of personal distress, consistent with other NHS staff groups.

Tackling burnout

Fortunately, the need for remedial action has been acknowledged within the NHS (2011), with the introduction of a 'Health & Well-being Improvement Framework'. This places the onus on services to develop an approach to support the health and well-being of their staff, such as promoting healthy options, supplemented by prevention, intervention and rehabilitation services. The NHS recognizes that staff well-being is a key indicator of organizational performance and enhances patient outcomes; it is accepted that the care of staff translates into care for patients. Helpfully, the NHS (2011) has proceeded to detail how the different employee roles should be tasked with improving well-being. Of most relevance to our focus on restorative supervision, line managers and supervisors (often one and the same person, at least in the UK) have a responsibility to look after the health and well-being of their staff. Specifically, they should "take the well-being of their staff seriously, listening and responding to their needs and helping them alleviate, as far as reasonably practicable, workplace stressors" (p.6). Additional responsibilities are to encourage staff in need to contact occupational health and well-being services (e.g. counselling) or employee assistance programmes. Similar guidance has been provided in the USA (Lyndon, 2016; NIOSH, 2014).

Tackling burnout through supervision: example

To illustrate these points on burnout, we now describe a representative study by Edwards *et al* (2006), which considered the role of supervision in reducing burnout. In this study, two hundred and sixty community mental health nurses working in 11 NHS units in Wales, UK, responded to a burnout survey (a response rate of 32%). Burnout was measured by the Maslach Burnout Inventory (MBI) (Maslach *et al,* 1996), while supervision was measured by the Manchester Clinical Supervision Scale (MCSS) (Winstanley & White, 2014). Burnout was found to be high, with 36% of these nurses reporting emotional exhaustion, and 12% reporting depersonalization. Conversely, 10% of these staff reported low levels of personal accomplishment. When related to supervision (the MCSS data), correlations suggested that feeling supported and being able to discuss sensitive issues with the supervisor were associated with less burnout (less emotional exhaustion and depersonalization). However, an association was also reported that undermined these findings: making time for supervision in a busy work schedule was associated with increased levels of burnout, a somewhat unfortunate but typical example of the kind of problems that arise in large healthcare organizations.

We will consider solutions to such paradoxical situations throughout this book, especially in the next Chapter, but one option is to enhance the value to supervisees of supervision through better meeting their restorative needs. For example, in studying burnout among IAPT therapists, Steel *et al* (2015) concluded that clinical supervision might prove most valuable to supervisees (the therapists) when focusing on their emotional reactions to clients, as addressing therapists' in-session feelings of anxiety may mitigate the burnout risk. Increasing its value may make it easier for therapists to make time for supervision.

Occupational excellence

So far in this problem statement we have outlined the consequences of stressful and unsupportive workplaces for staff, as well as noting the accompanying problems that can occur at the organizational level. If more proof were needed, consider too the failure to get the best out of staff and thereby move towards a virtuous organizational cycle with numerous positive benefits. Serious institutional failures are often marked by an organizational culture that does not reflect critical values in prizing high-quality patient care, and which feature corresponding breakdowns in the behaviour of clinicians (Wood, 2016). A healthy organization not only minimizes burnout, it also maximizes well-being. This can be promoted by a sustainable workload, giving staff feelings of choice and control, ensuring that they receive appropriate recognition and reward, and making sure that staff work in a supportive community (Begat & Severinsson, 2006). Other qualities include fairness and justice, together with work that is meaningful and valued. This is acknowledged by the NHS, for example, in recognizing that staff should be encouraged to show greater 'engagement' with their employing organization. Engagement goes beyond being satisfied at work to fostering among staff a deeper sense of commitment, attachment and organizational citizenship. Engagement also refers to social, physical and psychological well-being (e.g. having positive relationships with colleagues; experiencing positive emotions about one's work). It is also correlated with improved work performance (e.g. greater vigour, dedication, and absorption).

The links to supportive supervision become evident when one considers the kind of workplace factors believed to promote organizational engagement, such as having a sense of purpose, communicating effectively, managing work overload, and gaining social support. There is evidence that interventions such as supervision that improve psychological well-being among staff lead to improved outcomes for the organization (Boorman, 2009). Therefore, in addition to addressing burnout, this book is also intended to contribute detailed, concrete and actionable solutions to foster healthy workers and supportive workplaces.

5. Plan for the book

Our aims

Although there is good reason to invest in supportive clinical supervision, it is often scarce or superficial in practice, due to insufficient resources and a traditional emphasis on formative clinical supervision (e.g. Novoa-Gomez *et al,* 2019). Paradoxically, this can generate significant additional costs, in terms of staff burnout and organizational dysfunction. Growing awareness of the essential role that supervision plays has yet to embrace the restorative function. To help to remedy matters, this book aims to enhance and empower those who should be most interested in ensuring that supportive supervision occurs by summarizing the best available research, expert advice, and the most relevant theory on how to help individual staff members cope with the demands encountered in healthcare. This book builds on the foundations laid by our supervisor training manual, which detailed five complementary strategies for implementing supportive supervision, and included aids such as comprehensive guidelines, and associated video demonstrations (Milne & Reiser, 2017). We also draw on illustrative studies, helpful training materials, and practical examples (e.g. Wallbank & Woods, 2012; Wonnacott, 2016).

Supervisors are uniquely well-placed

Building on these foundations, our aim in writing this book is to convert supportive supervision from the most neglected and least understood aspect of clinical supervision, into a properly articulated and evidence-based sphere of professional competence. The current Cinderella-like status of supportive supervision is particularly frustrating because it is actually uniquely well-placed to address problems such as burnout. This is because effective supervision provides a space where the primary needs of the healthcare professional can be comprehensively considered by one person. Unlike anyone else, the supervisor can consider the organizational context to help alleviate depression; raise professional issues to relieve stressors and boost well-being; provide training and education to improve personal accomplishment; and offer social support to lower emotional exhaustion. Note that these functions address the features of burnout measured by the MBI. At the heart of this unique role is the way that the supervisor combines multiple roles in addressing such needs, playing many parts in one formally endorsed role (trainer, mentor, colleague, manager, evaluator, social supporter, etc) (Knudson *et al,* 2008). Another important strength of the supervisor's position within the organization is relative impartiality: when the supervisors are not the line managers, they can more readily understand and take the side of the supervisee.

Our objectives

i) We will present a summary of the best available evidence

Evidence-based practice (EBP) is increasingly important within modern healthcare. Arguments for this growing emphasis include cost-effectiveness and heightened fidelity. It follows that interventions such as supervision that are intended to encourage EBP should themselves be evidence-based, so that they are also cost-effective and carefully delivered. But terms such as 'evidence-based practice' are often used loosely.

Our approach to 'evidence' is to, **first**, review and summarize the best available research literature in order to clarify the research findings and methodological status of the experimental evidence. An example of research addressing the assumed link between supervision and well-being are the 27 studies that were analysed by Mor Barak *et al* (2009), who concluded that social support from supervisors was associated with well-being, organizational commitment, and job satisfaction. Although the great majority of the literature we summarize comes from clinical supervision, we also refer to neighbouring literatures when helpful or where the quality of the evidence is strong (e.g. extrapolating from research within education on corrective feedback; drawing on therapy research in relation to the supervision alliance). We also embrace evidence about other leaders, such as mentors and preceptors, when the evidence is scarce or the overlaps seem clear. Partly of necessity, but largely of conviction, we adopt a broad and inclusive perspective on research (Milne & Reiser, 2017). For instance, we do not believe that the only trustworthy knowledge comes from randomized controlled trials (RCTs), unlike some commentators (Alfonsson *et al*, 2017). Rather, we believe that we need a wide range of research methods if we are to develop a truly evidence-based approach to supervision (see Chapter 3). This is clear from considering the steps entailed in taking an evidence-based approach, as set out in Figure 1.1. For example, we need qualitative approaches to clarify expert consensus and to test the resulting guidelines and we need equally 'soft' reaction evaluations by supervisors if we are to succeed in providing them with acceptable forms of training. What is more, we do not even regard the RCT as the most valid or persuasive demonstration of how supervision works (efficacy research), preferring, at this early stage in supervision research, the intensive quantitative analysis of a few representative supervisors (i.e. 'n=1' or 'small n' research: Milne 0, 2012). Parallel qualitative methods, such as 'case studies' (e.g. Pereira & Barkham, 2015) and 'episode analysis', also carry weight in our scheme of evidence (e.g. Milne *et al*, 2011a).

Secondly, we draw on relevant theories, models and concepts to help us to comprehend the implications of research findings and to guide practice. An illustration of a relevant theory is 'social exchange theory' (Blau, 1964).

According to this theory, healthcare professionals who receive support (including task assistance, emotional support, and effective supervision relationships) reciprocate with positive feelings and behaviours toward their patients, which can in turn improve the clinical outcomes. Unfortunately, the research evidence indicates that, at least in mental health, the link between supervision and clinical benefits is not so straightforward (Milne 2014; Reiser & Milne, 2014). Using relevant theories, we can explore some plausible explanations for this complex pathway.

Thirdly, as a complementary form of evidence we will also draw on expert opinion (especially expert consensus statements and formally developed supervision guidelines). To illustrate, the Begat and Severinsson (2006) review, noted above, is in effect an expert consensus statement, albeit a rather informal statement, and one that involved two experts and three studies. More typically we refer to formal statements, developed following systematic consensus-building methods, such as the one by Falender *et al* (2004). These supervision experts included these supervision competencies in their framework: 'Knowledge of the immediate system and expectations within which the supervision is conducted', and 'awareness of the socio-political context within which the supervision is conducted'. The APA (2015) supervision guidelines also encouraged attention to the institutional, legal and regulatory contexts, while the Roth and Pilling (2008) competences framework noted that supervisors should 'take into account the organizational context for supervision'. Likewise, in considering depression and suicide among physicians in the USA, the consensus statement by Center *et al* (2003, p3165) recommended transforming negative attitudes and institutional policies so as to encourage physicians to seek help:

> *"Medical schools (should) educate medical students and residents about depression and suicidality, encourage them to seek help, and offer social support for any student or resident who seeks help."*

As illustrated in Figure 1.1, EBP entrenches these three forms of evidence within a system made up of 10 inter-connected and complementary steps for continuously developing the quality of healthcare practice (Parry *et al,* 1996). In this sense, EBP is the evidence system for supportive supervision, the process through which we can develop and apply the knowledge needed to guide supportive supervision. These steps take place within the workplace context (Box 11). In addition to depicting this system, through these 11 boxes Figure 1.1 indicates (through one or two examples per box) some of the specific ways in which these EBP steps can be applied to supportive supervision. For instance, Box 1 in Figure 1.1 ('Judging how to support supervisees') records that this step can be completed by conducting a needs assessment (e.g. does a supervisee avoid discussing emotional aspects of their clinical work?). Overlaid in Boxes 2 and 3 is a diagram of a tandem cycle, intended to show how this supervision model (part of the support model outlined in Chapter 2) links the supervisor's and supervisee's activities. For instance, the supervisor may pose questions, in order to encourage the supervisee to disclose anxieties about their clinical work. Figure 1.1 is therefore a means of considering how an evidence-based system provides a vital framework or context for supportive supervision, indicating how we believe that supervision should develop within healthcare. To the best of our knowledge, this is the first book to develop supportive supervision by applying this EBP process systematically.

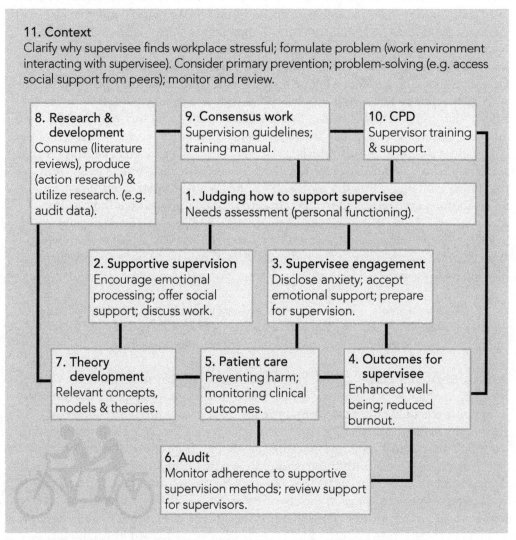

Figure 1.1 Legend: Supportive supervision within the context of evidence-based practice

ii) We will increase awareness of critical contextual factors

Fourthly, we will draw attention to the main influences affecting supportive supervision. Just as supervisors need to attend to contextual factors when working with supervisees, a book like this needs to identify those factors that might influence its success. For our suggestions to work, organizational leaders, managers and supervisors must be alert to: the personal and organizational influences on supportive supervision (e.g. supervisee characteristics that foster effective supervision; why some workplaces are toxic); the latest data on work-related distress (e.g. occupational burnout); identifying the positive benefits of sound supervision (e.g. personal growth and excellence), while being mindful of the boundaries with harmful or unethical supervision; the essential role of social support (informal help), linking it to their supportive supervision; how supervision arrangements can be adapted for challenging or novel situations (e.g. the use of tele-supervision in rural contexts).

iii) We will offer practical suggestions and a detailed action plan to address these problems

The book also aims to recommend actions for the various stakeholders, within relevant organizations. We do this by setting out how supervisors can best offer support to their supervisees, but we also note implications for supervisor trainers and supporters, managers, administrators, and relevant others. Drawing on the different forms of evidence detailed above and our own practical experience, we aim to help readers to make the most of supportive supervision. We will do this by providing detailed summaries of the best available supervision methods and processes, together with examples and other suggestions for supervisors and supervisees. Among other benefits, this will help readers to succeed in assessing supervisees' emotional needs, formulate why a supervisor neglects the restorative aspect of supervision, and understand a health professional's stress reactions or coping styles. This is a start, but we fully recognize that there is more to do to complete the full EBP cycle (as shown in Figure 1.1). Some of this EBP work has already commenced on supportive supervision, with the development of supervisor training materials and an initial consensus statement (e.g. the guideline in Milne & Reiser, 2017). We hope that others will undertake the remaining steps in EBP (e.g. conducting research; evaluating supervisor training; conducting audits, etc.). This work will further strengthen and deepen the practical suggestions for supportive supervision.

A final major objective for this book is to provide links to instruments and methods that allow others to review, monitor or evaluate the effectiveness of restorative work in supervision. This encourages and enables readers to decide whether their methods are working, and to refine and enhance them. For instance, a service manager within a healthcare organization should ensure that the training workshops, educational activities, and support arrangements for their supervisors and supervisees are achieving their objectives (e.g. by measuring the associated learning outcomes).

The book's chapters

Having now made the case for supervision, in Chapter 2 we define exactly what we mean by supportive supervision, and develop a fresh understanding of supportive supervision, to explain how it can minimize harm and maximize professional thriving. This understanding of our theoretical model is being our guiding logic or rationale for supportive supervision. Theoretical models should help us to make sense of individuals, enabling us to formulate why sometimes the same person experiences burnout, while at other times they flourish. Supportive supervision should draw on such models, and to help we will present an illustrative case study. In turn, a sound formulation provides the basis for success. In Chapter 3 we present the evidence on its effectiveness, linking this to the preceding theoretical material and to the definition below. Following Chapter 3 we adopt the approach taken in the research literature, in that Chapters 4 and 5 consider the role of individual differences (primarily in supervisors and supervisees), their organizational systems, and their interactions. We consider fundamental questions about the roles and responsibilities of those involved, and ask what can be done to reduce burnout and increase well-being at work. However, unlike the literature (and most of the professional literature), we examine the best available research, expert advice, and the most relevant theory from the perspective of supportive supervision. This enables us to present an evidence-based and systemic means of understanding personal distress among healthcare workers; review the ways that employing organizations create helpful and challenging environments for supervision; and summarize how supervisors and supervisees can affect the healthcare system (e.g. building teamwork or helping to foster social support). In Chapter 6 we scrutinize the range of supervision options what exactly can supervisors do to alleviate the stressors bearing down on their supervisees? How can they strengthen supervisees' coping strategies and clinical effectiveness? We describe 12 effective techniques in considerable procedural detail. Chapter 7 examines the supervisee's role in a similarly constructive fashion. Like supportive supervision itself, the supervisee has been much neglected in supervision, usually assumed to play a passive, minimal and insignificant role. In stark contrast, we take the view that supervisees must play an active and significant role in making supervision successful, and we provide guidance on how to make this happen. This includes the link to peer support and other coping resources, displaying reciprocal leadership, as well as ways of getting the most out of supervision. In this way, we further develop our formulation of successful supportive supervision. Chapter 8 continues our consideration of other neglected issues, this time focusing on how supervisors themselves should be supported (supervisors need training and can experience burnout too (Erera, 2008). We will detail the options for continuing professional development (CPD, including supervisor training), and the most promising support arrangements. By these means, Chapter 8 extends our systemic and inclusive approach to the managers and other stakeholders within the supportive supervision environment. We explain what such organizational leaders should be doing to facilitate the supervision system (e.g. ensuring that there is training and support for supervisees and supervisors; embedding policies and procedures to ensure that staff allocate time to supervision). Chapter 9 draws these themes together, listing the main conclusions and the key recommendations for action that follow from them.

6. Summary

Burnout is an alarming and growing problem within healthcare, but supportive supervision represents a particularly promising intervention. Although this type of restorative leadership is straightforward and can yield highly cost-effective results, to date there has not been an evidence-based understanding nor a linked procedural statement of how supervision should be provided. Therefore, this book will redress the neglect of supportive clinical supervision by: developing an empirical definition; constructing an integrative theoretical model; reviewing the best available research; formulating the healthcare system in relation to supervision; identifying suitable measurement instruments; listing evidence-based supervision methods (for supervisors and supervisees); clarifying how supervisors should be trained and supported; and concluding with recommended actions. In these respects, this book's thorough account of supportive supervision is unprecedented, and provides a practical, evidence-based and proven basis from which to address burnout and to foster well-being. This book is also distinctive in being:

- **extensive:** relevant to all healthcare professions and the associated training and support systems; the scope goes beyond mental health, whereas existing books tend to focus on one profession or client group (e.g. Wonnacott, 2016)

- **original:** it draws extensively on the latest research findings and concepts, bringing in valuable but often excluded material from neighbouring literatures, such as education (i.e. when necessary, we extrapolate carefully to the best available evidence)

- **scholarly:** founded on contemporary academic and applied psychology (especially clinical psychology), moderated by expert opinion and formal consensus, and informed by key theoretical concepts. The most relevant research is presented in detail to encourage critical thinking and problem-solving

- **practical:** evidence-based practices are specified in sufficient detail to encourage readers to apply the techniques effectively

- **deep:** existing books typically accord restorative supervision only passing mention (e.g. Bernard & Goodyear, 2014). This book will provide the most systematic, evidence-based treatment of the topic to date.

To make this book as helpful as possible, we will spell out the action implications from this and subsequent chapters in Chapter 9, where we will also draw the main conclusions from the book.

Chapter 2: Understanding Supportive Supervision

1. Introduction

A healthy organization minimizes burnout and maximizes well-being, and this book champions supervision as a vital part of achieving those objectives within an effective, caring organization. Although this affirmative view of supervision is shared in the professional and scientific literature, and at the governmental level (e.g. Department of Health, 2016), for many there is an accompanying discomfort that we do not really know as much as we should about supportive supervision (Avortri, *et al,* 2019): "There is an urgent need to develop interventions that address the high levels of stress, burnout, and dissatisfaction…" (Scottish Executive, 2006, p.57). Therefore, in this chapter we develop our understanding of supportive supervision to enable us to have a clear and evidence-based grasp of what it is and how it works. Supportive clinical supervision is a complex intervention within a highly complex healthcare system, so to achieve a proper understanding we will need to utilize the most relevant theories and the best available research, moderated by expert consensus. The term 'supportive supervision' has been used before, in relation to Social Work (Kadushin, 1976), and in the context of supervision in resource-poor countries (World Health Organization, 2008). As we will explain, our use of the term comes closest to its meaning in social work, first articulated by Dawson in 1926. We prefer the term 'supportive' to the popular term 'restorative' (as coined in relation to counselling by Proctor, 1993), as it better emphasises the greater scope that we accord supportive supervision. This includes a positive, 'strengths-based' emphasis; active prevention of stressors; and valuable personal development. However, we will use these terms interchangeably to ensure continuity with the restorative supervision literature.

By 'complex intervention' we mean that supervision consists of several intertwined parts (many people and multiple variables, such as the alliance and emotional support), parts which are all important when working with a supervisee (the intervention). To some extent, these variables all contribute to the success of supervision, though we do not yet know precisely how (e.g. several dynamic processes or multiple mechanisms may well be involved). In turn, the complexity of the intervention causes diverse outcomes for supervisees, and for their workplace too (see Figure 2.1 for examples; see Mor Barak (2009) for a summary of the research literature). This complexity requires us to develop a suitably detailed theoretical model, one that addresses in particular the fundamental questions surrounding burnout and well-being: why do some people struggle, when others thrive? Can we identify what it is about a workplace that creates distress, or that promotes well-being? We will also continue to develop our ideas as to how best to design and deliver the promising intervention that is supportive supervision: what should we do to minimize harm, and to maximize professional thriving?

So that we have some suitable guiding logic, our formulation of supportive supervision will be developed by defining supportive supervision empirically (i.e. based on research findings), and then by refining and integrating existing theories and models. This will help us to begin to answer the difficult questions in the preceding paragraph, and give us a proper rationale for supervision. Some readers may prefer us to swiftly move on to offering practical suggestions and quick fixes, but an evidence-based approach, as in professional practice in general, requires that we first have a firm theoretical foundation (as depicted in Figure 1.1 in Chapter 1). For instance, a model of supportive supervision will suggest the kind of information that matters most in supervision, the most promising course of action to follow, and how to judge whether progress is being made. But an evidence-based approach also requires research findings, as presented as the step after theory in Figure 1.1. Therefore, in the next chapter we outline the main research evidence on the effectiveness of supportive supervision. In essence, we use theory and research as complementary ways of understanding supportive supervision, both contributing towards our understanding, and guiding our supervision efforts. Also consistent with Figure 1.1, we add information from expert consensus where possible, treating it as a valuable moderating influence.

2. An empirical definition of supportive supervision

In making claims for the value of supervision, we should first explain exactly what we think it is. The original definition (Dawson, 1926) stated that clinical supervision in general had three parts or functions: educational ('formative'), administrative ('normative') and supportive ('restorative'). As set out in Figure 2.1, formative supervision focuses on the professional development of staff members, mainly skill-building and refining competencies. Normative supervision focuses on enhancing quality-control, effectively a management perspective on the workplace issues affecting the supervisee (e.g. managing waiting lists; policy or organizational change issues). Lastly, supportive supervision addresses the well-being of healthcare professionals, seeking to improve their morale and job satisfaction. It does this through protecting workers from excessive stress; by improving their personal coping strategies; and through validation and social support (Kadushin, 1976). Ideally, a supervision session will include attention to all three functions, since they should operate in a mutually beneficial, synergistic way. But there will be occasions when a supervisor will rightly judge that the session should focus on only one of these functions (e.g. to continue working in the supportive mode when the supervisee is distressed following an incident). More recent definitions build on Kadushin (1976). Clinical supervision is:

'a formal process of professional support and learning, which enables individual practitioners to develop knowledge and competence, assume responsibility for their own practice, and enhance consumer protection and safety of care in complex clinical situations' (Department of Health, 1993, p15).

This latter definition was endorsed and further enhanced in an empirically derived definition of clinical supervision:

'The formal provision, by approved supervisors, of a relationship-based education and training that is work-focused and which manages, supports, develops and evaluates the work of designated supervisees. The objectives are primarily: quality control (e.g. 'gate-keeping' and ethical practice); maintaining and facilitating the supervisees' competence and capability; and helping supervisees to work effectively (e.g. promoting quality control and preserving client safety; accepting developing own professional identity; enhancing self-awareness and resilience/effective personal coping with the job; critical reflection lifelong learning skills' (Milne, 2007).

A further revision and refinement extended these defining features to supportive supervision, based on a more recent review of the evidence (Milne & Reiser, 2017). This definition noted that we need to first understand the workplace (i.e. why is it being perceived as challenging by the supervisee?), then encourage the supervisee's adaptive coping with the workplace (e.g. processing emotional issues; seeking social support), in order to try and boost morale, motivation, and professional development. However, in that definition only brief attention was given to the role of supervision in attempting to also improve the workplace, such as working to ensure that supervision takes place regularly (e.g. Buus *et al*, 2011). Although this was the only example of improving the workplace mentioned in the restorative function of supervision by Milne and Reiser (2017), it did nonetheless indicate that seeking to change the workplace system was an appropriate goal of supportive supervision. This 'change agent' perspective assumes that 'the problem' sometimes rests within the healthcare system, rather than within the distressed worker. This perspective simultaneously discourages the supervisee from passively accepting and adapting to an unacceptable situation, or from taking responsibility for an unacceptable work situation. Therefore, this definition of supportive supervision (Milne & Reiser, 2017) went beyond the emphasis in Kadushin's (1976) original definition, and still retained in his later work (Kadushin & Harkness, 2002). Although both definitions included sheltering or protecting the supervisee from workplace stressors ('stress buffering'), the key difference is the active pursuit of organizational change, by the supervisee and/or the supervisor, in the definition by Milne and Reiser (2017). As such a change agent role is a logical possibility, and in some cases even an appropriate goal, we retain this 'change agent' emphasis in this book, suggesting a suitable extension to the definition in Milne and Reiser (2017, p191) to give equal emphasis to organizational change as a primary prevention or innovation strategy. Together with new material suggested by the research literature on restorative supervision reviewed in Chapter 3 (see Table 3.1), this then is our current, empirical definition of 'supportive supervision':

'Supportive clinical supervision addresses supervisees' emotional experience of their workplace, and their personal functioning in that context. It is a formal, case-focused, and intensive relational process, conducted by a trained, suitably experienced, and appropriate supervisor. Specific supervision techniques include problem formulation, coping strategy enhancement, facilitating peer support, and empathic debriefing. The primary mechanisms within supervision that enable these outcomes to be achieved are experiential learning, the supervision alliance, and social support. The main intended outcomes for supervisees are reductions in personal distress and enhanced well-being'.

An extended version of this definition, including also stress prevention and examples, is appended to this chapter. Some of the features that we have attributed to supportive supervision may occur in other forms of supervision, in response to other supervision events (e.g. feeling angry about feedback from a supervisor who is operating in the formative mode), and indeed in quite different activities (e.g. line management; therapy). We also acknowledge that 'experiencing' may occur more powerfully in response to certain events (e.g. a complaint or a physical assault by a patient). We believe that the above tandardiz makes supportive supervision suitably distinctive when it is considered fully, that is, including a combination of goals, content, methods and outcomes. For example, therapy enhances personal coping strategies through methods such as offering guidance and by challenging negative thought processes. But in therapy the goal is to help the patient resolve personal problems, whereas in supervision these methods are designed to improve patient care and work performance (reflecting this old wisdom: 'supervision is of the therapy, not the therapist'). The content of the two activities would also be expected to differ in corresponding ways (i.e. the supervision focus is on the patient or the workplace). There is another important distinction, which distinguishes supportive supervision not only from therapy but also from restorative supervision. This is the role that supportive supervision can play in primary prevention: addressing the workplace stressors experienced by supervisees (e.g. workloads; roles; communication; leadership). We discuss prevention in Chapter 5.

The outcomes of supportive supervision should also differ from therapy (e.g. feeling more valued and engaged at work). Other distinctions are that supervision includes a significant power differential (i.e. whereas therapy is usually optional, supervision is usually mandatory); supervision lasts throughout a career (at least in the NHS in the UK, however not in the US and many other countries); it includes evaluation (though only very minimally within supportive supervision); and supervision is primarily developmental (e.g. supportive or educational, not therapeutic). However, we recognize that the boundaries between such closely related professional activities can easily become blurred, and so they merit careful definition (e.g. in statements of departmental policies and procedures, with ongoing vigilance). The emphasis on vigilance is indicated by the alarmingly high frequency of inadequate, unethical, and harmful supervision reported in one survey (and replicated in a second), featuring multiple boundary violations (Ellis *et al*, 2014).

We are aware that the term 'supportive supervision' has also been used before in relation to developing health services in Africa. The World Health Organization (WHO, 2008) defined it thus:

'Supportive supervision is a process of helping staff to improve their own work performance continuously. It is carried out in a respectful and non-authoritarian way with a focus on using supervisory visits as an opportunity to improve knowledge and skills of health staff. Supportive supervision encourages open, two-way communication, and building team approaches that facilitate problem-solving. It focuses on monitoring performance towards goals, and using data for decision-making, and depends upon regular follow-up with staff to ensure that new tasks are being implemented correctly" (p1).

The associated WHO (2008) 12-item supportive supervision checklist addressed the normative and formative functions of supervision (e.g. problem-solving; data-collection; education), but ironically contained no restorative items. Therefore, although there are studies of the WHO approach that include some restorative element (e.g. supportive comments alongside feedback (McAuliffe *et al*, 2013), our definition of 'supportive supervision' seems to be distinct by virtue of prioritizing the restorative function, as opposed to practicalities such as task assistance (Avortri *et al*, 2019).

If required, greater precision and discrimination can be obtained by studying measurement instruments (e.g. MCSS & SAGE: see the Appendix on page 239 or www.pavpub.com/supportive-clinical-supervision-resources/). For instance, part of the Manchester Clinical Supervision Scale (MCSS) questionnaire concerns supervisees' perceptions of the supervisors' ability to discuss sensitive issues, and to offer support and guidance (White & Winstanley, 2014). In the case of SAGE, the manual that guides users of this observational tool (Milne *et al*, 2011) offers these examples of experiencing:

> *'Supervisee recognizes / identifies / labels own feelings; is aware of emotional or sensory accompaniments to activity (whether in relation to the experience of supervision, or to discussing their work in supervision); discriminating among sensations; regulating or managing emotions (positive or negative ones)'.*

The empirical definition of supportive supervision above examines the three common perspectives on burnout in the wider literature (and in this book): the personal characteristics of healthcare professionals, especially individual differences in the way that people try to cope with these stressors; the workplace as an organizational system, the environmental setting that influences these professionals (especially the inherent stressors); and the manner in which these individuals and environments interact, influencing one another. We realize that some authors define such environmental features as belonging to the normative function of clinical supervision, but in our extended definition we wish to incorporate organizational change within restorative supervision. This is because it overlaps with normative supervision, representing a logical and potentially valuable opportunity for professionals to consider how they can best contribute to more effective workplaces.

3. An integrative model of supportive supervision

A theoretical or scientific model is a valuable guide to the theory and practice of supportive supervision. Such a model requires us to be precise about the factors that we believe to be important, such as stress, coping, social support and burnout. In addition, a conceptual model predicts how such variables relate to one another, indicated on a model diagram by connecting arrows (e.g. indicating that stress does not lead straight to burnout, but first interacts with social support and coping). In this sense, a model helps supervisors understand the underlying structure of supportive supervision and also provides a framework that enables us to formulate why an individual supervisee is experiencing burnout within a specific workplace. In supervision research, a model aids us in integrating a diverse literature (both research studies and reviews of research help to generate hypotheses), deciding what needs to be measured, in making predictions that can be tested, and in interpreting the findings. For example, the 'tandem model' of clinical supervision, to be described shortly, indicates that the supervisor can help the supervisee to cope with an emotional upset by encouraging experiential learning ('experiencing', as described above). A verbatim illustration of the kind of process that would be expected to occur is provided in James *et al* (2004).

However, research and practice can and unfortunately do proceed without this kind of explicit model, which creates profound difficulties, including vagueness about the important variables; absence of definitions; limited understanding of cause and effect; and the impossibility of formulation. To illustrate, an exhaustive review of 144 supervision studies by Ellis *et al* (1996) indicated that only 20% of the studies involved explicit tests of relevant theories. This situation has been likened to assembling an ever-increasing number of bricks (i.e., study findings) without having an architectural plan (i.e., model) to guide the placement of the bricks so as to produce a solid and useful edifice (Barker & Hunsley, 2013). In their review of 25 supervision studies, Barker and Hunsley (2013) judged that only 12 of these studies specified a supervision model, indicating that there was still a fundamental problem with supervision research.

When a model is used to guide research, and it survives repeated testing, it gradually becomes established as a theory. In clinical supervision there are over 50 different models (Simpson-Southward *et al,* 2017), but nothing we can yet describe as a theory. For this reason, in this book we integrate theories from well-established, neighbouring fields, such as coping theory (see Table 2.1). In supportive supervision, we do not even have any evidence-based, testable models. Therefore, given the vital role played by models, in Figure 2.1 we use a diagram to set out our model. We believe that models like ours are a valuable aid to supervision ('nothing as practical as a good theory'), as demonstrated in Table 2.1. We next review the current models, before developing a novel integration that meets our requirements: a suitably detailed, support-specific, testable, and evidence-based model of supportive supervision.

a) Existing supervision models that include support

There are several models concerning organizational behaviour, typically indicating how supervision is thought to work, based on large-sample correlational studies of diverse industrial workers. These represent an example of our strategy of scrutinizing neighbouring literatures, from which extrapolation may be helpful in developing our 'support model'. Therefore, we will integrate them in this chapter, and refer to them throughout the book. In particular, we are interested in popular models that include supervision as a 'support' or 'resource' factor and where supervision methods are specified , especially the Conservation of Resources (COR) model (Hobfoll *et al*, 2018) and the Job Demand-Resources (JD-R) model (Schaufeli & Bakker, 2004).

TABLE 2.1: 'Nothing as practical as a good theory': Practical examples of the importance of theoretical models from the integrative model of supportive supervision

Model or theory	Practical implications for supportive supervisors
Coping theory	■ Understand that the supervisee's distress is best explained by the use of poor coping strategies (especially escape and avoidance-based coping), rather than by a stressful event ■ In particular, look for cognitive distortions (e.g. a self-serving bias) in how the supervisee is appraising the stressful event ■ Encourage the supervisee to access and optimize social support from colleagues (e.g. helpful involvement in peer support groups)
Tandem model	■ Emphasise 'experiencing', while balancing the emphasis on the other modes of experiential learning ■ As the leader, the supervisor must steer the supervision content and process (e.g. helping supervisees reappraise stressful events and improve personal coping strategies) ■ Ensure that your supervision alliance is experienced by the supervisee as a 'safe base', feeling safe to express and discuss doubts, anxieties, incompetence, etc.
Organizational (force-field) theory	■ Educate the supervisee to grasp and manage 'barriers and boosters', especially when involved at the organizational level (e.g. staff support). ■ In turn, ensure that as a supervisor you are 'boosted' by effective support and development arrangements (e.g. mentoring with like-minded colleagues) ■ Encourage managers and other leaders to play their full part (e.g. organizing supervisor training; scheduling preceptorship)
Systems theory (context)	■ Feedback maintains a healthy system, improving effectiveness ■ Monitor how impacts in one part of the supervisee's work affect other area (cause and effect are not one-directional or linear)

Unfortunately, it is rare for supportive supervision to be studied in relation to these models, although there are welcome exceptions. For example, Weigl *et al* (2016) used the COR model and operationalized supervision through two instruments, one being focused on social support from the supervisor through two items from

The Copenhagen Psychosocial Questionnaire (Pejtersen *et al,* 2010): 'How often do you get help and support from your immediate superior?' and 'How often is your superior willing to listen to your work-related problems?'. Answers ranged from 1 = never/hardly ever, up to 5 = always). We will draw on these rare exceptions, as, unlike the bulk of organizational behaviour research, they specify the supervision methods. They also have a second rare quality in this research literature: conceptual clarity (Hobfoll *et al,* 2018). But because these supervision studies are scarce, and the key concepts in these popular models are somewhat opaque, we mostly need to look elsewhere for a suitable model of supportive supervision.

We have only located one explicit model that is entirely devoted to supportive supervision, as we have defined it in Chapter 1, which we will describe shortly (Wallbank & Wonnacott, 2015). However, most general models of clinical supervision include a specific supportive aspect, so we can build on that thinking. An example from nursing is the 'growth and support model' (Faugier, 1992), which utilizes psychoanalytic psychotherapy to suggest good practice guidelines on developing and maintaining a supportive supervision relationship (e.g. the importance of 'working through' supervisees' issues). Similarly, Hawkins and Shohet (2007) drew on psychoanalytic psychotherapy as the basis for a 'process model' of supervision, with attention to supervisees' self-awareness and 'internal processes' (e.g. counter-transference). Although these accounts provide a deep and fascinating perspective, they are not presented as formal theoretical models, they are not supervision-specific, nor are they compatible with an evidence-based or testable approach.

A further model is supervision-specific, in the sense that it has been developed explicitly with supervision in mind (rather than being an extension of therapy to supervision). Prominent ones that include support as a major objective are those outlined by Heron (1991), Proctor (1991), and Wonnacott (2016). Heron (1989) distinguished between 'authoritative' and 'facilitative' aspects of supervision. The authoritative aspect included prescribing what a supervisee should do (e.g. suggesting or recommending actions), informing (e.g. educating), and confronting (e.g. challenging a supervisee statement). In the facilitative mode, a supervisor could offer 'catharsis', enabling the supervisee to discharge feelings; could encourage a 'catalytic' phase, facilitating reflection and problem-solving in the supervisee; or could be 'supportive', by approving, valuing and affirming the worth of the supervisee. The Proctor model (Proctor, 1991), shown in Figure 2.1, highlights the need for supervision to address 'normative', 'formative' and 'restorative' topics in a balanced way, so that these basic functions of supervision are achieved. We have also noted in Figure 2.1 the main roles that correspond with these three functions. For example, when seeking to serve a restorative function according to the Proctor model, the supervisor enacts a 'supporter' or counsellor-like role, using a range of methods to enable emotions to be managed, and to ensure that the supervisee feels supported. All three roles are considered necessary for effective supervision, as measured by the MCSS (Winstanley & White, 2014). Although Proctor (1991) did not follow an evidence-based approach in developing her model (see Chapter 1, Figure 1.1 for a summary of the steps entailed), there is coincidental empirical support from research (Mor Barak *et al*, 2009).

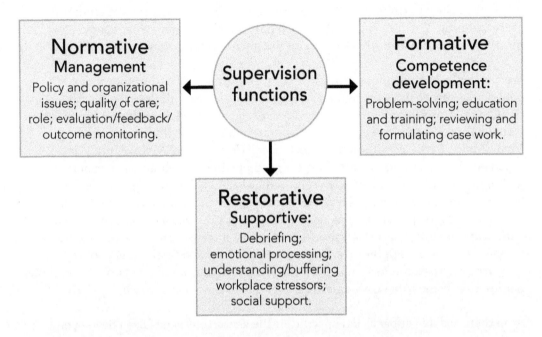

FIGURE 2.1 A summary of 'Proctor's model' (Proctor, 1991), emphasizing the need for supervision to achieve normative, formative, and supportive (restorative) functions

Supportive supervision is intended to be approximately one-third of the supervision agenda within Proctor's model (1991), and a content analysis of 52 supervision models indicated that it was indeed a prominent function (62% of these models identified a restorative function within supervision, compared to 89% of models including a formative function, and 58% a normative function (Simpson-Southward *et al*, 2017). But surveys of supervisors suggest that it plays a significantly smaller role in practice. Kadushin and Harkness (2002) reported a survey of over 500 Social Workers in the USA, which indicated that supportive supervision represented 24% of the supervision session (formative was most prominent, at 44% of the session, followed by normative at 32%). A more recent USA survey (Dorsey *et al*, 2017) indicated that only 8% of sessions were concerned with supportive supervision, with much greater emphasis on the formative function (70%), followed by the normative aspect (13%: presumably the remaining proportion was taken up with other kinds of discussion).

In stark contrast, supportive supervision is the entire agenda within the '4x4x4' model. Originally developed by social worker Tony Morrison (Morrison, 2005), it forms the basis for the single most extensive investigation and application of restorative supervision, which is with midwives in England (Wallbank & Wonnacott, 2015). It has been most recently and fully described by Wonnacott (2016). This 4x4x4 model is actually more of a practical framework, or a list of suggested supervision topics, than a formal theoretical model. But it usefully extends Proctor's model (1991) by adding 'mediation' with partner organizations to the restorative, formative, and normative functions. The 4x4x4 model also includes the requirement to give due attention to the four main stakeholders in supervision (i.e. clients, staff, the employing organization and partner organizations), and the four elements of Kolb's (1984) experiential learning cycle (i.e. the process by which the supervision functions are achieved: reflecting, conceptualizing, experiencing and planning). The aim of this 4x4x4 model is to emphasize the need to pay equal attention to all four functions, especially to accord restorative supervision overdue attention. The model also alerts us to potentially unhelpful situations, such as the provision of restorative supervision by managers (usually unhelpful because organizational issues may dominate supervision; and because supervisees may be reluctant to reveal their support needs to their boss).

In this book we appreciate the range of topics and functions within these support models, and value the belated attention to supporting staff systematically. To their credit, these models also treat supervision as a distinct professional specialization, rather than simply extending therapy models to supervision, and they undoubtedly include many useful ideas and valuable suggestions. However, on a more critical note we have to state that they are not what we require, as they have not been set out as formal theoretical models, and they also lack an evidence base. In keeping with our evidence-based origins, a suitable restorative model needs to have significant research support, and meet other tests of a good model, such as precisely articulating the factors that are of most interest (e.g. appraisal of stressors; emotional functioning; maladaptive personal coping strategies). However, thankfully, there are general models that subsume supportive supervision and which do pass these tests (e.g. Mor Barak *et al*, 2009; White & Winstanley, 2010). Therefore, our plan is to combine the best available models in order to create an integrative model of supportive supervision.

Among the many general models available, we begin with one that can help us to create a complete framework for supportive supervision as a complex intervention, namely the all-embracing systems model, which we will outline prior to describing the subsystems that are needed to complete our integrative model of supportive supervision. Each of these subsystems are also good models, with a sound evidence base, and a sufficiently detailed specification (e.g. coping theory). Therefore, our hybrid model is an original composite of previously disconnected systems, an integrative theoretical model that specifies the parts (variables) and processes needed to explain and to provide supportive supervision, as defined in Chapter 1. That we have to assemble it from separate theories is unfortunate, but it is not itself unusual or inherently problematic (see, for example, Mor Barak, 2009). It is our hope that future research will find our model helpful, and will refine it as necessary.

b) Systems theory: an overall framework

In order to provide a framework for this integration, systems theory will help us understand the complex nature of supportive supervision, especially the notion of multiple layers of mutual influence, as depicted in Figure 2.2. Each layer should affect how we understand every other layer, leading to a comprehensive awareness of what is going on within supportive supervision. Systems theory offers a comprehensive framework, in addition to some key assumptions about how a complex intervention such as supervision can best be understood. Although originating in biology, von Bertalanffy (1968) considered how systems theory could enhance the way we study human behaviour. To illustrate, he defined an open system as one that exchanges matter and energy with its environment, as in how a supervisor interacts with a supervisee within a context (as depicted in Figure 2.2). Subsystems are the parts that make up a larger system, and the ones that we will be describing behave just like open systems, albeit operating at different levels. For example, the supervisor shown in Figure 2.2 will be described shortly as utilizing coping strategies to manage interactions with the supervisee, involving exchanging words, feelings and actions in order to help maintain a stable interpersonal system.

Subsequently, Bronfenbrenner (1979) continued to promote open systems thinking, labelled as an 'ecological system', which became the best-established theory within the health field. According to this ecological reasoning, individuals are regarded as being embedded within successive and interacting systems, organized as a hierarchy of sub-systems and super-systems. For our purposes, these systems include:

1. The 'intrapersonal system' (our most immediate or proximal system, such as a supervisee's personal coping strategies)

2. The 'interpersonal' system (e.g. the supervision relationship)

3. The 'organizational' system (e.g. the workplace unit, including colleagues, patients, and physical resources)

4. The 'contextual' system (the most distal system, being the wider environment, including national organizations and cultural influences, such as national standards for professional practice, or the law of the land).

We illustrate these systems in Figure 2.2, using successive layers to help us understand how these dynamic interactions shape supervision. These systems are seen as inter-connected, exerting mutual influence, as in the interactions that occur between supervisor and supervisee. Other features of an ecological system, as described by Bronfenbrenner (1979), include the notion of 'synergy', namely that the whole is greater than the sum of the parts (i.e. systems are dynamic, having emergent, unpredictable properties, as in the supervisee's experiential learning and growing confidence); that there exist many cause-effect relationships, including non-linear, circular causal pathways; and that feedback enables the system to remain stable (homeostasis). In this sense, systemic thinking is holistic, dynamic, and complex.

Bronfenbrenner's (1979) theory of ecological systems was initially applied to help understand childhood development, but it has subsequently enjoyed such acceptance that we can now regard this kind of systemic thinking as the natural, accepted way to understand complex human relationships (as in Family Therapy). Therefore, it is not surprising to find that this theory has also been applied to clinical supervision, where it is the foundation of the systemic model of supervision (e.g. Rigazzio-DiGilio *et al*, 1997), as well as a more general systems approach to supervision (e.g. Holloway, 2014). More recent accounts have extended Bronfenbrenner's (1979) theory, in the form of 'dynamic systems theory', which was taken from physics to better understand human development (e.g. how we learn to walk (Smith and Thelen, 2003)), emphasising how such complex systems are self-organizing and have the capacity to create adaptive change (i.e. such systems can create improved processes, behaviours, or outcomes through their own activity). We believe that dynamic systems theory helpfully elaborates and verifies the earlier systems models, such as Bronfenbrenner's.

In this book, we include the general systems model (including dynamic systems theory) as the super-system that unifies the subsystems that follow, as well as to embrace these concepts as part of our definition of supervision. The definition itself affirmed that supervision should take due account of the interpersonal and organizational systems, when addressing the supervisee's emotional functioning, working towards a balanced system (homeostasis). The integration of systems concepts and theory is our first example of what we mean by 'evidence-based' supportive supervision, because we are using relevant theory as one form of evidence. As outlined in Chapter 1, a second type of evidence that we value is expert consensus, and we note here that the Roth and Pilling (2008) competencies framework includes two relevant generic supervision competencies. The first states that supervisors should demonstrate the 'Ability to take into account the organizational context for supervision'; the second that they should have the 'Ability to use a range of methods to give accurate and constructive feedback' (being necessary for maintaining the balance in a system). Models of organizational behaviour in particular emphasise the workplace system and its complex, dynamic nature (e.g. Hobfoll *et al,* 2018; Schaufeli & Bakker, 2004). These models include the 'job demands' (e.g. work overload; conflict with colleagues) and the 'resources' that can enable workers to cope with these demands (e.g. social support; supervision; participative decision-making). Consistent with systems theory, these models also recognize the complex interactions that can arise between such variables, naming them 'positive gain spirals' and 'negative loss spirals'. This is also consistent with coping theory, where the terms 'virtuous cycle' and 'vicious cycle' are used (see below). The key point is that the variables within these models operate in a cumulative, iterative way, so that they change with repeated cycles (e.g. an adaptive coping strategy becomes more frequent or powerful following repeated use, steadily reducing the strength of the associated distress).

In Chapter 3 we will consider our third main form of evidence, when we review the most relevant research studies. Before this, however, we will continue to build our integrative model of supportive supervision by adding complementary theories for the sub-systems included in Figure 2.2.

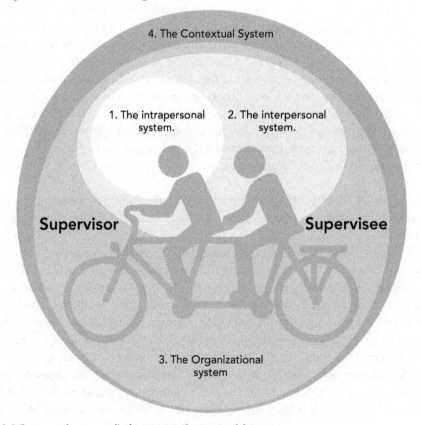

FIGURE 2.2 Systems theory applied to supportive supervision

In summary, systems thinking provides us with an overall framework that enables us to make sense of a concept as complex as supportive supervision. But within this all-embracing systems framework, we also need to record how the subsystems work to enable us to provide the clear guidance needed by supervisors and others in order to intervene skilfully. To paraphrase von Bertalanffy (1968, p35), 'the proper study of supportive supervision lies in the order and organization of its parts and processes, at all levels of the system' (we have substituted 'supportive supervision' for 'biology'). Following this reasoning, we will detail what we believe to be the parts and processes of supportive supervision, starting at the smallest 'intrapersonal' sub-system (personal coping strategies) and working outwards, layer-by-layer, to the contextual system. We should add that, in depicting our subsystems in Figure 2.2, we are following systems theory by defining the boundaries between these subsystems in a functional way. That is, we are drawing boundaries at the places where each unit (subsystem) effectively begins and ends, representing a coherent entity for our practical purposes.

c) The intrapersonal system – a theory of how we cope with our emotions

By contrast with the supervision-specific models outlined earlier, the theory of individual human coping has an extensive research pedigree (Folkman & Nathan, 2010), with highly relevant applications to healthcare settings internationally, dating back decades (e.g. Lazarus & Folkman, 1984). Although rarely linked explicitly to restorative supervision (for welcome exceptions see: Wallbank, 2013; and Weigl *et al*, 2016), the coping model has a clear and immediate relevance, together with a record of successful extension to diverse human situations. For instance, it is recognized as 'a key personal resource' within the field of organizational behaviour (Weigl *et al*, 2010, p143). In addition, coping theory (enhanced to primarily address emotional reactions, to fit our definition) provides the necessary detail to guide supervisors on the intrapersonal system (e.g. how to understand how people respond differently to workplace stressors). For these reasons we will use the coping model to understand how healthcare professionals function at work. The representation of the intrapersonal system in Figure 2.2 places the supervisee in a central position in the diagram to emphasise that it is the supervisee's coping that is a major focus in supportive supervision. We will return to the coping model in Chapter 4, where we consider how individuals contribute to their own functioning, as well as to the functioning of their work system. Before this, we need to identify something equally helpful in relation to the 'interpersonal' system that is also illustrated in Figure 2.2. This is how we might best understand how people interact, in relation to supportive supervision.

d) The interpersonal system – the tandem model

The tandem model of supervision (Milne & James, 2005) is a graphical metaphor for the evidence-based clinical supervision programme (Milne, 2018), and like any model it makes a number of key assumptions. Firstly, the supervisor is regarded as a leader, and so occupies the front seat of the tandem, where all the controls are located (steering, brakes and gears). As the leader, the supervisor is ultimately responsible for the direction and pace of supervision (e.g. through managing the supervision agenda). This assumption of supervisor authority is fundamental to all that follows, and is one reason we authors disapprove of the practice of 'peer supervision' (Martin *et al,* 2017). In supportive supervision, leadership has a restorative style.

As leadership implies that others follow, it is understood that riding a tandem is a highly interactive process, where the supervisor and supervisee influence one another's behaviour in a mutually beneficial, transactional process. This includes practical 'task assistance' that is managed by the supervisor, including instruction, co-working, and problem-solving discussions (according to the review by Mor Barak *et al,* 2009). But it also entails supervisee involvement in creating and sustaining a working alliance, a collaborative bond enshrined in expert consensus statements (e.g. Roth & Pilling, 2008; APA, 2015). We utilize these frameworks to define the supervision alliance, and to detail how the supervisor should strive to build and maintain the alliance. The supervisor should fundamentally seek to establish a collaborative bond. This is based on mutual caring and engagement, and working towards agreed goals (Roth & Pilling, 2008). In this relationship building effort, certain additional qualities are considered essential by experts, including genuineness (openness and honesty), supportiveness, empathy, warmth, encouragement, validation, and the creation of a 'safe base' (i.e. the supervisee feels respected, secure and valued; the supervisor is considered responsive). The supervisory relationship also benefits from the supervisor taking a professional approach to supervision, emphasising its importance and instilling confidence in the supervisee (Barak *et al,* 2009). Therapy research supports this conception of the supervision relationship (Beinart, 2014), as does organizational behaviour research ('relational' leadership works best (Cummings *et al,* 2010)). In Chapter 6 we will describe how supportive supervisors, as leaders, can build and sustain this alliance.

As a professional role, enacting the alliance within supportive supervision entails playing the role of a supporter, caring ally, or counsellor (with suitable qualifications). In particular, the most suitable counselling model is the 'person-centered' style of counselling, as developed by Carl Rogers (1957). Our qualifications are that, unlike person-centered counselling, the supervisor is directive (e.g. giving feedback and expressing approval, rather than being non-directive); provides some forms of social support; and focuses on the supervisees' work (rather than their personal or private issues).

To date, the tandem model has explicitly included the alliance and restorative supervision, but they have only played a minor role, overshadowed by attention to the formative function of supervision. For example, although the tandem model emphasized a 'balanced experiential learning cycle, especially addressing affective and restorative aspects of supervision... [and] ... support systems' (Milne, 2018, p79), the instruments used to measure the tandem model only included one or two restorative items (e.g. 'relating' and 'experiencing' in the 23-item observational tool SAGE, as appended to this chapter). Also, although latterly much more attention was given to the alliance and to restorative supervision in the manual for training supervisors (Milne & Reiser, 2017), it remained a secondary focus (i.e. they were two of six guidelines for the practice of evidence-based clinical supervision). Therefore, to our knowledge this book provides the first use of the tandem model (including the evidence-based clinical supervision approach) that is exclusively focused on supportive supervision. This presents a new challenge to the tandem model, since many of the issues that supportive supervision must address are not explicit within the model, especially personal distress (e.g. how burnout should be addressed). However, when examined against the overall restorative agenda, we believe that the tandem model remains entirely relevant. To illustrate, there is nothing in the guideline on restorative supervision, in our manual (Milne & Reiser, 2017), that cannot be addressed through applying the tandem model (and addressed just as readily as a formative issue). Rather, recommendations within this guideline, such as 'encourage emotional processing and personal growth', simply indicate a different focus, based on the same supervisory methods. An example would be the use of the supervision alliance to facilitate the supervisee's experiencing of emotions or the use of listening and discussion to facilitate experimenting. Therefore, we believe that the tandem needs to take a different track in order to cover many restorative issues. But to cover all such issues we still need to factor in organizational and contextual influences on burnout and psychological well-being.

e) The organizational (environmental) system

In this book, the healthcare workplace is the organizational system of interest, made up most obviously by the facilities within a unit or service (e.g. built environment; equipment) and the individuals within the system (patients, administrators, managers, professional staff, etc). It also includes the supporting departments (e.g. HR: Human Resources; OH: Occupational Health), the national or international organizations that govern the local units, together with related subsystems (e.g. service purchasers; the surrounding community). Such individuals and groups have the power to help or hinder whether or not supervision occurs within a system, and to influence the form that it takes (Buus *et al,* 2011; Gonge & Buus, 2010). For example, the style of leadership and the availability of social support are critical determinants identified within the organizational behaviour literature (e.g. Hobfoll *et al,* 2018; Schaufeli & Bakker, 2004). In addition to people, the environmental system includes moderating factors, such as the organizational culture, ambience, or atmosphere. This is the feeling one gets about working in a place (e.g. the flow of information; the tone of personal interactions: see Holloway, 2014, for a detailed account). We discuss the organizational system again in Chapter 5.

To illustrate social support, here are some examples provided to us by a senior female supervisor: the flexibility shown by managers in aiding work-life balancing (e.g. rota changes); colleagues providing information on interesting jobs, together with words of encouragement towards career progression (and words of caution – 'not wise to apply'); the availability of 'mentors' in relation to an initial professional training programme; encouragement for a trainee to mix with the team during the lunch break; seeking support and guidance over tricky clinical decisions from the multidisciplinary team; allowing staff members time during work to attend counselling sessions to aid their well-being. These examples are underlined by negative alternatives: lack of compassion for difficult personal circumstances (e.g. family member hospitalized), in that no interest shown (so left feeling isolated); not feeling welcomed into a supervision group (feel like an interloper; feel more could have been done to prepare group).

In Figure 2.2 we have depicted the tandem as overlapping with this organizational system, including social support. Whereas the supervisor and supervisee represent the interpersonal system in our support model (especially through their supervision alliance), their tandem journey together entails interacting with the organizational system at every stage. For example, the supervisee's progress along their developmental path will include junctions involving colleagues and patients, and negotiating the social support terrain. Social support plays a vital role within supervision (e.g. boosting coping skills and building confidence (Barak *et al,* 2009), but supervision can also empower supervisees to gain and reciprocate support within the workplace, especially from peers. As we proceed out from the organizational system, we should also factor in the wider context.

f) The contextual system

By 'context' we refer to the more distant factors that influence our organizational unit or service, such as the built environment (roads; cities), politics (e.g. professional groups; government policies), resources (e.g. national funding streams), society (e.g. the local community; professional bodies, cultural context of work), national and international organizations (e.g. the NHS), and technological developments (e.g. new assessment equipment and treatments). As shown in Figure 2.1, these contextual factors act as moderating influences on the proximal sub-systems, such as the workplace. This definition is consistent with the 'systems-contextual' thinking about healthcare (Beidas & Kendall, 2010). An example of the moderating effect of national policies can be found within the Improving Access to Psychological Therapies (IAPT) programme in England (e.g. payment by results). Recall from Chapter 1 such challenging workplace stressors and high levels of burnout, associated with IAPT, driven by an NHS agenda. Consistent with this business-like context, although staff well-being is mentioned in the IAPT supervision guidelines (Turpin & Wheeler, 2011), restorative supervision is not included as one of the functions of clinical supervision. The cultural context of work is further explored in the following vignette.

Vignette

Cultures differ in their attitude toward work, with important implications for work-related stress and burnout. Even in cultures that share many common features, such as the US and the UK, there are distinctly different attitudes towards the role of work and work-life balance. For example, in the US it would be extremely rare to take four weeks of vacation every year, but this is an accepted practice in the UK and other European countries. Studies in Japan into 'Karoshi' ('death due to overwork') give a good example of the power of contextual systems and culturally determined factors. As a result of studies indicating that life expectancy for males in Japan at 78.4 years was considerably lower than for females (at 85.3 years years: Health and Welfare Statistics Association, 2004), the Japanese government convened a taskforce to review the effects of overwork on mortality and morbidity and to make recommendations as to preventative measures to reduce Karoshi. A second systemic factor driving this change was a series of Supreme Court decisions granting compensation for work-related illness in Japan. The taskforce reviewed expert evidence, leading to the explicit recognition of a causal link between overwork and illness. This resulted in a comprehensive industrial health programme designed to prevent Karoshi, by addressing the problem at several levels (including government, employers, labour unions, and individual employees). Recommendations at the government level included shorter working hours, longer paid holidays, a nationally subsidized system for occupational health examinations, in addition to strengthening preventive medical care. Recommendations at the employer level of the system included limiting overtime, improving participation in medical exams, and creating a more comfortable work environment. Recommendations at the individual level included recognizing fatigue and practicing prevention.

Despite this commendable systemic approach, it appears that the problem continues to be deeply embedded within Japanese culture. In 2017, Reuters reported on the death from heart failure of a 31-year-old female journalist, who had worked 159 hours of overtime in the month before her death. In this case, the overwork culture appears to continue to be part of the Japanese context, a 'super-system' that powerfully influences workers and their well-being. It should be noted that the overwork culture is certainly not restricted to Japan, as the United States also struggles with it, particularly in the context of Silicon Valley, a culture that prizes long work hours and immediate availability on email and social media in its employees, even when they are not at work.

4. Summary

We now have the necessary conceptual basis for a new, integrative model of supportive supervision, which we christen the 'support model', one that can withstand the main tests of a model (Milne & James, 2005). In particular, this new model is theoretically-grounded, evidence-based, internally consistent, elaborated (a detailed specification), testable, and has clear practical advantages over competing models. In place of the plethora of 'murky' definitions (Avortri *et al*, 2019), it also illuminates the key parts of supportive supervision, allowing us to better answer the question we raised at the start of the chapter: what should we do to minimize harm, and to maximize professional thriving? According to the support model, to succeed we need to: attend to the contextual and organizational systems, to protect workers from excessive stress (e.g. Karoshi) and to ensure that communication and leadership is effective (including goals, roles and feedback); develop social support at work (e.g. peer support groups; informal social support; the supervision alliance); and enhance supervisees' personal coping strategies (e.g. empathic debriefing to improve relationships). There is already some research evidence behind these interventions (e.g. Mor Barak *et al*, 2009), and also strong endorsement for the support model from expert consensus statements (especially the vital role of the supervision alliance (Roth & Pilling, 2008; APA, 2015; Falender *et al*, 2004)). The support model is also consistent with popular organizational behaviour models (e.g. Hobfoll *et al*, 2018; Schaufeli & Bakker, 2004; Weigl, 2016). Within supervision practice the support model helps us to better understand the causes of supervisees' distress, better formulate an action plan, more precisely judge whether progress is being made, and know the kinds of instruments that would furnish the most appropriate feedback. But we should also test the support model against the best available research on supportive supervision, the focus of the next chapter.

Chapter appendix: The full empirical definition of supportive clinical supervision

Supportive clinical supervision addresses supervisees' emotional experience of their work (including supervision), especially in relation to their workplace (e.g. work overload; staff relationships and morale; leadership), and their personal functioning in that context (burnout, well-being, personal growth, morale and job satisfaction). It is a formal, case-focused, and intensive relational process, conducted with due authority by a trained, suitably experienced, and appropriate supervisor (e.g. skilled in the type of work that is being supervised). Specific supervision techniques include coping strategy enhancement, advice and guidance, facilitating peer support, challenging thinking processes, feedback, debriefing (e.g. gaining perspective; emotional ventilation: expressing concerns), problem formulation (e.g. interpersonal problems), processing troublesome emotions (e.g. by discussing and clarifying feelings), plus empathy, encouragement, and validation. The main intended outcomes for supervisees are reductions in personal distress (e.g. less burnout, anxiety, depression), enhanced well-being, confidence, and personal growth, as well as improved morale (better cooperation; trust; relationships with colleagues), job satisfaction, and job commitment (to employing organization and to own profession). Additionally, supportive supervision sometimes attempts to improve the workplace, either directly, through the actions of the supervisor (e.g. liaising with service managers), or indirectly, through guiding and empowering the supervisee (e.g. jointly formulating environmental stressors; discussing and enacting plans to reduce stressors). The primary experiential learning mechanism within supervision that enables these outcomes to be achieved is engagement in the 'experiencing' mode (i.e. increased self-awareness; better management of emotional experiences (Kolb, 1984; 2014)). The primary relational mechanisms are the supervision alliance and the provision and receipt of social support (emotional, practical, informational, and companionship support, from the supervisor and from peers). Supportive supervision may take place as a discrete, distinctive intervention (individually or in group formats), or more commonly will form part of general clinical supervision (or related activities, such as mentoring or preceptorship), complementing the formative and normative parts. Supportive supervision can be measured by questionnaire (e.g. The Manchester Clinical Supervision Scale: MCSS, White & Winstanley, 2014) and by direct observation (e.g. Supervision: Adherence and Guidance Evaluation: SAGE, Milne *et al*, 2011).

Chapter 3: Research on Supportive Supervision

1. Introduction

Supportive supervision has long been recognized and promoted across the health and social care professions (e.g. Craik, 1988; Kadushin, 1976; Proctor, 1991), but research studies have only recently begun to appear. How then can we build a research foundation for supportive supervision? Clinical supervision in general has a notoriously weak empirical basis (Ellis & Ladany, 1997), so what might we do to complement the theoretical foundations (Chapter 2) and expert consensus statements? As noted in Chapter 1, in order to create an evidence-based approach, we need to:

- **discriminate,** by focusing on the small seam of studies that are 'good enough' (i.e. plausible and interpretable), rather than exclusively considering the most rigorous studies

- **extrapolate,** by bolstering this seam of good research with high-quality studies conducted in neighbouring literatures

- **diversify,** by judging the success of supervision in relation to multiple outcomes (some probably negative).

In the past, these coping strategies have allowed us to define a sound, evidence-based approach to clinical supervision in general (Milne & Reiser, 2017), one that has gained some acceptance in both scientific and professional circles (e.g. our review approach by Gosselin *et al*, 2015; our supervision guidelines by supervisors (Milne & Dunkerley, 2010)). Contrast this with approaches that find nothing by either sampling too narrowly from the available research (e.g. Pollock *et al*, 2017), or by sampling too exclusively (e.g. Alfonsson *et al*, 2018).

Therefore, in this chapter we will conduct a literature review based on sampling more broadly and inclusively, with the objective of building a plausible research foundation for supportive supervision. We will supplement this literature review by also extrapolating from high-quality research within neighbouring literatures. In addition, this chapter will consider the wide range of supervision outcomes, listing the positive and the negative effects. We will attempt to map these outcomes onto the support model developed in the last chapter (an empirical test of the model); we also offer a critical review of research and outline the action implications.

2. The multiple outcomes of supportive supervision

Although the widely accepted purpose of supervision is 'to promote safe and effective clinical practice' (Milne & Watkins, 2014, p7), most researchers ignore the 'safe' aspect and concentrate instead on the clinical and other intended effects, even when citing this overall purpose (e.g. Alfonsson *et al*, 2018). But safe clinical practice is an essential part of healthcare, and so merits proper attention. Its importance is indicated by the Hippocratic oath taken by physicians ('I will abstain from all intentional wrong-doing and harm'). More dramatically, the tragic consequences of harmful care are evident in healthcare scandals internationally (e.g. Department of Health, 2016; Department of Veterans Affairs, 2014). And although supportive supervision is a means of reducing such harm, and of promoting safe care, we also have to acknowledge that supervision can itself cause significant harm (Ellis *et al*, 2014). We should not be too surprised by this finding, as complex interventions into complex environments can cause unintended harm and other side effects (Medical Research Council, 2000). This is a truth exemplified by ecology, and by the systems theory that forms part of our support model (Chapter 2). Our logic is that, just as supported staff are more likely to support their patients (according to social exchange theory (Blau 1964)), unsupported or harmed staff may be more likely to harm their patients. In this way, among other things, we use our sample of research studies to assess the concern that "the deleterious effects of harmful supervision on supervisees may parallel the detrimental effects of harmful therapy to clients" (Ellis *et al*, 2014, p433). This neglected angle (safe clinical practice, on the basis of caring for the clinician) will strengthen the guidance that we are able to offer in this book, and will hopefully complement the theoretical understanding of supportive supervision that we developed in Chapter 2.

In addition to considering the likelihood of harm, we also need to recognize that supportive supervision has multiple intended outcomes associated with safe practice, involving multiple participants, practising in diverse workplace settings. To illustrate, a review based on 27 studies and including a total sample of over 10,000 social and healthcare staff (Mor Barak *et al*, 2009), cited the positive outcomes of supervision for staff (the supervisees), including personal well-being, job satisfaction, and empowerment (e.g. sense of competence and personal accomplishment). Mor Barak *et al* (2009) also reported reductions in negative outcomes (e.g. job stress, anxiety, depression, and burnout).

> **Vignette**
>
> Another way in which things can go wrong is when supervision is omitted, especially when it is an essential part of initial professional training. In one example, a supervisee turned up at work to find a junior colleague in distress: she was due to see a client in the next hour, but her supervisor had failed to appear, so she felt totally unprepared. As she was new to the clinical speciality, the junior supervisee had no real idea what she should do with this client, and was understandably panicking. By contrast, the senior supervisee had experience in this line of work, so offered some suggestions, as there was no other help available. This lowered the junior supervisee's distress, and helped her to see her client as planned. In a second example, the supervisee avoided supervision altogether, despite repeated tactful efforts to engage him in supervision. He appeared to take the view that it was unnecessary, as he was completing his training with an 'elective' placement, and felt confident in his abilities. In both examples there was a real risk of harm to the patients concerned. But the training systems behind these examples were also failing, and they were duly alerted. Thankfully corrective actions were taken, in that the absent supervisor was ultimately fired from his post, and the absent supervisee was allocated to a different placement.

3. Research review

We now summarize the 25 quantitative studies that we were able to locate that met our inclusion criteria. We located research through electronic searching, from suggestions made by supervision experts, and through references within the located literature (ancestry). Our inclusion criteria were that studies:

- were published in the past 20 years (i.e. from 1999–2019)

- were published in peer-reviewed scientific journals, in English

- included healthcare workers (clinicians) in the sample

- specified at least one supportive supervision method (as stated in the definition of supportive supervision in Chapter 1, or otherwise were clearly evaluating restorative supervision, as defined in Chapter 1)

- used a support-related instrument or objective evaluation procedure, one that included a relevant quantitative outcome (e.g. MCSS: Winstanley & White, 2014)

- were naturalistic (studies of existing staff and services, as opposed to researcher-contrived 'laboratory' experiments); and that

- demonstrated that supportive supervision was mostly effective or positive (it mainly achieved or was positively correlated with its intended purpose, such as reduced burnout or increased job satisfaction, though there may also be some negative findings, such as causing harm or aggravating the situation). There was no restriction on research designs, save that they provided interpretable findings and were at least partly quantitative.

These are conventional inclusion criteria for a review, with the exception of the last one: excluding studies of ineffective supervision (or those with negative outcomes). We took this decision in keeping with the logic of the 'best-evidence synthesis (BES)' method (Petticrew & Roberts, 2006; Slavin, 1995). The BES logic is that, in a field with a weak research base, focusing on effective interventions can answer pressing pragmatic questions about what works, providing some valuable practical guidance in the short term. This strategy enables us to write this book and offer advice, but we fully recognize that the BES approach would be inappropriate as a way of judging the status of the whole literature on supportive supervision. Although we will not include ineffective supervision interventions in our research review sample (e.g. Osman *et al*, 2019), we will carefully note any negative findings associated with the sampled studies, and consider what they have to tell us about supportive supervision. We will also study the results of more inclusive literature reviews, alongside ineffective supervision interventions or analyses (e.g. surveys of harmful or abusive supervision (Ellis *et al*, 2014; Mackay *et al*, 2017)). In this way, we will try to generate an accurate and balanced list of the negative, unintended effects associated with supportive supervision. However, we do not intend to conduct the typical BES review, dominated by quantitative details. This is because the available studies lend themselves better to a largely descriptive summary or 'qualitative overview'. In this description, we nonetheless aim to extract the essential information that we need to evaluate supportive supervision as best we can. In the strongest tradition of healthcare evaluation, we take the essence to be information on the structure, process and outcome (SPO) of supervision (Donabedian, 1988). 'Structure' data include the time and other resources used in providing supervision, 'process' refers to what was done in the name of supervision (the methods used), while 'outcome' concerns the obtained results (Table 3.1 provides examples). We also attend to the research context through adopting a naturalistic inclusion criterion, and by noting evidence of contextual factors as moderating influences. These features make our approach compatible with 'realist-informed inquiry', which can be helpful in explaining how complex interventions succeed under naturalistic conditions (Rycroft-Malone *et al*, 2018).

Narrative review of studies of supportive supervision

We next review the 25 included studies chronologically, using a narrative, descriptive style. The questions we plan to address concern the methods used within supportive supervision and their effectiveness plus any side-effects or indications of harm. We will also summarize the participants and study contexts (e.g. settings; professional groups), alongside a consideration of the validity of the studies (the research methodology).

The oldest study in our review was conducted by Berg and Hallberg (1999). They used questionnaires within their pre-post research design to evaluate the effectiveness of group supervision for 22 psychiatric nurses. The supervision sessions lasted for three hours every fortnight for a year, and focused on the participating nurses' patients. The most explicit supportive aspects of this 'systematic' approach to supervision was that each nurse described the kind of feelings that the patient evoked, and the quality of their relationship. The results indicated that supervision significantly improved creativity at work, as well as the organizational climate (more trust, fewer conflicts), but did not quite achieve significance in relation to perceived strain ($p<0.08$). There were few signs of an adverse reaction to supervision, though some of the nurses perceived problems or did not appear to benefit on some of the measured aspects. For instance, after twelve months of supervision five of the seven nurses who responded to the question: statement 'Supervision has increased tensions in the team' agreed that this had happened. On a personal level, five of the 19 nurses who replied to the item 'Supervision has resulted in my personally feeling better in my work' indicated that they were uncertain after six months of supervision (this improved to 16 of 18 nurses reporting feeling better after 12 months). As acknowledged by Berg and Hallberg (1999), this pre-post research design does not rule out other possible explanations for their findings, so caution is warranted in interpreting their study and others with the same design.

Positive findings were also obtained for supportive supervision in a correlational study involving 201 mental health nurses who worked within one large English NHS Trust, a response rate equivalent to 30% of the Trust's registered nursing workforce (Bowles & Young, 1999). Of these, 161 nurses were currently actively engaged in clinical supervision. Using an ad hoc, 21-item questionnaire to measure the normative, formative and restorative functions of supervision, comparisons were made between the 161 nurses' perceptions of the supervision that they received. This survey indicated that relatively high ratings were given for questionnaire items such as 'Supervision makes me feel more supported in my practice', and 'Supervision has helped me to cope with difficult situations'. However, some items indicated that supervision had had a minimal effect. Among the lowest rated items was 'Clinical supervision reduces my work-related stress', though it still received the equivalent of 68% endorsement (the highest rating was 81%, for the item 'Clinical supervision has helped me look more objectively at my work'). Overall, the supportive aspect of supervision was endorsed as much as the other functions.

However, we should note that the questionnaire developed by Bowles & Young (1999) only included positively phrased items, which may have reduced the likelihood of detecting harm or other negative outcomes (this is a recurring problem with the questionnaires in this review). This possibility is increased by the finding that only a minority of participating staff had a supervision contract, which would normally spell out the relationship boundaries. Also, their study was correlational, making valid causal inferences impossible. Another type of research design that does allow inferences about the effect of supervision to be drawn is the 'small n' or 'n=1' methodology (Shadish *et al,* 2002). Although the small number of participants means that external validity is low (i.e. very limited generalizability to other healthcare staff is possible), this design is exceptionally strong with respect to judging whether supervision caused the obtained outcomes (i.e. high internal validity). With colleagues, we evaluated whether one supervisor's general CBT supervision led to observable outcomes for the three supervisees (all mental health nurses (Milne & Westerman, 2001)). A supervision manual and observational instrument guided the supervision, and among the content were several specific supportive supervision items (e.g. 'supporting', 'self-disclosure', and 'feedback' this manual was the basis for Milne & Reiser, 2017). The effectiveness evaluation of supervision was through direct observation, using audio-tape recordings of supervision, and also included ratings of the supervisees' satisfaction with supervision. The results indicated that the supervisor was highly supportive throughout the eight-month longitudinal study (e.g. only one of the 16 items that was observed, the item 'listening', was more frequently observed than 'supporting'). The observational tool also studied the supervisees' reactions to the 30 hours of supervision that took place during this eight-month period, and the most relevant item, 'experiencing', was also the second most frequently observed. Perhaps this strongly supportive supervision explains why the supervisee satisfaction ratings were also very high. Four other n=1 studies have produced similar findings, indicating also that supervisors could be trained to provide supportive supervision through a consultancy approach ('supervision-of-supervision': see Milne, 2018, for a summary).

Another study, which belongs in this select group explicitly addressing supportive supervision, was conducted with 569 nurses (supervisees) in Finland by Hyrkas (2005, p 552), who concluded from her cross-sectional, questionnaire-based analysis that:

> "...the findings of this study demonstrate that efficient clinical supervision is related to lower burnout, and inefficient supervision is related to increasing job dissatisfaction in mental health and psychiatric health care professionals".

Also in Scandinavia, Begat and Severinsson (2006) reflected on three of their correlational studies, involving a total sample of over 250 Norwegian nurses (we count all three in our review total of 22 studies). Their findings indicated that these nurses became more satisfied with their workplace following supervision in that, overall, they reported reduced anxiety, less physical symptoms and fewer feelings of not being in control. However, a small number of these nurses still reported physical symptoms and anxiety, and feelings of not being in control. This was associated with concentration difficulties and sleep problems; and we note that the worst problems occurred in those receiving the least supervision. However, as with the above studies, these negative findings were only reported by a few nurses. Overall, Begat and Severinsson (2006) attributed this generally positive link between supervision and well-being to the confidentiality and validation inherent in supervision. This promoted in nurses an enhanced ability to create relationships through cooperating and giving priority to the building of a trusting relationship with the patient. In turn, nurses were of the opinion that they provided good care in situations where they felt they had succeeded in creating such a relationship, encouraging the patients' cooperation and recovery. This suggests how the link between the well-being of the healthcare professional can directly influence the well-being of the patient. The time to reflect on their work in group supervision allowed such opinions to be clarified and supported by others. As noted by Begat and Severinsson (2006), in this nurse–patient relationship the nurse becomes a significant part of the patient's environment.

Social support from a supervisor was also found to correlate positively with job satisfaction and negatively with burnout in a study of registered nurses working in three different care units in an academic medical unit (Hall, 2007). The greater the nurses' perceived the supervisors' support to be, the greater the effect. The mechanism was unclear, but other research studies to date suggest that supervision can have this kind of beneficial effect on supervisees' well-being by reducing the negative impacts of therapeutic work and through preventing emotional exhaustion, one of the indicators of burnout (Edwards *et al*, 2006; Knudsen *et al*, 2008), although the precise mechanisms and outcomes vary.

Sterner (2009) examined some of these associations with a random sample of 71 American counsellors, working in a range of private and public-sector organizations. Correlational statistics were used within a cross-sectional survey design. The study was based on questionnaire data concerning the supervision working alliance (SWA) and its association with work satisfaction and work-related stress. The SWA includes a narrower concept than the supervisory relationship, in that it focuses on the relational bond within supervision, which is regarded as a mechanism of change. It also differs in focusing on the supervisees' goals. Therefore, topics such as evaluation and feedback from the supervisor were excluded in SWA work. On average, supervisees received one hour of supervision per week. The results indicated that supervision played an important role in how the supervisees perceived their work; as supervisees' perceptions of the quality of the SWA increased, their work satisfaction also increased, while their work-related stress decreased. Also, Sterner (2009) reported that the supervisor's focus on patient issues (i.e. fostering the supervisees' professional development) and on building rapport were highly positively correlated with counsellors' perceptions of feeling satisfied with their work environment.

White and Winstanley (2010) conducted one of the very few RCT studies of supervision, this one in Australia, with 24 mental health nurses acting as supervisors (following four days of experiential training in supervision). The authors attempted to establish a set of causal relationships between clinical supervision, quality of care, and proxy measures of client outcomes (i.e. quality of care and patient satisfaction). Participants were 168 multidisciplinary therapists and 82 clients, in community or inpatient settings. Comparable numbers were recruited in relation to the control group, who did not receive supervision, and the two staff groups did not differ significantly on demographic variables. The study used the MCSS alongside other questionnaires, plus interviews and diary records. White and Winstanley (2010) found that there were no changes over the 12-month long study in the control group. By contrast, the supervisors regarded themselves as becoming significantly more competent in supervision (as measured by the MCSS), which was maintained through the study period. They also reported a non-significant reduction in their personal distress (on the General Health Questionnaire). Their supervisees perceived the supervision that they received from these 24 supervisors as becoming significantly more supportive by the end of the study, which was associated with reduced personal distress (supervisees receiving poor supervision, by contrast, reported greater distress). But save for the one private-sector setting, there were no significant changes in the quality of care that they provided, nor in client satisfaction, which was attributed by the authors to 'unhealthy (organizational) cultures' (p161: e.g. non-involvement of service managers). From the interviews with senior managers and the supervisors' diary records, White and Winstanley (2010, p159) concluded that: 'The personal disposition of individual middle managers emerged as the central factor which substantially influenced, if not determined, the outcome of the entire clinical supervision enterprise'. Specific problems indicated by interviews and diary records were suspiciousness, low levels of staff commitment, and an organizational context for non-involvement.

Wallbank (2010) also conducted an RCT, but this one had a rare focus on restorative supervision. Thirty midwives and physicians in England's NHS were randomly allocated to either a restorative supervision group or a control group. Those in the supervision group received six one-hour long sessions on an individual basis from a clinical psychologist. The supervision was described as providing 'containment' (a method of processing anxiety and emotions so that the ability to 'think' is restored in the person), and encouraging 'reciprocity' in key relationships with colleagues and patients. Specifically, supervisees were reported to use their six sessions to discuss and process their workplace experiences, and the impact that these were having on their ability to think and make decisions, and to reflect on and cope with their workplace experiences. In a later paper (Wallbank, 2013, described below), she added that this supervision was intended to support staff with the emotional demands of their work roles, to strengthen their professional resilience, and to improve their health and well-being. All 30 participants completed two self-report questionnaires to assess their symptom levels (The impact of event scale by Horowitz *et al*, 1979), and their professional quality of life (ProQol by Stamm, 2008), including burnout, compassion fatigue and compassion satisfaction. The results indicated that supervision led to highly significant improvements in the participants' well-being: distress symptoms, burnout and compassion fatigue scores reduced markedly, while the compassion satisfaction scores increased. There were no significant changes in the scores of the control group members over the same period. While acknowledging that the small sample size limited inferences about whether the positive results would extend to other staff groups, Wallbank (2010) concluded that restorative supervision had been effective in this study. She also noted that supervision normalised personal distress, was relatively inexpensive, and represented a more appealing source of help than occupational health services. Due to this demonstration that restorative supervision was effective, Wallbank (2013) was encouraged to develop a sustainable supervision approach within the same NHS organization, including the training of supervisors and a large-scale dissemination programme. However, although this 2013 paper presents the favourable results of two staff surveys, we have not treated this as a second study for the present sample, since it is unclear whether the dissemination of restorative supervision was associated with these favourable results.

Koivu *et al* (2012) endorsed the importance of establishing effective workplace interventions in order to promote well-being among clinicians. They surveyed 14 medical-surgical hospital units in Finland where group supervision with a restorative element had taken place. The 74 nurses in the sample who rated their supervision as effective reported reduced burnout, especially in terms of improved personal accomplishment. By contrast, no such findings were reported for their 156 colleagues who either did not attend a group, or for the 74 nurses who rated their supervision as ineffective. There were no adverse findings for supervision reported. Koivu *et al* (2012) conjectured that this positive association between personal accomplishment and effective supervision indicated that guided reflection on past action was the mechanism through which supervision enhanced well-being at work, aiding learning from emotionally challenging work experiences that can create feelings of failure and incompetence. However, supervision also correlated positively with better job engagement, so the authors acknowledged that well-being at work may be an antecedent (i.e. well-being enables staff to make good use of supervision), and a consequence of effective supervision. They concluded that management should develop a workplace culture that ensured effective supervision to encourage self-reflection, coping with work experiences, and to generate new ideas about quality improvements.

Livni *et al* (2012) also evaluated group supervision with a restorative element, comparing it with 1:1 supervision within a randomized controlled design for multi-disciplinary staff (a waitlist control group). Ten supervisors and 37 supervisees working in drug and alcohol services in one Area Health service in Australia were randomly allocated to either group, 1:1 supervision, or a combination of these formats. Another strong feature of this study was that the supervisors received didactic and experiential training in supervision, featuring supportive, 'coaching' relationships, working collaboratively towards supervisee-selected supervision objectives. A further strength was that participating supervisors were invited to monthly support meetings. A battery of psychometrically sound questionnaires was administered at three time-points to the supervisees, such as The Maslach Burnout Inventory (Maslach & Jackson, 1981). Correlational analyses at time three (i.e. after supervision) indicated that the more time that supervisees had spent in supervision, the greater the benefits. Especially for the staff in the 1:1 format, these benefits included stronger alliances, seemingly the basis in turn for reduced burnout and work-related stress. However, the findings were varied: following six months of supervision, supervisees in the waitlist control group had higher levels of burnout and lower levels of well-being, and no effects were found on the measures of psychological well-being or job satisfaction. The authors conjectured that this might be due to workplace factors (e.g. some workplaces were relocated during the study, and there were staff shortages); or factors outside work (life events); or were simply due to the introduction of supervision itself (for the first time, demanding more staff time and so increasing stress).

Livni *et al* (2012) noted that there had been logistical and emotional reasons for the limited participation in supervision. An analysis of causal pathways explaining participation was conducted through a survey of 136 mental health nursing staff in Denmark (Gonge & Buus, 2011). The authors' main interest lay in clarifying the links between supervision participation (measured by the supervisee-reported frequency: 'How many clinical supervision sessions have you attended within the last 6 months?'), supervision effectiveness (as measured by the MCSS (Winstanley & White, 2014)), and any related benefits of supervision (measured by a package of validated questionnaires, including The Maslach Burnout Inventory (Maslach *et al,* 1996)). The expected pathway was found, in that there was a significant positive correlation between attending effective supervision and benefits (greater job satisfaction and vitality, more frequent rational coping strategies). Conversely, there were also the anticipated negative correlations between attending effective supervision and adverse consequences (less 'stress', reduced 'emotional exhaustion', and reduced 'depersonalization'). Gonge & Buus (2011) noted that high scores on the MCSS (i.e. more effective supervision) are traditionally associated with lower levels of burnout, and this was corroborated by their findings. We should also note that their study was one of the few supportive supervision studies to introduce any control, due to the ability of multivariate statistical analyses to control for some potentially confounding variables. However, as they acknowledged, their correlational research design does not exclude the possibility that staff with positive well-being participate and profit more from supervision (as per Koivu *et al,* 2012).

In a subsequent RCT (Gonge & Buus, 2014) primarily concerned with improving participation in supervision, comparisons between experimental and control groups again indicated significant differences on the MBI scale (for 'emotional exhaustion' and 'depersonalization', both favouring the experimental group; there were 23 mental health nurses in each group). However, the findings were generally weak and the authors were unable to replicate the links to changed coping or other explanatory variables, with the exception that again supervision participation was necessary for a reduction in reported burnout. Also unexpected was an overall decrease in the supervisees' rating of the effectiveness of their supervision (as measured by the total score and all six subscales of the MCSS (Winstanley and White, 2014)). These disappointing findings may be due to the rather narrow focus of supervision, which only consisted of encouraging the supervisees "to systematically reflect on how they could overcome the individual and organizational constraints they experienced, as limiting the effectiveness of their own clinical supervision" (p3). The authors concluded that individual and organizational barriers to involvement in clinical supervision should be addressed.

The relationship between supportive supervision and one possible explanatory variable (professional status) was studied by Kristofferzon *et al* (2013). They focused on the differential effectiveness of three different clinical supervision roles that were occupied by one profession – nurses who were preceptors, head preceptors or clinical lecturers. Within a nurse training programme based in a Swedish university, 107 students rated the relative supportiveness of these three roles (nursing specialization not stated, perhaps as this was a generic foundational course). These students rated the supportive function of supervision as the most highly valued aspect, which they judged as coming least from the head preceptors (who played an administrative role), while the lecturers were significantly more challenging than the preceptors (i.e. encouraging critical thinking, reflection, and the discussion of clinical experiences consistent with their role as a university teacher). Together, the supportive and challenging elements of supervision explained 39% of the variance in the learning outcomes (including confidence) reported by the students. A significant association was also found between support and learning; the higher the students rated the support that they received, the higher was their rating of their achievement of the programme's learning outcomes. Having different roles that prioritize support or challenge makes good practical sense and simplifies supervision. Typically, students will only have one supervisor at any one time and that individual faces the classic task of striking a difficult balance between support and challenge, as both are necessary in developing healthcare professionals. This balancing act is complicated by the supervisees' personalities and support-seeking behaviours, in that individual supervisees may also play different roles with respect to seeking or avoiding support for their learning (Moked & Drach-Zahavy, 2015). We return to this study and say more about such individual differences in the next chapter.

Gonge and Buus (2011) are to be commended for their attention to supervision itself, reasoning naturally enough that we can only expect an effect to emerge from supportive supervision if supervisees actually participate in it (and it is then effective). As indicated by Moked and Drach-Zahavy (2015), for personality reasons even participating supervisees may actually be more or less motivated to seek or use support. A further consideration is whether the supervisor is effective in providing support, given that many supervisors never receive any training in supervision (Milne et al, 2011c), and others practice supervision in an unethical way (Ellis et al, 2014; and see summary below). Thankfully, specific training for supervisors in restorative supervision has been developed and evaluated (Wallbank, 2012; 2013; Wallbank & Woods, 2012). This is a rare initiative, as most supervisor training is generic, and probably focused largely on the formative aspect (Milne et al, 2011). It is also rare for any such training to be conducted on a large scale, with even the most rudimentary evaluation. Sonya Wallbank's supervisor training programme (Wallbank, 2012; 2013; Wallbank & Woods, 2012) is a one-day workshop, plus a manual to support subsequent learning. Additionally, the trained supervisors are supported in cascading restorative supervision to their colleagues within a group format. These six-session restorative supervision groups have reached over 2,500 healthcare professionals in England, including health visitors; midwives, doctors and general nurses working in obstetrics and gynaecology (Wallbank, 2013). Questionnaire-based evaluations have indicated that six sessions in the restorative supervision group is associated with reduced burnout, together with positive impacts on the workplace (it is this study that we count towards the 22 reviewed evaluations). However, the impressive scale of this staff support programme needs to be considered alongside the provisional nature of the evaluation, which does not allow the findings to be attributed to the groups, as the research design was an uncontrolled pre-post group comparison.

In a research design that did allow inferences about causality to be drawn, Knudsen et al (2013) surveyed 934 counsellors. They concluded from a regression analysis (including control for some demographic and professional variables, such as qualifications) that the counsellors' commitment to their employing organization, and their commitment to their profession, mediated the link between supervision and burnout (emotional exhaustion). That is, provided that the counsellors experienced these two forms of commitment, then higher-quality supervision was associated with significantly reduced exhaustion (quality was measured by an ad hoc, single-factor 17-item rating scale). It appeared that high-quality supervision had an impact on these two forms of commitment, as they were significantly positively correlated with supervision.

The quality and quantity of supportive supervision was also considered in a large-sample correlational study by McAuliffe *et al* (2013), with 1,561 mid-level obstetric staff working in Malawi, Tanzania and Mozambique. These countries were included because of a serious shortage of skilled and motivated staff, and supportive supervision was selected because it was seen as valuable in ensuring appropriate task delegation, raising motivation, and ensuring that clinical performance is of the required quality. In their introduction, McAuliffe *et al* (2013, p2) stated that:

"several studies of mid-level healthcare workers suggest that supervision is frequently absent and that even when present supervision may be solely corrective in nature."

By 'corrective', they meant that supervision for this neglected group was "a fault-finding exercise derived from a coercive 'inspection and blame' model of supervision" (p6). These circumstances had been found in prior studies to lower job satisfaction, demotivate staff, and create problems over staff retention. This was replicated in the study by McAuliffe *et al* (2013). By contrast, across all three participating countries they found positive correlations between regular, formal, and supportive supervision, and staff motivation and retention. The findings were based on multi-level data analysis (i.e. regression analysis) that adjusts for demographic and occupational factors, as well as for facility characteristics. They concluded that "improving and expanding healthcare services in resource-poor settings requires more attention be paid to the provision of formal supportive to healthcare workers" (p7).

For example, they found that some supervisees only received negative feedback, which was associated with reduced work motivation and intentions to leave their job. It may conceivably also have lowered their sense of well-being at work. Evans and Marcroft (2015) also described a system-wide supervision initiative, but theirs was in an English social enterprise service, designed to provide community nursing and health visiting. Early work had indicated to these authors that group supervision was highly valued by the nursing staff, emphasising professional support, reflection and learning. But attendance had been dropping. This was a concern, as among other things there was a need to meet the standards of external assessors, such as the Care Quality Commission (CQC), which requires healthcare organizations to ensure staff receive "appropriate training, professional development, supervision and appraisal" (CQC, 2010). Therefore, Evans and Marcroft (2015) undertook a staff consultation process, conducted through surveys and focus groups. This led to a menu of supervision options (partly to overcome scheduling barriers to participation) and a staff survey suggested that supervision was again valued and attended. For example, when staff were asked how clinical supervision helped them in their practice, the supportive and reflective elements of supervision were most highly appreciated (over 85% of staff valued these elements, more than double the endorsement of the educational element). Although weak on evaluation, this study is strong on addressing supervision problems through organizational change.

Related to the Milne and Westerman (2001) n=1 study described above, we also conducted a mixed design analysis of the audio-tapes from one of these n=1 supervision studies (Milne *et al*, 2014). This corroborated the supportive aspect in Milne and Westerman (2001). This 'episode analysis' (Ladany *et al*, 2005) combined qualitative and quantitative analyses, finding that among the 31 episodes that were observed there were 208 different kinds of supervisor utterances (speech units), of which 53% were supportive (35% 'feeling reactions'; 18% included a 'counselling focus' (Milne *et al*, 2011a)). In these n=1 studies, the principal outcome has been treated as the supervisees' reactions to supervision ('mini-outcomes', such as 'experiencing'), but supervisee satisfaction was also always assessed by questionnaire, and was always very high (including items specific to supportive supervision). In addition, within the episode approach the 'resolution' is the qualitative outcome. In the Milne *et al* (2011a) study, 10 of the observed resolutions were supportive (32%: heightened self-awareness; valuable supervision alliance). If we include the 16 skill-enhancement resolutions (admittedly probably closer to a 'formative' resolution), this rises to a total of 84% of observed resolutions. Interviews were conducted separately with the supervisor and the supervisee after the intervention, which included a question about the negative effects of supervision. The supervisee noted that supervision sessions could be "rushed, as there was so much to fit in" and could also be taxing, including "raising anxiety levels" (p161). The supervisor agreed that supervision had been 'challenging' and that he too experienced some anxiety. However, both construed this arousal as desirable and productive. On a few occasions supervision had not been conducted correctly – for example, CBT supervision including a focus on insight or counselling, although this did not appear to cause any harm, as the supervisee's ratings of her satisfaction with supervision remained very high throughout the study period.

Yeun and Kim (2015) conducted a survey of 190 nurses, employing a regression analysis of the data to determine the extent to which supervisor support contributed to the reduction of high nursing staff turnover in university hospitals in two South Korean cities. Support was measured with The 9-item Supervisor Support Questionnaire (Shinn *et al*, 1989) and the findings indicated that those nurses with the highest perceived supervisor support reported the most positive job outcomes (e.g. personal accomplishment) and the least negative outcomes, including less occupational stress. Yeun and Kim (2015) concluded that supervisor support had an important influence on the turnover intentions of these nurses (though emotional exhaustion had the largest influence). For example, younger nurses were at particular risk of emotional exhaustion, due to a combination of low status, a heavy workload, a low sense of personal accomplishment, and with low supervisor support.

A similar correlational approach was employed by Shanafelt *et al* (2015), who related the self-reported burnout and satisfaction with the employing organization of nearly 3,000 physicians working in a range of specialities in a large US healthcare organization. This was related to the help provided by their 128 immediate 'physician supervisors'. The 12 'leadership qualities' of these supervisors were rated by their supervisees, and included affirmative ratings of several questionnaire items that were consistent with a restorative aspect to the supervision (e.g. showing personal interest; empowering). Highly significant correlations were reported between these qualities and burnout and job satisfaction, in the predicted directions (i.e. a negative association between burnout and supervision; a positive correlation between supervision and satisfaction). Furthermore, through multivariate analyses Shanafelt *et al* (2015) were able to quantify the strength of these associations. Overall, they found that each 1% increase in the quality of supervision (the composite leadership quality score) was associated with a 3.3% decrease in the likelihood of burnout, and a 9% improvement in job satisfaction. When the data were analyzed at the more specific level of the work unit, it was found that 11% of the variation in burnout and 47% of the variation in satisfaction was explained by this supervision rating. These authors concluded that supervision of adequate quality appeared to impact the well-being and job satisfaction of the participating physicians to a 'remarkable' extent (p436), especially given the many other factors present in the workplace. Encouraged by these findings, they drew out the implications for selecting and training supervisors in the future.

An unusually sophisticated study surveyed a total of 313 general nurses in two different settings at two different time points, also controlling for possible confounding effects of general well-being (as well as age, gender, leadership position, and part-time work (Wiegl *et al,* 2016)). These fully qualified German nurses worked either in inpatient wards (e.g. intensive care unit, operating theatre, radiology, and the emergency unit), or in day care. The second group were comparable nursing professionals, with similar professional backgrounds to the inpatient group. This second group served as a test of the consistency of the findings across different healthcare settings and time. The surveys used questionnaires to assess the links between burnout, depression and supervision, in particular the relationship between work overload and supervisor support. Consistent with the model outlined earlier in this book, the authors treated work overload as a stressor (which is associated with depression) and supervisor support as a buffer (protecting supervisees against stressors through social support, performance feedback and the development of work competencies). The questionnaires included these items: 'How well does your supervisor understand your job problems and needs?'; 'How often do you get help and support from your immediate superior?' and 'What are the chances that your supervisor would "bail you out" at his or her expense?' A 5-point response scale was used (e.g. 1 = not a bit; 5 = to a great extent). To clarify the interactions between these variables, the authors used a statistical procedure called regression analysis, which allowed them to examine associations in a stepwise way. This analysis indicated that burnout (emotional exhaustion) and depression were lowest for nurses reporting high supervisor support and who were experiencing low work overload. Supervisor support was positively associated with well-being (less depression). By contrast, highly exhausted nurses appear to have coped poorly by not seeking supervisor support when they were struggling, thereby failing to reduce their workload (i.e. a vicious cycle). These correlational findings were consistent across times, settings and samples, and remained robust after adjusting for general well-being and other possible confounds, increasing our confidence in the results.

The most recent and final study that we located was a survey of the effectiveness of supervision (Gardner *et al*, 2018), which included 100 participants from a wide range of allied health disciplines in Australia (AH: physiotherapy, occupational therapy, social work, speech pathology, dietetics, psychology, podiatry, exercise physiology, audiology, and allied health assistants). Supervision was measured by the MCSS questionnaire (Winstanley & White, 2014). However, there was difficulty finding time for supervision and differences between the professional disciplines. Between-group statistical comparisons indicated that, for the full MCSS, respondents from occupational therapy rated their supervision as very significantly more effective than their colleagues within physiotherapy. For all respondents, restorative supervision was rated slightly more highly than the normative and formative aspects, at 78%. There were also statistically significant differences between the 30 occupational therapy and the 25 physiotherapy respondents in both the restorative and formative domains; both of the MCSS restorative subscales ('trust/rapport' and 'advice/support') were rated significantly more favourably by the occupational therapists. The 7-item 'trust/rapport' subscale measures the supervisees' perception of the supervisors' ability to discuss sensitive or confidential issues. The 6-item 'advice/support' subscale assesses the extent to which supervisees' feel supported by their supervisors, and also measures the level of advice and guidance received. The authors attributed these differences to the supervision received, with occupational therapists having more formalised (e.g. supervisors were trained), frequent, and better-structured supervision (e.g. supervision contracts were used), due to a longer history of engaging in supervision. Therefore, although participating physiotherapists

TABLE 3.1: A summary of the supervision methods and outcomes for supervisees, as described within the reviewed sample of 25 quantitative studies

Model or theory	Examples of supportive supervision methods (the 'process')	Examples of positive outcomes
Coping theory	■ Develop the supervisees' personal coping strategies and professional competencies by offering advice and guidance	■ Improved confidence ■ Greater self-awareness ■ Skill enhancement
	■ Encourage supervisees to access and optimize social support from colleagues	■ Better relationships (less isolated) ■ Greater group cohesion
Tandem model	■ Build and strengthen the supervision alliance (e.g. engaging in shared activities; discussing supervisees' feeling reactions to stressors; enhancing rapport; and focus on patients)	■ Stronger cooperation ■ Valuable alliance
	■ Provide social support (protecting/buffering supervisee from stressors)	■ Feeling more supported ■ Enhanced well-being ■ Decreased stress and burnout
Organizational (force-field) theory	■ Facilitate peer support	■ Increased honesty and openness ■ Greater commitment to workplace
	■ Challenging thinking errors & clarifying feelings ■ Monitor caseload	■ Enhanced capacity for critical thinking ■ Higher job satisfaction
Systems theory (context)	■ Provide constructive feedback on the supervisees' work performance	■ Feeling more valued ■ Improved work efficiency
	■ Build relationships and address interpersonal problems ■ Be sensitive and sympathetic ■ Discuss feeling reactions (to clients & to colleagues); express concerns	■ Greater trust ■ Emotional processing (through 'experiencing' reactions) ■ Increased commitment to profession and to job (reduced intention to leave/ improved job retention)

and occupational therapists all valued supervision, only the occupational therapists believed that it improved their skills and the service that they provided (because they were supported to reflect on their practice, and were able to discuss sensitive or confidential issues with their supervisor).

The theoretical elements of the support model are listed in the left-hand column of Table 3.1, and it can be seen that this model provides a good framework for capturing the multiple supervision methods and supervisee outcomes that were reported in the sampled studies. This test represents a partial validation of the support model in that it 'fits' with the reviewed research literature (more below). Also, the methods that were used by supervisors (see column 2) are consistent with our definition of supportive supervision, as are the diverse outcomes (column 3). These findings indicate that supportive supervision, when done properly, achieves a valuable range of positive outcomes.

Harmful aspects of supportive supervision

For simplicity's sake, we have not included in Table 3.1 the few negative, unintended, often harmful outcomes of supervision that we located within our literature review, but in principle the support model could accommodate these too. This is because the elements in this model all assume a spectrum of associated outcomes, ranging from the desirable to the harmful. For example, coping theory recognizes that supervisees' personal coping strategies may be maladaptive and cause personal distress. Not surprisingly, having been selected as examples of effective supportive supervision, the above studies suggest that there are few indications of negative or harmful outcomes for staff, and none at all for their patients. Specifically, two studies in our review indicated some harm associated with supportive supervision, in terms of raised levels of distress (anxiety; sleep problems; concentration difficulties; burnout (Hyrkas, 2005; Berg & Hallberg, 1999)). Two further studies suggested a decrease in well-being (Livni et al, 2012; Yeun & Kim, 2015). However, these were counterbalanced by positive findings for other participants in these self-same studies (e.g. for more experienced staff with lower workloads and a sense of greater work accomplishment), as well as by the positive results from the remaining 18 studies. Furthermore, these study authors noted that it may not have been supportive supervision that actually caused the harm, but rather that it may have been due to concurrent workplace stressors (e.g. Livni et al, 2012; McAuliffe et al, 2013) or due to a failure to participate fully in supervision (e.g. Gonge & Buus, 2011; Weigl et al, 2016). In other cases, the supervision may have intentionally included a degree of personal challenge that unfortunately raised the supervisees' anxiety levels temporarily, coinciding with the assessment of outcomes (e.g. Milne et al, 2011a). While it is unfortunate that anxiety arises in supervision, there is theoretical reason and practical examples to indicate that some emotional turbulence is a necessary condition for experiential learning (Vec et al, 2014). Therefore, it should not automatically be construed as harmful.

To ensure a balanced view, we should also consider neighbouring literatures, especially extrapolating from reviews that have used more inclusive searches. Do these reviews provide a more alarming picture? Scrutiny of all 10 relevant systematic reviews of which we are aware indicated that there were very few clear indications of negative outcomes (i.e. Addo *et al*, 2012; Aronsson *et al*, 2017; Bailey *et al*, 2015; Ke *et al*, 2017*; McCann *et al*, 2013; Mor Barak *et al*, 2009; Pollock *et al*, 2017; Snowdon *et al*, 2017; Wheeler & Richards 2007; Windley *et al*, 2015*). These reviews were not restricted to sampling effective or positive studies, and they related supervision to relevant restorative outcomes. We found only one exception involving supervision, noted in the review by McCann *et al* (2013), which indicated that counsellors who received more group supervision (or more case consultation) scored higher on a questionnaire measure of burnout than those who received less supervision. The authors of that study hypothesized that these counsellors may have been more aware of their work stresses and therefore sought out more supervision, rather than the supervision itself actually being harmful.

4. Critical review of research

These positive conclusions about the outcomes of supportive supervision within the 25 reviewed studies above need to be considered in relation to other key aspects of their validity (i.e. their methodological quality: see Shadish *et al*, 2002). A strength of this sample of studies was the wide range of research designs and investigative methods used (in the rare cases of mixed designs, this summary counts the design most relevant to the findings that we reported). There were ten correlational studies; three group designs (pre-post between-group comparisons); five regression analyses (controlling for some demographic and professional variables), four randomized controlled trials (RCT); two studies that relied on descriptive statistics; and one n=1 analyses (we could have included four more n=1 analyses, as summarized in Milne, 2018, but the one we included was the most specific to supportive supervision). There were only ten studies in our sample which could be regarded as in any way 'controlled' (i.e. the RCTs, the regression analyses, and the n=1 study), in the sense of providing a reasonable causal demonstration that supervision led to the reported outcomes. That is, we judged that the validity threats that were present were minimal, making the selected studies interpretable (i.e. permitting an inference that supervision caused the obtained outcomes). An example of such a threat to validity, and a further reason for caution, is that the cross-sectional (correlational) and regression research designs relied entirely on self-report questionnaires, often exclusively positively phrased. This is highly likely to introduce significant distortions to the data through various responder biases (particularly as the surveys ask about sensitive aspects of work performance and because many supervisors are also the managers of the survey participants). Furthermore, the correlational statistics that were applied to the questionnaire data can only suggest associations between variables such as supervision and burnout: they cannot demonstrate a causal link (though many authors employ language implying a causal link).

For the majority of our selected studies, we cannot conclude that supervision is responsible for the associated outcomes (e.g. reduced burnout), the extent to which response biases or artefacts are involved, or whether it is other ('third') variables that are responsible. Furthermore, only one of these 25 studies focused exclusively on supportive supervision (Wallbank, 2010), as it was typically only one of several elements within clinical supervision (usually having a primary focus on formative supervision objectives, such as competence development). Another major concern is that supervision as an intervention was usually described loosely if at all, and was rarely measured; only six of the 25 studies assessed supervision directly, mostly using the MCSS questionnaire. Furthermore, only two of these six studies used direct observation to quantify supervision (and its mini-outcomes for the supervisees), using audio tapes and a supervision competence rating scale, administered reliably (Milne & Westerman, 2001; Milne *et al,* 2011a).

This lack of measures designed to directly observe and describe supervision means that we are not certain about what exactly happened within the intervention termed 'supportive supervision' (i.e. unknown frequency, duration, methods or fidelity). This further undermines our confidence in the causal link and significantly limits our ability to specify how it works, a view that is consistent with the methodological weaknesses and conclusions from larger-scale reviews of clinical supervision research in general (e.g. Buus & Gonge, 2009; Ellis & Ladany, 1997) and in relation to preceptorship (Ke *et al,* 2017). We should also note that this review was not a formal, quantitative systematic review but more of a descriptive summary or 'qualitative overview', meaning that we should also be cautious about our conclusions (Ryan & Hill, 2016). For example, we did not evaluate specific quantitative aspects within the studies independently, nor assess the reliability of the above summary. Another reason for caution is that our sample included only a small handful of studies concerned with the supervision alliance, indicating that we may have missed an important seam of research. As far as we can tell, our small sample appears to be due to a heavy reliance within this literature on student participants, a focus on clinical practice rather than supervision, and a large volume of studies from within social work and child welfare services. These studies did not meet our inclusion criteria, which emphasised naturalistic evaluations of supervision within healthcare. Another indication that we did not miss a seam of relevant research is borne out by a recent search for experimental evaluations of the supervision alliance using other study inclusion criteria (Milne & Reiser, 2017) and by scrutinizing major reviews performed by alliance experts (e.g. Beinart, 2014; Watkins, 2014).

However, information on the resources used to provide supervision – the 'structure' data – was sadly lacking in these 25 studies. About one-third of these studies contained no information at all on the frequency, duration, or other resource aspects (e.g. experience, qualifications, or pay grade of supervisors). Of the other studies, the most commonly mentioned detail was that supervision lasted for approximately an hour per week, often in a group format, and many pointed out that such supervision was regular through the study period. However, other studies reported markedly less frequent supervision, equating to about an hour per month (as far as we could ascertain from the brief or vague descriptions). Furthermore, bearing in mind that all but one of the 25 studies concerned general clinical supervision, the implication we draw is that the restorative focus of this supervision may only have averaged approximately 15 minutes per fortnight. This lack of information on the intervention undermines our ability to infer what resources are required for supervision to achieve its outcomes, preventing a sound evaluation. As another example, aside from the supervision itself, very few other resources were mentioned in the 25 studies and then only sketchily (e.g. brief introductory meetings or workshops; questionnaires and written materials; video recordings and video coding; consultancy support for supervisors). Unfortunately, this is not unusual; even much-cited clinical trials have reported such information 'inconsistently' (only 16 of 27 studies specified the frequency of supervision), and then only in outline (Roth *et al,* 2010).

Therefore, these 25 studies appear to be representative of the field of supportive supervision and provide grounds for moderate confidence that established supervision methods, when applied correctly, achieve consistently positive outcomes (Avortri *et al,* 2019: see Table 3.1). This confidence is also based on a wide range of complementary research designs and measurement instruments that were applied across nations and service contexts, with different kinds of participants (in effect an extension of the generalizability logic in Wiegl *et al,* 2016). This suggests that supportive supervision has a 'real' effect, as the various confounding factors that were inevitably present across each of the 25 studies did not prevent it from always yielding positive results. We should also take into account the mixed samples and the spectrum of complementary research designs, the lack of side-effects (when supervision was done correctly), the apparent cost-effectiveness, and other relevant considerations (such as those bulleted below). Therefore, we conclude that the evidence of effectiveness falls into the 'moderate' category within the GRADE system (Ryan & Hill, 2016). We expect that future research is unlikely to alter our confidence in supportive supervision. Another implication of judging the evidence to be moderate is that the guidance that we offer in this book justifies us in recommending that the methods suggested 'should' be used, following the guideline development reasoning (NICE, 2012). This suggestion is also influenced by noting that supportive supervision is

unanimously endorsed by all stakeholders (i.e. it is socially valid), that given
the option supervisees would choose it, and that its benefits when done properly
clearly exceed any harm.

Our confidence is bolstered by other relevant forms of evidence, as per our evidence-
based strategy. This includes:

- **Extrapolation from neighbouring empirical research** (e.g. general clinical
  supervision research: Watkins & Milne, 2014; qualitative research on supportive
  supervision, such as Cutcliffe & McFeely 2001; Whitehead *et al*, 2016)

- **Research on the effects of unsupportive or harmful supervision** (Nelson
  & Friedlander, 2001; Ellis *et al*, 2014)

- **Systematic reviews** (e.g. Mor Barak *et al*, 2009; Edwards *et al*, 2006; Michie &
  Williams, 2002; Mimura & Griffiths, 2002; Rhodes & Eisenberger 2002; Rowe *et
  al*, 2005; Snowdon *et al*, 2016; 2017; Wheeler & Richards, 2007)

- **Expert consensus statements** (APA 2015; Falender *et al*, 2004; Roth & Pilling,
  2008)

- **Relevant theory** (see Chapter 2).

These other forms of evidence afford strong support for upgrading our confidence
in the defined methods of supportive supervision and the validity of its outcomes.
To express it differently, there is a 'web of evidence' (Elliott, 2002) to corroborate
our sample of 25 supportive supervision studies. An example from related empirical
research may help to demonstrate this kind of corroboration. This is the much-cited
study by Butterworth *et al* (1997), excluded from our sample because it was not
published in a peer-reviewed journal. However, this was one of the best-controlled and
largest longitudinal studies, involving 586 mental health nurses in the UK's NHS.
During this period, supervision (a new experience) with a supportive component
was provided to nurses in the experimental group, on average lasting 45 minutes
per month for 1:1 supervision, and up to two hours for group supervision. Those
nurses that received supervision reported decreased psychological distress arising
from their work, while nurses who did not receive supervision reported clear signs of
distress arising from their workplace (emotional exhaustion and depersonalization).
Furthermore, when the control group subsequently received supervision their
distress also decreased (the groups did not differ significantly on the assessed
demographic characteristics: gender; work setting; nursing grade). A sample of the
participating nurses were interviewed at the close of the study, and stated that they
personally valued peer support, honesty and openness, plus the help with personal
coping strategies. There were also perceived organizational benefits, including
stronger relationships, and an increase in staff morale.

Although we regard the reviewed sample of research as providing useful data on the effectiveness of supportive supervision, much more needs to be done to make the research more rigorous and relevant. Specifically we urge researchers to:

- base study designs on sound theory and relevant conceptual models
- select research designs that can capture the complex nature of the studied phenomena
- qualitative methodologies are a case in point, and in general merit greater inclusion
- utilize multiple measures of the structure, process and outcomes of supervision
- include direct observation as one type of instrument (especially as an adherence check)
- administer such instruments repeatedly over time, within research designs that allow causal inferences to be drawn (i.e. longitudinal, controlled research)
- small n ('n=1') research represents a sensible and accessible way to clarify
- promising interventions, providing a firm foundation for large-group designs
- interventions should be fully specified and quantified to be high-fidelity, convincing, informative, and replicable
- the workplace environment should become the primary intervention focus, as the assumed main cause of burnout
- well-being and other positive consequences of the way that staff manage to cope with workplace challenges also merit attention.
- Limiting or preventing harm also deserves research attention.

In this sense, we believe that a 'harm test' should be applied alongside evaluations of benefit, such as the established 'acid test', though both tests should be based on a stepwise succession of equally important criteria (e.g. cost-benefit, as per Reiser & Milne, 2014).

These recommendations on measurement and designs could contribute to clarifying and boosting the profound process of 'social exchange' (Blau, 1964). This theory explains the recurring observation of a trickle-down of positive interventions in healthcare; the causal pathway linking supportive supervision to its outcomes. For example, Begat and Severinsson (2006) reported that nurses felt they provided good care in situations where they felt that they had themselves received support within supervision. Similarly, supportive supervision appears to increase professionals' commitment to their work and their employing organization (Gonge & Buus, 2011; Kilcullen, 2007; Knudsen *et al*, 2013). In short, healthcare staff "...need to be healthy in order to care for other human beings..." (Addo *et al*, 2012, p.2). As a further stimulus to action, bear in mind that the converse also appears to be true (Mor Barak *et al*, 2009).

5. Summary

The studies we have just reviewed point to several ingredients of sound supervision (see column 2 of Table 3.1). These instances are broadly consistent with the evidence-based CBT supervision approach (Milne, 2018) and are also corroborated by the related supervision guidelines (Milne & Reiser, 2017). One of these guidelines concerns the supervisory working alliance, and by referring to this guideline we can illustrate how the alliance might underpin the supervision methods listed in column 2 of Table 3.1. For example, an alliance featuring mutual understanding and collaboration would be expected to contribute to the supervisee's personal coping strategy enhancement; while showing interest, being approachable and constructive might help to address interpersonal problems. That is, we can regard the alliance as a relationship process that consists of micro-competencies (e.g. collaboration), which enable the larger supervision competencies to benefit (e.g. coping strategy enhancement).

What do these studies tell us about our model of supportive supervision? As indicated by Table 3.1, the examples of supervision provided map on well to the support model (see Chapter 2, Table 2.1). The associated supervisees' reactions in Table 3.1 can be clustered readily and completely around the four theories (our thematic synthesis: Chapter 2, Table 2.1). In particular, we take the view that social support is the single most fundamental process underpinning supportive supervision, and that it shows itself in one way or another through the diverse supervision methods and supervisee outcomes that are detailed in Table 3.1. The fact that we were able to readily fit all the main findings from the sample of 25 studies into the model suggests to us that the supportive supervision model has passed this empirical test. That is, the variables in the model match those in this literature (the precision and specificity tests), the study outcomes validate our claims for the models effectiveness (a corroboration test). The fourth and final test of an empirical definition is that the model can be measured (operationalization). We have noted instruments that can measure supportive supervision alongside the definition in Chapter 1, such as the MCSS, used in several of the 25 studies in our review sample. This repeats the approach used to develop an empirical definition of clinical supervision (Milne, 2007). It also provides a test of the definition of supportive supervision we provided in Chapter 1, allowing us to refine that definition to match the findings from these 24 studies (we redrafted that definition retrospectively, following this test).

In summary, we found that supportive supervision confers consistent, strong and diverse benefits. As summarized in Table 3.1, supportive supervision helps healthcare staff to feel supported, to cope better with stressful workplaces, to access more social support from peers, to become more consistent and competent, and to minimize their distress (usually measured as burnout). In turn, such improvements contribute to better organizational functioning, again in terms of multiple outcomes (improved staff morale and relationships; peer support; enhanced organizational climate and work satisfaction; feeling in control at work; retention). Furthermore, these studies indicate that the higher the quality of supervision, the better it works. There is only rare and weak evidence that supportive clinical supervision, when it is done correctly, causes any kind of harm to supervisees or their patients. Conversely, poor-quality or non-existent supervision is associated with maladaptive coping and increased burnout among staff (and other problems, such as high turnover). Not surprisingly, given these generally positive outcomes, supportive supervision was also unanimously valued by supervisees, and by the different participating professions and countries. Some of these studies also reported moderating workplace factors (i.e. antecedent or contextual influences), such as organizational commitment (indicated by the supervision that was provided), the availability and participation in supervision, workplace relationships among staff (conflicts; trust), and work overload. These conclusions are consistent with the wider literature on clinical supervision, in terms of both benefits (e.g. Reiser & Milne, 2014) and harm (Ellis *et al*, 2014). Expert consensus statements also corroborate this summary (APA, 2015; Falender *et al*, 2004; Roth & Pilling, 2008). In conclusion, the intended, positive effects of supportive supervision clearly outweigh the weak, negative effects, not least as there was no indication of any harm to the supervisees' patients.

Chapter 4: Individual Differences and Supportive Supervision

1. Introduction

In the next two chapters we turn our attention to the most popular understanding of well-being at work. This is the view that well-being is the result of workers' ability to cope with the demands of their job, by virtue of their individual characteristics and personal qualities, in interaction with the job factors and interpersonal challenges that they face in their workplace. Why should we give it our attention; is it not a personal matter, best left to the individual worker? We believe that personal characteristics of staff that affect their work should not simply be left to staff to resolve. Supportive supervision involves attending to concerns collaboratively, with the aim of improving how individuals cope at work. Specifically, as we described in Chapter 2 (see Figure 2.1), relevant theory indicates that supportive supervision means working intrapersonally by offering support and validation to supervisees, which is effective through techniques such as debriefing, and through mechanisms such as emotional processing. Because of the interaction with the workplace environment, supportive supervision also means improving supervisees' peer support, and ensuring their group membership. According to the 'conservation of resources' theory (Hobfoll *et al*, 2018), personal characteristics represent important individual resources that enable us to cope with workplace demands and develop additional resources (e.g. peer support). When we reviewed the best available research in Chapter 3 (see a summary in Table 3.1), we emphasised the importance of social support and relationship-building, extending our understanding to also include developing the supervisee's personal coping strategies and professional competencies (by offering advice and guidance); building and strengthening the supervision alliance (e.g. by being sensitive and sympathetic); challenging thinking errors and clarifying feelings; monitoring the supervisee's caseload; and providing constructive feedback on the supervisee's work performance. These supervision methods will be described and discussed in this chapter, in addition to Chapters 6 and 7, where we adopt different perspectives on these crucial methods. Here we focus on the role played by individual differences in shaping supervisees' personal coping strategies and in influencing supervision.

There is ample reason to believe that problematic coping occurs when workers 'bottle up' their concerns and do not share their job struggles. A likely consequence is that matters will worsen; they will tend to spiral downwards in a vicious cycle of ever-worsening coping and personal distress (e.g. burnout). For example, doctors perhaps tend not to expect themselves or their colleagues to be ill, which is reflected in only one-third of junior doctors in the UK being registered with a general practitioner (Montgomery et al, 2011). This is of concern, as it may well lead to less adaptive coping (e.g. abuse of alcohol or the use of recreational drugs) and ultimately to serious personal distress (Lizano, 2015; Pan et al, 2017). This is worrying enough, but such circumstances can easily deteriorate further, disrupting other parts of the organization such as the team culture (Willard-Grace et al, 2014). In turn, this can disrupt the quality of patient care, and result in safety risks, clinical errors, accidents and harm (Salyers et al, 2016). For example, therapists with burnout achieve significantly less clinical success than their peers, perhaps as they disengage to reduce work stress, struggle to offer empathy, and form weak alliances with their patients (Delgadillo et al, 2017). This link between burnout (especially emotional exhaustion) and harm is a major concern, as evidence suggests that burnout plays an important role in both workers' mistakes and their provision of sub-optimal care (Montgomery et al, 2011). How might we best understand the interaction between workers and their work? That is, which individual characteristics help us to understand why some staff members thrive in an environment that their colleagues find distressing? Why do some healthcare staff have good days at work when others experience the reverse, even though the work remains the same? Why do some colleagues become cherished buddies, while others become alienated? In determining our answers, we will focus primarily on the supervisee, the healthcare worker struggling to cope with the daily demands of the job, aided by a supervisor. To return to our basic tandem analogy, we are now turning our attention to the supervisees' highly individual struggle to cope with the journey, influenced by their personal characteristics. We are concerned with understanding their individual experience of the emotionally-charged journey through the workplace terrain, and how the supervisor in particular can provide support and guidance during the inevitable ups and downs, through good moments as well as the inevitable mishaps and accidents.

Chapter plan

We start to develop our understanding of the interaction between workers and their work by considering personal characteristics, those 'individual differences' that make people distinctive. Our perspective will be to adopt an evidence-based and pragmatic approach, one that appreciates the ways that we all try to cope with stressors in the workplace. Our focus on the use of evidence-based methods marks the beginning of a more practical emphasis in this book, now that we have a firm theoretical foundation (the support model in Chapter 2) and an understanding of the research evidence (the literature review in Chapter 3). By the end of this chapter, we will have addressed the above questions on workplace adaptation, showing the role played by individual differences in the supervision methods and outcomes summarized in Table 3.1. In the following chapter we consider the related question: how can individuals influence their workplace to better meet their needs? In both chapters, we aim to clarify the best available evidence-based methods for improving matters, related to supportive supervision.

2. Individual differences that matter most in supervision

What are the main personal characteristics that we should consider, and how do they influence our experience of the workplace? We will structure this chapter mainly by using elements of the coping model (stressors, coping strategies, social support, etc.). For each element, we will specify the best practical options, including ways of measuring and intervening. Our aim is to empower supervisees (with further information in Chapter 7) and to strengthen and invigorate supportive supervision by considering individual factors (e.g. neurotic or perfectionistic personality traits). Within the supportive supervision literature, researchers have primarily studied demographic variables (e.g. gender, age, education, job experience & tenure), personality characteristics (including attitudes, values and motivation) and personal coping strategies. These are understood to interact with workplace characteristics such as job stressors, supervision, and social support.

Demographic variables

Contrary to popular opinion, research indicates that demographic variables tend to play an insignificant role in explaining workers' effectiveness (Chow et al, 2015; Gonge & Buus 2010; Maslach et al, 2001; Rhoades & Eisenberger, 2002; Westwood et al, 2017). This view is further supported in a systematic review of therapist training (Beidas & Kendall, 2010) and in analyses of therapists' personal contribution to outcomes (Green et al, 2014). In surveying nurses regarding supervisor support and turnover intentions, Yeun and Kim (2015) did find significant correlations related to the nurses' age and experience; younger and less experienced nurses had a greater intention to leave their job. Being younger does appear to be one of the few consistently important demographic factors (Simionato & Simpson, 2017), reflecting a greater likelihood of burnout attributable to less experience, weaker coping strategies (immaturity), less social support, less satisfying work, and more unrealistic expectations (Rupert et al, 2015). Supervision can help to mitigate inexperience. When Teasdale et al (2001) surveyed 211 qualified nurses who were working in the NHS in England (using questionnaires and a qualitative, critical-incidents analysis), they found that the nurses who had received supervision reported better coping at work and greater access to social support from peers (to discuss clinical issues). This association was greatest for the more junior nurses.

However, the overall link between demographic characteristics and burnout or well-being is weak. This is illustrated by a meta-analysis of the association between long working hours, heart disease and stroke based on a prospective sample of over 600,000 people (Kivimaki *et al*, 2015). The findings indicated that individuals who worked 55 hours per week or more had a higher risk of a stroke or coronary heart disease than those working standard hours. This association was found to be the same for men and women.

Practical implications

Although the research evidence is weak, it makes practical sense for supervisors to take an interest in demographic factors, such as their supervisee's age and experience, as they will probably have an important relationship to the supervisee's coping skills, emotional resilience, and general response to supervision. For instance, developmental approaches to supervision have emphasised the value of providing more practical suggestions to novices, anticipating higher anxiety and a greater need for structure and support (Stoltenberg *et al*, 2014). Taking such typical developmental differences into account, supervisors should vary their relationship style accordingly, starting with a didactic and supportive stance early on in a supervisee's career and gradually becoming more experiential and challenging. In practice, this means altering the alliance to suit the supervisee's needs, agreeing work objectives that make developmental sense, and varying techniques like feedback sensitively (e.g. more positive, frequent and affirming feedback for novices).

Another important demographic consideration is cultural and diversity competence, the ability of supervisors and supervisees to relate to one another effectively, regardless of any diversity issues or contextual differences. According to the supervision guidelines from The American Psychological Association (APA, 2015), competent supervision entails responding sensitively and affirmatively to relevant individual differences (e.g. valuing differences in race, ethnicity, culture, religion, sexual orientation, disability, language, and socioeconomic status). The APA (2015) also encourages supervisors to consider diversity in relation to the supervisee's clinical work and the supervision itself. In particular, they should strive to be self-aware, and reflect routinely with the supervisee on key dynamics, such as bias, stereotyping, power differentials, disempowerment, oppression and privilege. A similar emphasis exists within the supervision competence framework in the UK (Roth & Pilling, 2008).

Measurement

Detailed examples of cultural competence can be found in the numerous checklists and instruments that measure it, such as a questionnaire that was developed through expert consensus by The Royal Australasian College of Physicians in

2012. Consistent with peer review, this questionnaire was intended to provide a framework for healthcare professionals to identify and exceed their standards for cultural competence. This scale includes items that are rated for frequency and concerned with communication (e.g. 'I use interpreters appropriately and effectively'), responding to difference (e.g. 'I show sensitivity towards different patients' backgrounds, cultural beliefs or attitudes'), and supporting colleagues (e.g. 'I give credit for tasks performed well, irrespective of team members' backgrounds or cultures'). It can be found at: https://www.racp.edu.au/docs/default-source/default-document-library/cultural-competency-questionnaire.pdf?sfvrsn=3dc32c1a_4.

Summary

Although demographic factors typically play a minor role in supervision, they should be discussed respectfully and regularly, and supervision should be adapted accordingly. Not least, the supervisor should ensure that the supervisee's work is moderated by an awareness of the role of demographic factors and differences in the supervisee's clinical work. Joint reflection and discussion should be a routine feature of supervision. Supervision that upholds and cultivates cultural competence is an excellent opportunity for the supervisee to develop their own awareness, personal coping strategies, and professional competencies, consistent with the goals of supportive supervision (summarized in Table 3.1). A video demonstration of cultural competence can be found in the CBT supervision manual (Milne & Reiser, 2017). A review of culturally competent supervision can be found in Tsui *et al* (2014), including some powerful and extended illustrations of the role played by personal characteristics.

Personality characteristics

Personality characteristics that have been studied in relation to supervisees' work experiences include neuroticism, hardiness, poor self-esteem, 'Type-A' behaviour, and avoidant coping styles (all of which have been associated with burnout: Maslach *et al,* 2001). According to a more recent and systematic review of studies by Simionato & Simpson (2017), the personality factors associated with burnout include neuroticism, a rigid thinking style, excessive conscientiousness, over-involvement in client problems, perfectionism (a tendency to strive to meet high self-expectations), 'disagreeable' traits (e.g. egocentrism, less compassion, more competitiveness), low extraversion, and high introverted traits (e.g. shyness). These reviewers attributed the links to less interpersonal connection with clients, limited avenues of collaboration with colleagues, fewer opportunities for social support, and fewer intrinsic rewards (e.g. less effective at helping clients). By contrast, Table 4.1 provides an illustration of some of the generally positive personality characteristics that researchers have reported as correlated positively with supervision and work. In supervision, it is necessary to find the right balance between supporting and challenging the supervisee. This balancing act is partly influenced by the supervisee's personality (e.g. support-seeking behaviours) and partly by the supervisor's agreeableness. To illustrate, Moked and Drach-Zahavy (2015) surveyed 178 students and 66 of their clinical mentors in Israel, finding that the nursing students who rated themselves as more competent and as having a more independent attachment style sought the least support from their supervisors.

TABLE 4.1: An illustrative sample of the diverse personality factors that have been associated with worker performance, related to supportive supervision	
Personality factor (definition)	Relevance to supervision (example study)
Supervisee 'perfectionism' (Maladaptive perfectionism is the determined pursuit of personally demanding, extremely high self-imposed standards despite adverse consequences, linked to rigid rules and an overdependence on self-evaluation for feelings of worth. Fears of being revealed as an imposter may drive the perfectionism)	Supervisees who believe that they must pursue excessively high standards will tend to lack self-confidence, procrastinate, and experience personal distress, e.g. anxiety (Chand et al, 2018)
Supervisee 'resilience' (Ability to find ways to cope despite adverse, challenging circumstances, as in managing setbacks)	A personal style associated with being proactive, flexible, open, prepared & organized (e.g. Green et al, 2014; Delgado et al, 2019)
Supervisee 'extroversion' (Extroverts are relatively excitable, sociable, talkative, assertive, and emotionally expressive. Extroverts love being around other people, which makes them feel energized and excited)	This personality type may dispose supervisees to be 'supervision ready', by contrast with supervisees who are more defensive and reserved (e.g. Rieck et al, 2015)
Supervisor 'workaholism' ('The most rewarded addiction in Western culture' – working long hours, with a compulsive work mentality that results in setting high standards, seeking out more work, and staying perpetually busy. Some	A supervisee who works long hours may appeal to supervisors and managers, and may benefit from favourable treatment. Also, long hours alone may not be distressing for the supervisee, especially if they →

Personality factor (definition)	Relevance to supervision (example study)
may feel anxious and guilty when not working, others will enjoy switching off. Consequently, little attention paid to rest and recovery, with a higher risk of personal and interpersonal distress)	have effective coping strategies, and if they find their work meaningful, engaging and satisfying. The 'engaged' workaholic may flourish. By contrast, 'non-engaged' workaholics struggle to cope, feeling guilty and anxious (e.g. Brummelhuis et al, 2017)
Supervisor 'agreeableness' (Concerns qualities such as trust, straightforwardness, altruism, compliance, modesty, and tender-mindedness)	More disagreeable supervisors are detached, critical, sceptical, analytical, and directive. Surprisingly, this personality style may actually boost their supervisees' clinical success, based on a more questioning approach to case discussion, and more directive feedback (e.g. Rieck et al, 2015)
Manager 'relatedness' (Emotionally intelligent, considerate, interpersonally engaged; vigorous and motivating; influential and transformative; charismatic)	A relationship-focused leadership style benefits the workplace environment and the workers, improving productivity and effectiveness. Key relationship qualities are empathy, understanding, trust, support, and responsiveness (Cummings et al, 2010)

Included and defined in Table 4.1 are 'extraversion' and 'agreeableness', two of the factors within the five-factor model that has become the most popular approach for measuring personality, known as 'the big five' (Costa & McCrae, 1992). The other factors are 'neuroticism', 'openness to experience' and 'conscientiousness', leading to another popular acronym for the big five: OCEAN. 'Neuroticism' is a personality trait featuring sadness, moodiness, and emotional instability. Those low in this trait tend to be more stable and emotionally resilient. 'Openness to experience' is characterised by imagination, creativity and insight. People high in this trait are adventurous and curious about the world and other people, and eager to learn new things and enjoy new experiences. 'Conscientiousness' features high levels of organization, thoughtfulness, firm impulse control, and consistent goal-directed behaviours. Highly conscientious people tend to be reliable, plan ahead, think about how their behaviour affects others, and are attentive to details and deadlines. All five personality factors are thought to range on a continuum, from one extreme to the other. This variation provides the basis for individually distinctive personality profiles.

The 'big five' personality factors were studied in a naturalistic sample of supervisors, supervisees, and patients from a training clinic in the US (Rieck et al, 2015). The extraversion and openness to experience personality factors were positively correlated with effective supervision, explaining around 30% of the variance. That is, supervisees whose questionnaire replies indicated that they were relatively more open to experience and extraverted by nature perceived themselves as having stronger supervisory alliances and more positive supervision interactions. Rieck *et al* (2015) interpreted this personality profile as indicating that these supervisees were 'supervision ready', by contrast with those supervisees in their sample who were more defensive or reserved. More surprisingly, supervisor 'agreeableness' was significantly negatively correlated with outcomes. That is, the more disagreeable supervisors were associated with better supervision, in terms of helping their supervisees to achieve greater clinical success. This was unexpected, since low agreeableness indicates a detached, critical, sceptical, analytical, and direct personality style. Rieck *et al* (2015) hypothesised that this more challenging style of supervision may actually have benefitted therapy, in that it may have consisted of a more questioning approach to case discussion, and more directive feedback.

Personality features such as the 'big five' are stable and famously hard to change, being strongly tied to character traits and temperamental dispositions that are acquired through our genes and our conditioning from early childhood. Throughout our working lives, these personality factors can be regarded as a personal filter through which our job experiences are processed (Rieck *et al,* 2015). In effect, this means that the influence of our personality profile may sometimes be negligible, outweighed by other environmental factors. To illustrate, Gonge and Buus (2010) predicted that extraversion and introversion would play a role in supervisees' engagement in supervision. They assumed that lower neuroticism would correlate with less anxiety, and so result in greater engagement in clinical supervision. They expected that greater extroversion would facilitate the kind of self-disclosure needed to engage fully in a reflective process. But their results indicated that neither personality factor was related to participation in supervision, nor indeed were the other individual characteristics that they measured (i.e. gender, age, education, and experience). Rather, it appeared that it was the characteristics of the workplace that determined the extent of staff participation (e.g. shift-work, work demands, and peer support).

On other occasions the workplace may enable personality factors to flourish, as reported from an examination of therapist effects within an Improving Access to Psychological Therapies (IAPT) service in England. Green *et al* (2014) found that the supervisees with the greatest resilience achieved the best outcomes for their patients, and were also more proactive, prepared and organized at work. These more effective workers were more confident, flexible and made better use of supervision. These findings and qualitative observations were consistent with the concept of resilience, which concerns effective coping with work stressors, as in bouncing back from setbacks or adversity. In addition, supervisors' accounts of these more resilient and clinically effective supervisees indicated that they were more willing to discuss their work difficulties and more willing to engage in experiential learning. Green *et al* (2014) believed that resilience could best be understood as a coping process, and therefore as something that was amenable to change, rather than regarding it as a fixed personality trait. Consequently, they encouraged efforts to train and facilitate resilience. On this logic, we now consider coping as the individual difference of greatest relevance to supervision.

Measurement

The big five personality factors can be measured by a self-report questionnaire, the Neuroticism, Extraversion, and Openness to experience Five Factor Inventory (NEO-FFI) (Costa and McCrae, 2004). The NEO-FFI is a reliable and valid version of the original questionnaire, shortened to 60 items (12 items per personality factor), that were clarified in this study. The items are descriptive statements (e.g. 'I am not a worrier'; 'I really enjoy talking to people') rated on a 5-point Likert-type scale (1 = strongly disagree to 5 = strongly agree). Respondents rate how much each item describes them at the present time, relative to their peers.

Practical implications

Supervision should be adapted so that the personality of the supervisee is an acknowledged element just like a demographic difference. This means that relevant personality factors are addressed when appropriate, and that supervision is tailored to the individual supervisee. For example, in relation to a 'perfectionistic' personality, supervisors can help by challenging faulty thinking patterns (e.g. selective attention to failure at work), by modifying maladaptive coping at work (such as continuous self-criticism), and by supporting stress management efforts (Chand *et al,* 2018). In relation to the 'workaholic' personality, the supervisor can encourage their supervisee to find more personal meaning, fulfilment, rewards and satisfaction in their work to reduce guilt and anxiety or whatever is driving over-working (Arnold *et al,* 2007). Practical steps can include ensuring that the work goals are challenging but achievable, reducing barriers, increasing boosters (e.g. additional feedback, resources or help), and reflecting together on the supervisees' professional development in relation to their work (e.g. identifying opportunities to gain greater recognition, or to develop their career).

Supervisees need to play their part, and those of a particularly conscientious, neurotic or perfectionistic nature may need to protect themselves from over-work. Clear rules, standards, and setting maximum hours of work can help, especially if combined with the monitoring of achievements and well-being (as individuals will naturally differ significantly in what works best for them). Supervisees who discuss ongoing coping efforts with their supervisor and peers can gain valuable perspective and excess can be prevented. Difficulty winding down after work, enjoying leisure pursuits, or sleeping are signs that they are struggling to cope (Brummelhuis *et al,* 2017). Disclosing such problems and associated worries to supervisors represents a healthy openness to the inevitable difficulties in professional life and will help to elicit comforting disclosures in return.

As these examples indicate, leadership style can have a strong influence on the supervisees' well-being (Cummings *et al,* 2010; Skakon *et al,* 2010). For example, leaders such as clinical managers are likely to be more effective and motivating if they possess the kind of 'relational' or charismatic personality that enables them to empower staff by building supportive, responsive, and trusting relationships. This entails taking the time to listen to staff concerns with empathy, attending to emotional needs (e.g. validation, respect), and responding to staff members as individuals (as opposed to focusing on the tasks that require attention). Leadership is further considered in the following chapter.

Summary

One of the goals of supportive supervision is to 'build relationships and address interpersonal problems' (these goals are summarized in Table 3.1). The respective personalities of the supervisor and supervisee are critical to achieving this goal, aided by managers and other leaders. For example, resilient and extroverted supervisees make it easier to provide supportive supervision, especially if the supervisor is agreeable and the manager is charismatic and trusting. But personality characteristics are elusive and hard to change, making the more observable and responsive coping strategies a more promising focus for one and all. We summarize the role of coping once we have considered the factor that triggers coping, i.e. stressors.

Stressors

In this book, we regard 'stress' as synonymous with personal 'distress' or occupational 'strain', as in someone being 'stressed out' or suffering from 'work/ occupational stress'. By contrast, a stressor is something that an individual perceives as requiring a response, a stimulus, demand or challenge, such as a patient posing a question, or a manager asking for a report. A stressor will vary in potency, depending on its nature, and whether it is perceived as exceeding our coping abilities and personal resources (Lazarus, 1991). A worrying example of a stressor is workplace bullying (reported in a survey by 27% of junior doctors, especially female doctors (Pan *et al,* 2017)). The most common and taxing stressors in the healthcare context are listed below, based on research studies (Butterworth *et al,* 1997; Jenkins & Elliott, 2004; Sarafis *et al,* 2016; Walklet & Percy, 2014; Woodhead *et al,* 2016; Yoon *et al,* 1996), systematic and other reviews (Bhui *et al,* 2012; Maslach & Leiter, 2016; Michie & Williams, 2002; Panagioti *et al,* 2017) and an expert consensus statement (Health and Safety Executive, 2009):

- Inadequate control: poor job design; unclear roles and responsibilities; sense of low control or discretion; loss of autonomy

- Excessive demands: workload exceeds coping and support resources (e.g. high numbers of patients or other work pressures, such as challenging targets or standards; not enough time, so long hours worked; role complexity); managing the distress and behaviour of patients, such as aggression, contact with suicidality and death (e.g. dementia sufferers; those with a personality disorder); inefficiencies and bureaucracy (e.g. certification, computerization, audit, and training demands)

- Insufficient support: lack of emotional and companionship support from peers; lack of practical or emotional support from managers

- Weak relationships: negative team dynamics; peer conflicts and other relationship struggles; negative attitudes; high turnover

- Inadequate resources: not enough staff; no help with the endless paperwork; lack of training

- Ineffectual leadership: management issues (e.g. bullying; unfairness); endless changes and reorganization; inadequate communication or participation in decision making. Lack of work incentives and encouragement

- Impacts outside work: disturbing the work-life balance; inability to detach from work; harming personal relationships

As this list indicates, healthcare workers face a wide variety of exceptionally challenging stressors in their jobs. A good example is again the Increasing Access to Psychological Therapies (IAPT) service, introduced by the UK government in 2009 to better enable people with moderate anxiety and depression to access evidence-based therapies. In 2012, a competitive market strategy was introduced, featuring targets for clinical outcomes and payment by results in IAPT services. Local tariffs were set by commissioners but may have been set too low to enable clinical supervision, or indeed other forms of professional development, to be effectively implemented. In the study of the IAPT Service by Steel *et al* (2015) work demands and autonomy were identified to be the stressors which predicted therapist burnout, while distress was indicated by in-session feelings of anxiety. As a result, the authors concluded that clinical supervision could usefully focus on these factors.

Another illustrative study of the IAPT programme in England's NHS indicated an exceptionally challenging cluster of stressors, featuring a target-driven culture, constant organizational change, long waiting lists, a high volume of patients, insufficient resources, and difficult team dynamics (Walklet & Percy, 2014). In addition, a fairly unique stressor within IAPT programmes is what was referred to as 'high-tariff training', which refers to how most IAPT staff are contracted to concurrently complete and pass a rigorous postgraduate professional qualification in the first year or two of their new job (i.e. if they fail the course they lose their employment). In addition, demanding performance indicators, such as ensuring that clients access therapy within 28 days of referral and achieving recovery rates comparable to those achieved in clinical trials (i.e. in excess of 50%) were identified as exceptional stressors. Due in part to these stressors, their replies to a questionnaire measuring psychological distress indicated that an alarming 30% of these IAPT workers were themselves in need of psychological help (The General Health Questionnaire, GHQ-12 (Goldberg and Williams, 1988)). This rate of distress is similar to the prevalence rates reported for mental health nurses, but lower than the figures reported for mental health social workers, and for clinical psychologists (Hannigan *et al*, 2000).

Measurement

Stressors can be measured by The Coping Responses Questionnaire (CRI) (Moos, 1993), which – although first published some years ago – is still used in research. The CRI starts qualitatively by inviting the respondent to describe the most important stressful problem experienced in the past 12 months. It then asks for that problem to be rated quantitatively, in terms of 10 considerations that tend to make situations stressful. These include the problem's unfamiliarity, unpredictability, and uncontrollability (e.g. exceeding the individual's coping repertoire). Personal considerations which may further compound the stressor are also included in the CRI, such as negative appraisal (e.g. exaggeration or 'catastrophization'), self-inflicted stressors, bad timing, the threat value, and whether or not the problem was resolved (e.g. were benefits achieved?). Other useful sources of data noted by the Health and Safety Executive (HSE, 2009) are sickness s absence data; staff turnover figures; exit interviews; the number of referrals to occupational health; and information from staff forums.

Practical implications

Some stressors are perceived as unacceptable by everyone, (e.g. 'excessive demands') but there are large individual differences between people in their personal judgement of stressors ('appraisal': see below). Staff who have experienced extreme or traumatic events at work (e.g. the threat of violence, or the death of a patient) will tend to react negatively. Natural reactions include a heightened sensitivity (hypervigilance), persistent avoidance, poor concentration and irritability in relation to the stressor. These and multiple related reactions can vary on a continuum, from minor increasing to the symptoms of Post-Traumatic Stress Disorder (PTSD) (American Psychiatric Association, 2013), though most stress reactions in healthcare will tend to be at a low level. The nature of the stressor will influence these reactions but so will individual differences, as described in this chapter (e.g. personality factors, such as 'hardiness', will tend to reduce the perceived challenge presented by a stressor).

Therefore, it is important that supervisors initially clarify how the supervisee perceives the stressors that they find challenging at work. We cannot 'second guess' such personal perceptions, as individual differences and life experiences will make individual supervisees respond in distinctive, unpredictable ways. One scenario is that the challenging stressor is being exaggerated by the supervisee, perhaps due to a fairly traumatic prior encounter, leading to some dysfunctional thinking (e.g. exaggerating the threat posed; minimizing their ability to cope). A second scenario is the opposite, in that the supervisee may perceive a stressor accurately (in the supervisor's opinion), but assume an unreasonable level of responsibility for addressing it (e.g. perhaps because of deeply held values about providing high-quality care, even at a high personal cost). It follows that a supervisor should review stressful events with supervisees, helping them to become more aware of how their own personality (and other individual characteristics) influence their appraisals and reactions. Supervisors can also develop a supervisee's ability to distinguish diverse situations, guiding them to realize that they should not automatically accept personal responsibility in every situation at work (e.g. uncontrollable stressors, such as equipment failures or other factors outside their control). Sometimes a supervisor may wisely judge that a supervisee should be protected from a particular stressor, as in intervening supportively with management regarding an unacceptable workload. Peer support can be vital, validating a shared perception that some stressors need to be addressed at an organizational or higher level (such as government policy or funding).

Another important conclusion is that stressors are not all bad, and indeed should ideally be reframed as an opportunity for personal development. This is because, in coping adaptively with stressors, the supervisee has the opportunity to increase their self-esteem and job satisfaction, developing professional proficiency (e.g. resilience; hardiness). In this sense, stressors are an opportunity for coping strategy enhancement, a greater sense of well-being, and also an opportunity for recognition or promotion. Supervisors should seize these opportunities to promote the supervisee's personal development and well-being. They should even cultivate in supervisees the habit of favourably reframing stressors (and coping reactions) in this manner. This will strengthen their working alliance and contribute to further improvements (e.g. by increasing the trust that the supervisee can place in the supervisor, aiding disclosure of problems and concerns).

Managers and service leaders should detect and correct misunderstandings among their staff, preferably in the early stages before stressors cause damage or harm, by monitoring supervisees' perceptions of inadequate or harmful supervision, perhaps through regular, confidential surveys. They should also ensure that their organization's policies are explicit regarding the required or acceptable standards of interpersonal behaviour, by detailing clearly what is expected of supervisors and supervisees. This can be supplemented by an anonymous telephone hotline or a mailbox that links to the organization's human resources (HR) or Occupational Health (OH) department. Such arrangements can make it easier for inexperienced or unassertive staff to report instances of unreasonable stressors or unacceptable behaviour (e.g. workplace bullying). These measures assist in creating a culture that makes it OK to seek support (Pan *et al*, 2017). Other ways that HR or OH can help include confidential coaching, counselling and mentoring services (Mackay, 2017). More constructively, managers can help their staff with their work engagement by emphasising the intrinsic value or meaning of their work (e.g. recognizing the benefits to society), regular positive feedback, satisfying relationships with colleagues, and challenging tasks, all within a supportive work culture (Brummelhuis *et al*, 2017). Particularly stressful factors should be addressed, such as poor job design and vague job descriptions (e.g. unclear or conflicting roles and responsibilities), and ineffective communication or insufficient resources (Lizano, 2015). Enhancing team culture is a fundamental way to address such issues and cultivate an empowering workplace (Willard-Grace *et al*, 2014). Burnout contributes to high staff turnover, so the costs of addressing work stressors may be offset by cost savings due to improved staff retention and reduced sickness absence, etc. (Westwood *et al*, 2017). Chapter 5 contains more detailed emphasis on the roles that managers, administrators, and other clinical leaders can play.

Summary

As this example of alliance development illustrates, addressing stressors with supervisees contributes to several of the aims of supportive supervision (as summarized in Table 3.1). Protecting supervisees from unmanageable stressors is a case in point, achieved by methods such as monitoring the workload and goal-setting collaboratively. Manageable stressors can be regarded as positive or negative, depending on how they are perceived by the individual supervisee. When we are coping effectively, many people actually enjoy responding to stressors, and may even seek them out, as they allow us to exercise our judgement and ability and thereby flourish (e.g. volunteering for particularly demanding tasks). In contrast, when we are struggling, we can become highly sensitive to repeated stressors, making strenuous efforts to escape or avoid them.

The IAPT programme exemplifies the increasingly business-like nature of modern healthcare in Western or developed societies, but the challenges faced by IAPT staff are essentially the same as those faced by healthcare professionals everywhere. Indeed, dealing with stressors is a basic, inescapable human task. Although the original theory behind such coping is somewhat dated (Lazarus & Folkman, 1984), it remains the best available theory, now so widely-accepted that it is regarded as 'common-sense' and sometimes not even specified any longer (e.g. Michie & Williams, 2003).

Appraisal

Another aim of supportive supervision is to challenge thinking errors, to help supervisees engage in more balanced, rational thinking (for a summary of these aims, see Table 3.1). As noted earlier, errors arise through the way that people appraise the events that happen to them at work (e.g. assuming too much responsibility). Appraisal is the mental process of judging the personal meaning of events as they happen, in order to decide if they are important for our well-being (Lazarus & Folkman, 1984; Lazarus, 1999). Within milliseconds, our brains typically classify events as threatening or harmless, which triggers emotional reactions and coping efforts to suit. The emotional consequences of appraisal make it an essential part of understanding how individuals view stressors, together with the ways that they react to them. Individual differences play a significant role and so supervisors need to take this into account in reviewing supervisees' appraisals.

There are three stages to this appraisal process, each capable of illuminating emotional reactions that merit discussion in supervision. Firstly, 'primary' appraisal concerns the instant judgement that we automatically form about a stressor that has just occurred – a kind of innate, automatic brain reaction. We perceive events as either threatening (associated with burnout), or challenging but potentially under our control (associated with well-being) (Tomaka *et al*, 2018). Threat appraisals involve a physiological reaction (heightened arousal; the 'flight or fight' response), leading immediately and automatically to initial negative emotions (e.g. fear, anxiety, and worry). For example, in the verbatim material reported and interpreted by James *et al* (2004, p.51), the supervisee responds with anxiety to a tough question from the supervisor. By contrast, appraising a stressor as a challenge signals the potential for gain, personal growth, or mastery. Positive emotions are produced, including feelings of eagerness, excitement, and exhilaration. What follows these emotions is 'secondary appraisal', where we decide whether and how we can cope with the event. Individuals who appraise the situation as too overwhelming for their coping skills will tend to continue to perceive the stressful event as threatening, and engage in avoidance-based, emotion-focused coping strategies (e.g. repeated rumination over what happened or emotional discharge, such as repeated complaining). But if individuals believe that they can cope with the situation (i.e. that they have the necessary coping skills and feel in control of the situation), then the stressful event continues to be perceived as challenging and individuals will employ approach-based coping strategies (Tomaka *et al*, 2018).

The third and final stage of this appraisal process is reappraisal, which occurs once the episode has closed. Here we take account of available feedback to judge what happened and to identify any lessons (e.g. Was the stressor truly threatening, or did I overreact? How well did I cope?). This account indicates the emotionally charged nature of appraisal, and a valuable role for supervision in heightening awareness and challenging supervisees' negative appraisals. All three stages are affected by our personal belief systems, our habitual ways of perceiving events (technically termed our 'schema'; for a burnout example, see Kaeding *et al*, 2017). For example, the schema of 'unrelenting standards' (thinking that nothing one does is good enough, i.e. perfectionism) creates a tendency to reappraise one's coping as deficient.

Relevant research supports this account of appraisal. For instance, Gomes *et al* (2016) studied more than 2,000 general nurses (i.e. working in medical specialties, emergency and intensive care, and surgical specialties) within Portugal's national health service. The authors found that the way that these nurses appraised their jobs affected their psychological health – perceiving events as threatening was associated with burnout, whereas perceiving events as challenging but controllable had the opposite correlation. However, they also reported that some "specific work conditions can impair professionals' well-being regardless of how they appraise the conditions and their professional activities" (p24). This indicates that there are limits to the power of appraisal, underlining the need for supportive supervision as a mechanism for preventing unmanageable workplace stressors. Similar findings on the appraisal process have been consistently reported in the research literature (e.g. high challenge and control appraisals were correlated with less exhaustion and depersonalization, but more accomplishment) (Ben-Zur & Michael, 2007). By contrast, trying to avoid or ignore low control appraisals has been found to predict absenteeism (Bond *et al*, 2011).

Measurement

Primary and secondary appraisal can be measured by questionnaires and an example is the Cognitive Appraisal Scale (CAS) (Gomes and 2016). The CAS evaluates primary appraisal in terms of threat perception (e.g. 'My job… is not disturbing to me/ is disturbing to me') and challenge perception (e.g. 'My job… is not exciting for me/ is exciting for me'). Secondary appraisal is assessed in terms of coping potential (e.g. 'To what extent do you think you are prepared to handle the demands of your job?') and control perception (e.g. 'To what extent do you feel that what happens in your job depends on you?'). Each item is measured using a 7-point Likert scale (e.g. for coping potential 0 = Not at all prepared; 6 = Well prepared for coping potential). A review of related appraisal measures can be found in Carpenter (2015).

Practical implications

Perceiving a stressor as a challenge that can be controlled is a major example of secondary appraisal and this is something that can be developed in supervisees. The ability to change appraisals carries significant implications for supportive supervision, as thinking errors can be reappraised at this stage (e.g. supervisees underestimating their coping skills or catastrophizing about the stressor).

Supervisees' confidence can also be boosted by helping them to realize that they can control a stressor. Supervisors should therefore ask their supervisees about how they appraise stressful work events in order to develop a better understanding of their supervisees' thinking processes. Appraisal is a promising area for improving the supervisee's personal coping strategies, as for example in helping to reframe a stressor as unavoidable, or in validating how the supervisee coped.

Summary

Appraisal activates our coping response to workplace stressors, drawing on our individual differences and social support (Ben-Zur & Michael, 2007). It is therefore a highly subjective and individual process, involving a rapid and at times automatic perception of stressors. Research suggests that we initially appraise stressful events as either threatening (associated with burnout), or challenging but controllable (associated with well-being) (Tomaka *et al*, 2018). However, there are definite limits to such positive appraisal, since some work stressors are perceived as overwhelming and so bypass our coping strategies, leading straight to distress (Gomes *et al*, 2016). This possibility underlines the need for supportive supervision as one mechanism for addressing unmanageable workplace stressors.

Personal coping strategies

Coping theory explains how individuals deal with stressors, including the adaptive and maladaptive strategies employed (Lazarus & Folkman, 1984; Lazarus, 1991) with highly relevant applications to healthcare settings internationally (Folkman & Nathan, 2010). Although rarely linked explicitly to restorative supervision, the coping model has clear relevance, as illustrated in the preceding discussion of appraisal, and in staff surveys that attempt to illuminate burnout (e.g. Pan *et al*, 2017; Delgado *et al*, 2019). It is also a practical theory that can greatly aid us in understanding and addressing problems such as burnout, or in fostering well-being.

Effective or 'adaptive' coping is usually based on tackling stressors with 'approach-based' strategies such as problem-solving, or through seeking advice and assistance. We define these as adaptive if they work, indicated by reduced distress or increased well-being. Maladaptive coping is usually based on 'avoidance-based' coping (e.g. postponing action or ignoring the problem). Avoidance-based strategies are popular because they can bring quick relief with minimal effort. Unfortunately, they tend to result in longer-term setbacks and contribute to growing distress. For example, Bourne *et al* (2019) described how physicians engaged in various 'defensive practices' to minimize their burnout (including over-prescribing, over-investigation, and avoiding certain procedures or more difficult cases). The optimal approach is therefore to develop and apply approach-based coping strategies. Table 4.2 is structured using the eight factors within the CRI the first four being adaptive, approach-based methods and the remainder being avoidance-based (Moos, 1993).

In Table 4.2. we have illustrated these eight CRI factors with the findings from a survey of how a sample of nearly 1,000 American counsellors reported coping with their work (Lawson, 2007).

TABLE 4.2: Eight major coping strategies, as measured by The Coping Responses Inventory questionnaire (Moos, 1993), with examples from a survey of American counsellors (Lawson, 2007)	
Personal coping strategies	Examples from a survey of counsellors
1. Logical analysis	Maintain objectivity; seek case consultation.
2. Positive appraisal	Reflect on positive experiences; gain a sense of control.
3. Seeking support	Access clinical supervision; peer support; personal therapy.
4. Problem-solving	Increasing self-awareness; Continuing Professional Development; reflection; read literature.
5. Cognitive avoidance	Put aside unwanted thoughts; avoid responsibility.
6. Acceptance/resignation	Take a vacation; turn to spiritual beliefs.
7. Seek alternative rewards	Use substances to relax; leisure activities.
8. Emotional discharge	Describe work frustrations to colleagues.

Research supports the validity of the coping model. For example, Maslach *et al* (2001) reviewed the early research on burnout, emphasising the crucial role played by coping. This early burnout research focused on care-giving ('people work'), where the essence of the job required staff to maintain an empathic relationship, despite experiencing the patients' distress. A research illustration is based on interviewing health professionals in England (Walklet and Percy, 2014), indicating the use of a range of coping strategies. Common examples were planning, positively reinterpreting events (positive appraisal), seeking social support (emotional and practical), and an acceptance of the stressors that could not be changed. These strategies are consistent with good, adaptive coping, according to coping theory (Lazarus & Folkman, 1984). Walklet and Percy (2014) reported that, while acceptance and active approach-based coping correlated with significantly lower levels of personal distress, emotional discharge was related to higher distress (as measured by the General Health Questionnaire (Goldberg and Williams, 1988)). Similarly worrying levels of distress were found among a sample of 482 Australian mental health nurses

(Delgado *et al,* 2019), though they also reported some adaptive coping strategies (e.g. actively seeking feedback and support at work). There was a positive association between clinical supervision and resilience, in that the nurses who engaged in clinical supervision had higher overall resilience. Delgado *et al* conjectured that supervision may have contributed as a work-related resilience-building strategy, helping the nurses to learn to manage the 'emotional labour' of their work and positively influencing their interpersonal relationships and well-being.

Action implications

Supervisors can start by recognizing and validating the valiant efforts that supervisees (especially trainees) make on a daily basis to cope with the seemingly endless and often extreme demands in healthcare. Staff are remarkably resourceful and resilient. Perhaps we should pause to applaud this effort more frequently, building on the coping strategies that work best for different individuals. Prime contenders for development in supervisees include their resilience and openness (i.e. a willingness to discuss and address difficulties), which can respond to training (Green *et al,* 2014). In essence, supervisors should aim to use advice and guidance to shift the balance from the maladaptive 'avoidance-based' coping strategies (e.g. procrastinating or denying the problem) towards the adaptive, approach-based coping strategies (e.g. thinking through the options for tackling a problem; seeking advice from a peer). These methods are consistent with the goals of supportive supervision as set out in Table 3.1 (e.g. 'Encourage supervisees to access and optimize social support from colleagues' and 'Develop the supervisees' personal coping strategies and professional competencies by offering advice and guidance'). As indicated in that table, such methods should improve the supervisees' relationships, confidence, self-awareness and competence.

Summary

The single most useful way to understand how individuals develop burnout or well-being is by considering the role played by personal coping strategies. Like personality characteristics, these are hugely diverse, reflecting individual differences. Some strategies are of short-term value but will ultimately prove maladaptive (e.g. avoidance and emotional discharge). According to the coping model, these maladaptive strategies lead to personal distress, usually following a negative downward spiral, the 'vicious cycle'. Supervisors and others should rather encourage adaptive coping strategies in supervisees, such as positive appraisal, support-seeking, and emotional resilience. Adaptive coping strategies enable us to thrive in our work, promoting personal effectiveness and well-being (they are in a positive upward spiral, a 'virtuous cycle'). Sometimes termed 'grit' or 'hardiness' when regarded as a personality trait, emotional resilience is more accurately seen as a facet of coping (Grant & Kinman, 2014; Delgado *et al,* 2019). That is, resilience is an ability to adapt and thrive despite adversity (e.g. working with particularly challenging patients; recovering from setbacks), a cluster of professional competencies that can be learned. The resilience cluster includes flexible coping strategies, good problem-solving skills, and a strong sense of purpose (Grant & Kinman, 2014). Helping supervisees to develop their adaptive coping strategies and resilience lies at the heart of supportive supervision, as indicated by our main summary of evidence-based methods in Table 3.1.

Social support

Personal coping strategies are closely linked to social support. As indicated by Table 4.2, coping can be seen to include attempts to gain social support. Sometimes social support takes the form of directly helping others to cope, for example by offering advice or by helping in a practical way. At other times social support entails protecting someone from specific stressors (the 'buffering' role of support) or helps simply because individuals feel generally supported (e.g. that there is someone who will help, if necessary). Supportive supervision should involve significant amounts of social support, as well as encouraging supervisees to access and reciprocate peer support. We say more about social support in the next chapter, and especially in Chapter 7, when we discuss how supervisees might best gain the support that they need. For now, here is a preview of Chapter 7: Social support can be defined as the perception of companionship and as referring to "emotional, informational, or practical assistance from significant others, such as family members, friends, or coworkers" (Thoits, 2010).

Such support takes myriad forms (see the classic High Street surveys by Cowen, 1982), but results in a few fundamental benefits for people, such as a sense of attachment and acceptance. Table 7.3 in Chapter 7 offers a summary of the links between the different forms and functions of social support.

Distress

Distress (also termed 'occupational stress' or work 'strain') is usually the negative consequence of maladaptive coping, consisting of unpleasant thoughts, feelings or behaviours (e.g. anxious thoughts about being judged incompetent; depressive symptoms, such as feeling low or useless; or burnout in the form of absenteeism). To illustrate, in the Walklet and Percy (2014) research, one-third of their sample of 44 staff were distressed at clinical levels, as measured on the General Health Questionnaire (GHQ) 12 (Goldberg & Williams, 1988). The GHQ encompasses depression, concentration, and self-confidence. Example items are, respectively: 'Been feeling unhappy and depressed?'; 'Been able to concentrate on whatever you are doing?'; and 'Been losing confidence in yourself?'. The items are rated on a 4-point frequency scale, ranging from 'More so than usual' to 'Much less than usual'. The GHQ is a widely used measure of psychological distress.

Burnout

We have already indicated (Chapter 1) the damaging societal consequences of burnout, so now we adopt a personal perspective. Burnout is the most frequently cited type of distress in the healthcare workplace. The most widely used definition and measure was published by Maslach and Jackson (1981).They developed a 22-item questionnaire, the Maslach Burnout Inventory (MBI), with items rated on their frequency, from 0-6 ('never' to 'every day'). Emotional exhaustion is the main dimension of burnout, a feeling of being emotionally depleted through chronic work stressors (e.g. coping resources drained by an excessive and unrelenting workload). An example item is 'Working with people all day is a strain for me'. Workers experiencing emotional exhaustion tend to cope by distancing themselves from patients and detaching from work. An example is depersonalization, which features negative feelings towards one's patients, such as taking a callous, cynical and dehumanising approach (e.g. the attitude that patients deserve their problems). An example item is 'I really don't care if my work is done well or poorly'. Impaired personal accomplishment refers to feeling ineffective and unproductive at work, which is associated with a tendency to evaluate oneself negatively and to find work unrewarding and unsatisfactory. An example item is 'I am confident that I am effective at getting my work done'. A high score on the exhaustion and depersonalization components of the MBI, and a low score on personal accomplishment, indicate burnout. Burnout as measured by the MBI was found to be distinct from job satisfaction and from depression (e.g. depression is more global, affecting all aspects of one's life; burnout is work-specific).

Study findings consistently point to the many negative impacts of burnout (Lizano, 2015). To illustrate, the review of research conducted by Naczenski *et al* (2017) indicated that high levels of burnout were associated with reduced self-confidence, poor sleep, decreased mental functioning, impaired work ability, and a higher risk of developing cardiovascular diseases. These review authors concluded that there were also negative consequences of worker burnout for employers too, such as 'presenteeism' and lost productivity, not to mention the healthcare costs to society at large. Although studies in this field are largely cross-sectional in design and therefore causal relationships are hard to determine, the review by Naczenski *et al* (2017) did include longitudinal studies. Burnout can take myriad forms, as effectively illustrated by a table of negative consequences in Dyrbye and Shanafelt (2016). They distinguished between professional and personal 'ramifications', the former including: decreased empathy and altruism; cheating/dishonest behaviours; inappropriate prescribing behaviours; decreased personal accountability regarding impaired colleagues; dropping out of training; suboptimal patient care and clinical errors. The personal ramifications cited from their review of research included suicidal ideation, a sense of stigma regarding mental health problems, and motor vehicle incidents.

Interventions for burnout should be based on applying the coping model, meaning that individual sufferers should be assessed by a suitably qualified professional in relation to the main contributing factors, leading to a personal formulation (e.g. assessments could include some of the questionnaires detailed above). It is not appropriate for the supervisor to undertake this work in a formal way, as it would represent therapy (i.e. a role boundary transgression). As indicated throughout this book, such a formulation may well indicate that the problem lies primarily within the workplace, indicating that a systemic intervention is most appropriate (see Chapter 5). But if the most appropriate intervention is at the individual level, then a range of options should be considered. As already noted in relation to stressors, HR and OH departments can help through arranging for confidential coaching, counselling and mentoring services (Mackay, 2017). Some individuals may require therapy, with cognitive-behavioural therapy (CBT) the most promising, evidence-based approach (Awa *et al,* 2010; Marine *et al,* 2009). Antidepressant or anxiety-reducing medication under medical review is a possible alternative in appropriate cases. Other options may play a more preventive or supplementary role and lend themselves to general implementation. These include stress management classes, groups intended to enhance personal coping strategies, advice on healthy living (e.g. balanced diet, reduced alcohol consumption), progressive muscular relaxation and mindfulness meditation, and participation in exercise and sport (Ochentel *et al,* 2018). A systematic review of such interventions for individuals concluded that they were successful in reducing burnout in over 80% of the reported studies, although booster or refresher work was necessary to maintain the gains made (Awa *et al,* 2010). These studies involved professional skills development training, communication training, in addition to clinical supervision.

Practical implications

The GHQ-12 and MBI are suited to repeated administration, making them a valuable aid in monitoring how an individual is responding to an intervention. A popular alternative to the GHQ-12 is the Outcome Questionnaire (Lambert *et al,* 1996), which measures subjective distress, interpersonal functioning and social role performance. In this sense, the preferred tool could be completed weekly by a supervisee who is addressing workplace distress to provide cumulative outcome data. If feasible, it would make good sense to also measure appraisal and coping strategy use, since this should indicate whether or not the intervention is having the intended effect on the supervisee's overall adjustment.

Summary

For the individual worker, burnout consists of emotional exhaustion, depersonalization, and ineffectiveness at work, but workers with burnout also negatively impact colleagues and employers (e.g. accidents and lost productivity). It is the main type of distress in the healthcare workplace, and reducing it is a core function of supportive supervision (see Table 3.1). As this table indicates, the main way that a supervisor can help to prevent or reduce burnout is by protecting the supervisee from excessive stressors through the personal provision of social support and by helping the supervisee to access peer support. In Chapter 1 we summarized a relevant study by Edwards *et al* (2006), which found that feeling supported by the supervisor, and also being able to discuss sensitive issues, were associated with less burnout (less emotional exhaustion and depersonalization).

Well-being

In direct contrast to burnout and other forms of distress, workplace well-being concerns emotions associated with work mastery and engagement. It is associated with feelings of choice and control, recognition and reward, fairness and justice, a supportive community, together with a belief that work is meaningful and valued (Begat and Severinsson, 2006). We discussed well-being briefly in Chapter 1, noting evidence that supervision can improve well-being among staff, leading to improved productivity and other benefits for the organization (Boorman, 2009). This is acknowledged by the UK's NHS in recognizing that staff should be encouraged to show greater 'engagement' with their employing organization. Engagement goes beyond being satisfied at work to fostering among staff a deeper sense of commitment, attachment and organizational citizenship. Engagement also refers to social, physical and psychological well-being (e.g. positive relationships with colleagues; experiencing positive emotions about one's work; greater vigour, dedication and absorption at work).

The links to supportive supervision become evident when one considers the kind of workplace factors believed to foster organizational engagement, such as having a sense of purpose, communicating effectively, managing work overload, and gaining social support. According to a review of the resilience literature by McAllister and McKinnon (2009), key practitioners (such as supervisors) can provide opportunities for colleagues to reflect on and learn from experience, as well as benefiting from the supervisors as role models. Supervisors can also share their experiences of engagement and thriving in health workplaces, mentor, lead, coach and motivate supervisees, so that a generative health professional culture is developed. Research on building resilience, reviewed by McCann *et al* (2013), compared four different healthcare professions. They found support for the value of reflection, a sense of humour (laughter), spiritual beliefs, and a sense of professional identity. Some of these may serve as mechanisms for resolving conflicts and improving communication. Begat and Severinsson (2006) summarized the well-being findings from three of their studies, based on a large group of Norwegian nurses' experiences and reflections. Well-being was associated with a supportive workplace in which the nurses were able to create trusting relationships with their patients, aided by supervision that offered 'containment' (supervision providing a 'safe base'), affirmation, reflection and empowerment. The nurses also regarded supervision as a place where they could process their experiences, another part of supportive supervision as summarized in Table 3.1 ('discuss feeling reactions; emotional processing'). Begat and Severinsson (2006) concluded that supervision positively influences well-being. Koivu *et al* (2012) studied supervision of 304 female medical–surgical nurses, involved in direct patient care. Group supervision was available to all, and satisfaction with supervision was assessed. Those who attended supervision and rated it as satisfactory reported the same level of job stressors, but fewer burnout symptoms and greater professional effectiveness than those colleagues who rated supervision as unsatisfactory. Compared with the nurses who did not participate in supervision, supervisees reported increased job and personal resources, especially experiencing greater job control. The perception of being in control is seen by some as the most vital antecedent for well-being at work (Dorman *et al*, 2006).

A rare and unusually large-scale dissemination of restorative clinical supervision has been described by Wallbank (2012). Specifically designed to support health visitors in the UK, this approach to group supervision has been subjected to a longitudinal evaluation (pre-post, plus follow-up). This evaluation indicated that six group sessions, attended by a sample of 174 Health Visitors, led to them reporting highly significant reductions in their work stress and burnout, together with improvements in their job attachment and compassion satisfaction (the pleasure they derived from their jobs (Wallbank & Woods, 2012)). Anecdotally, these supervisees also reported more energy, creativity, and clearer thinking. This group of studies indicates that supportive supervision is associated with well-being, although once more we must emphasise that this literature is mostly uncontrolled and generally of poor methodological quality.

Instrument

An example of a suitable measurement tool for well-being is the Connor–Davidson Resilience Scale (CD-RISC; Connor and Davidson 2003), a 25-item questionnaire addressing the characteristics of resilient people. These are hardiness ('grit'), a sense of control, job commitment, seeing stressors as a challenge, and perseverance.

Practical implications

According to a practice-focused review of positive psychology by Howard (2008), there are many ways that 'the typical day-to-day practice of clinical supervision' might contribute to well-being (and related positive outcomes, such as resilience). These include reflection on casework, so as to make it more understandable and effective; reviewing and adjusting workloads (numbers, tasks, or patient types); matching workplace goals to the supervisee's skills, while maintaining some stimulating challenge, resolving conflict with colleagues, and enhancing communication skills to encourage peer support or improve job resources. These supervision methods can foster professional effectiveness and a sense of personal accomplishment, and this appears to be particularly valuable in boosting job engagement (Koivu *et al,* 2012). For instance, these researchers suggested that guided reflection assists recovery and learning from emotionally demanding work setbacks, ones that induce feelings of ineffectiveness or incompetence.

Managers can help by encouraging staff to exercise choice (i.e. increase their autonomy), as well as by implementing job diversity and enrichment. A general 'tight-loose' approach to autonomy emphasises achieving agreed results ('tight' about the objectives), as opposed to focusing on the actions that produce those results ('loose' about the methods). Such an approach increases the staff members' sense of control by empowering them to be inventive and diversify their work routines (Yoon *et al,* 1996).

Summary

Enhanced well-being is a core function of supportive supervision (see Table 3.1), which can also improve job engagement and employee retention. As this table indicates, the main means by which a supervisor can help to foster well-being is by forming a strong alliance, protecting the supervisee from excessive stressors, enhancing coping strategies and competencies (e.g. through guided reflection) and through social support (e.g. by discussing supervisees' emotional reactions to work events). Supportive supervision is a particularly promising way to foster professional effectiveness and a sense of personal accomplishment, which can then boost job engagement and well-being.

Case study: Personal issues create conflict with the workplace

Background: The supervisee was a junior therapist, a male in his mid-20s undergoing a one-year post-qualification training programme in Cognitive-Behavioural Therapy (CBT). The supervisor was an experienced CBT therapist, a woman in her late 30s providing supervision within this university-based training programme.

Critical event: After six months of supervision (i.e. halfway through training), the supervisee had still not provided the supervisor with a video recording of his therapy, which is a standard expectation within the workplace.

Interaction sequence: The supervisee explains that he has been making recordings, but that "they are not up to my usual standard". He goes on to explain that he has high expectations and is a bit of a perfectionist. He is aware that time is passing, but is determined to provide a recording that demonstrates his competence in CBT. The supervisor challenges his thinking in a way that is consistent with CBT, saying that that she is a bit puzzled: You seem to be assuming that I am here to rubber-stamp your competence. But this is a training programme and you are here to develop greater competence. If you were to provide a recording demonstrating high proficiency, →

how could I give you corrective feedback?" She also points out that no one is perfect, and that even renowned CBT researchers have fallen short of best practice. The supervisee explains that he is concerned because he has been criticised in the past: "When I received that criticism, I felt that I was being punished. I can't let that happen again; I was pretty upset for a while."

Resolution: The supervisor notes that the supervisee's avoidance has been due to the supervisee's worries, and suggests that they discuss this barrier. She normalizes how people feel about recordings ("No one enjoys having their performance evaluated") and self-discloses that she didn't enjoy it at all when she was training, being "tortured" by the initial feedback that she received, but that in the end she found it really helpful. This encourages the supervisee to recognize that "maybe this is something we all have to endure". The supervisor goes on to suggest a coping strategy: recordings should be reframed as helpful feedback, i.e. that inevitably involves criticism but is well-intentioned and will help us to improve. It is part of being a professional working within a healthcare organization. Lastly, she asks how the experience can be made easier or more helpful. The supervisee suggests that, as a first step, they should together watch a section that he selects "to desensitize me", before doing anything more threatening. This reminds the supervisor of a suitable method ('interpersonal process recall' (Kagan & Kagan, 1997)), which she then describes and they agree to try that approach so that the supervisee feels more in control of feedback.

Discussion: This supervisee had some 'personal issues', in that he held perfectionistic beliefs that led him to avoiding furnishing his supervisor with a recording. Such beliefs and behaviours can lead to reduced work accomplishments and burnout. But instead of being punitive, the supervisor adopted a supportive stance, seeking to understand the problem from his perspective, and to share her experiences ('self-disclosure') together with her beliefs regarding the value of recordings. Continuing to adopt a CBT approach in her supervision, the supervisor negotiated a way forward that was ultimately suggested by the supervisee, which gave him a feeling of control. This reduced his worries and so indicated an end to the avoidance. This case study also illustrates how the personal characteristics of the supervisee can create tensions within the workplace which can be resolved through supportive supervision.

Chapter summary

This chapter has helped us to comprehend the complex processes that explain well-being at work and enables us to answer the main question we posed: How can we best understand the interaction between workers and their work? It is these individual differences that help us to understand why some staff members thrive in the same environment that their colleagues find distressing; why we have good days and bad days at work, even though the work remains the same; and why some colleagues become cherished friends and associates, while others become adversaries and strangers.

Chapter 5: Influencing Organizations Through Supportive Supervision

1. Introduction

So far in this book we have built an integrative model of supportive supervision, testing and validating that theoretically grounded model against the best available research evidence (see Chapters 2 and 3). What emerged was surprising and encouraging: a brief but effective intervention, revolving around the provision of social support to the supervisee, primarily from the supervisor. Furthermore, supportive supervision appeared to have several important benefits and no harmful side-effects. Therefore, this intervention is clearly worth developing. In Chapter 4 we moved on to consider the participants (individuals and groups), clarifying how their personal characteristics affected supervision. In particular, we focused on the supervisee's reaction to their workplace, identifying ways in which the supervisor could support and guide the supervisee's efforts to cope and develop as a resilient, effective and engaged professional worker.

We now turn our attention to the nature of the workplace system to consider in turn its characteristics and how that system might be influenced favourably through supportive supervision. In essence, a healthy workplace supports staff, with supervision playing a particularly valuable role in that process. Reflecting on a decade of England's innovative, large-scale IAPT programme, Clark (2018, p16) noted how the best-performing IAPT services had a more supportive environment, which he judged to be 'essential' to their clinical success. But many researchers have indicated that the workplace is often an unsupportive environment (e.g. Avortri *et al*, 2019) and even harmful. For example, Moran (2014) described how middle managers were hostile and resistant to the provision of supervision, while White and Winstanley (2011) reflected on how some managers 'thwarted' supervision arrangements for their staff. Other examples of adverse workplaces are not hard to find (e.g. Dorsey *et al*, 2017; Gonge & Buus, 2014), including harmful and unethical supervisors themselves (Tepper, 2000; Ellis *et al*, 2014).

How can supervisors contribute to a supportive environment? How might they empower their supervisees to influence the workplace? Our definition of supervision in Chapter 2 included this general answer:

"... supportive supervision sometimes attempts to improve the workplace, either directly, through the actions of the supervisor (e.g. liaising with service managers), or indirectly, through guiding and empowering the supervisee (e.g. jointly formulating environmental stressors; discussing and enacting plans to reduce stressors)... The primary relational mechanisms are the supervision alliance and the provision and receipt of social support (emotional, practical, informational, and companionship support, from the supervisor and from peers)..."

Therefore, in terms of our support model (for an illustration, see Figure 2.2 in Chapter 2) we are now focusing on the interface between the organizational system and the interpersonal system. By analogy, the supervisor and supervisee are turning their tandem on a journey towards addressing the environmental factors that are interfering with their professional development, tackling together the metaphorical road-blocks, risks and barriers that they encounter in their workplace. They are seeking out better routes and supportive allies, venturing towards their destination of personal well-being and professional satisfaction.

In this analogy, and in saying that 'supportive supervision sometimes attempts to improve the workplace' we take an unusually proactive position, viewing supervision as a preventive and constructive response to its environment, a form of problem-focused coping that is capable of influencing the workplace for the better by preventing or reducing stressors. This version of supervision overlaps with some of the organizational content within the 'normative' or managerial function of supervision (see Figure 2.1 in Chapter 2). However, our emphasis differs in seeking to change the way that the organization works, in particular to empower the supervisee to intervene at the level of the workplace system (e.g. influencing through feedback how managers lead staff; suggesting how jobs could be re-structured; how communication might be enhanced). An example is enhancing communication through group supervision. Indeed, the literature on burnout has tended to focus on interventions that address the personal functioning of the healthcare worker, as opposed to considering first the organizational system in which personal problems arise. This is indicated in the review by Michie and Williams (2003, p8), who stated that:

"Intervention studies...have focused mainly on staff training. There is a need for future studies to evaluate interventions based on employment practices and management style. This would represent primary prevention, reducing sources of psychological ill health, rather than secondary prevention, training individuals who are already experiencing work related stress to be more robust in the face of such pressures" (Michie & Williams, 2003, p8).

Our preventive position also extends beyond how other supervision authors have viewed supervision in the rare instances that they have considered its context (e.g. Hawkins & Shohet, 2000; Kadushin & Harkness, 2002). Secondary prevention reflects a traditional focus on 'fixing' or 'blaming' the individual – a reactive strategy which has dominated research on occupational stress, at least in the US (Hall, 2007; Shanfelt & Noseworthy, 2017). Illustrative examples include providing CBT to cure 'perfectionistic' student physicians (Chand *et al,* 2018) and training staff in mindfulness to reduce their burnout (Salyers *et al,* 2011). This gives little or no attention to primary prevention, omitting to acknowledge that such personal distress may sometimes have organizational origins. By contrast with fixing distressed workers, an expert consensus has recognized that we also need to transform the workplace (Joint Commission on Accreditation of Healthcare Organizations, 2002). This is increasingly supported through more recent research findings (e.g. Panagioti *et al,* 2017; West *et al,* 2016) and reflected in a greater emphasis on the improved management of burnout (e.g. Shanfelt & Noseworthy, 2017). This focus on social rather than purely personal action represents a logical if challenging option for addressing how supervisors may help clinicians to cope at work. While it is largely based on the same supervision methods as before, now they are focused on the workplace. The principle methods are also within the definition in Chapter 2:

"Specific supervision techniques include... advice and guidance, facilitating peer support, challenging thinking processes, feedback ... (and) problem formulation (e.g interpersonal problems)... plus empathy, encouragement, and validation."

A more specific answer to the chapter's question is now addressed (How can supervisors empower supervisees to influence their workplace?). As before, we will do this by drawing together the best available research and the most relevant theory, moderated by expert consensus. Before we can expect to have an influence on an organization, we need to have a sound understanding of the workplace system, so we will also discuss the roles played by others, in addition to the supervisee and supervisor. Therefore, in this chapter we initially consider the key factors or environmental characteristics that best describe the healthcare workplace, and how they might be assessed (such as leadership and communication). This complements the individual characteristics of the supervisee in the last chapter. Based on this description, we then consider how we might best understand how healthcare organizations work, a formulation task that should guide supportive supervision (e.g. the supervisee's working relationship with leaders or role in communicating with colleagues). Formulation should guide us into selecting the most appropriate supportive supervision interventions, from among the best available, evidence-based options (e.g. contributing to corrective feedback within the workplace, such as continuous quality improvement or clinical outcome monitoring). We describe and evaluate the most promising interventions. We will again conclude with an illustrative case study, followed by the action implications for the main stakeholders. Therefore, in taking these steps, we follow the clinical formulation and problem-solving cycle that supervisors and others routinely utilize and extend it to the workplace system, in what is sometimes called the 'quality enhancement process' (Rowe *et al,* 2005). In this sense we aim to offer a practical outline for enhancing supportive supervision.

2. Assessing the key organizational factors

Just as the individual healthcare worker has a personality, each workplace can also have distinctive characteristics. What are these main characteristics, and how are they associated with supervision? In a comparison of hospitals in the UK, rates of psychological problems among staff ranged from 17% to 33%. The lowest rates were found in the smaller hospitals, characterized by greater cooperation among staff, better communication, more performance monitoring and training, together with more staff control and flexibility in their work (Wall *et al,* 1997). Similar workplace factors and outcomes were reported in a systematic review of 49 studies concerned with work-related psychological problems (Michie & Williams, 2003), with comparable findings reported in a more recent systematic review (Bhatt & Ramani, 2016). These review samples included healthcare workers from several countries, alongside many other groups. Their conclusions were surprisingly consistent, regardless of the type of workers or the country of employment. The key work factors implicated in work-related psychological problems were found to be long working hours; work overload and pressure (and the knock-on effects of these on workers' personal lives); lack of control over work; lack of participation in decision-making; inadequate social support; and unclear and conflicting job roles. Role conflict and role ambiguity consistently showed a moderate-to-high correlation with burnout (Maslach *et al,* 2001). Role conflict occurs when conflicting job demands have to be met (or where professional groups compete for activities both deem to be 'their' work), whereas role ambiguity occurs when there is a lack of adequate information to do the job well (e.g. no specific work priorities or feedback). According to the review by Maslach *et al* (2001), lack of feedback to guide workers has consistently been related to burnout. However, the organizational resource that has been most studied is social support. There is now a consistent and strong body of evidence that lack of social support is linked to burnout. These authors added that a lack of support from supervisors is especially important. These research findings indicate that a pattern of recurring organizational factors contribute to the well-being of staff and that some of these workplace features could be influenced through supervision. For example, the results of the review of supportive supervision in Chapter 3 (see Table 3.1) indicated that greater trust and better working relationships among staff were associated with enhanced social support-seeking by the supervisees, itself part of the coping strategy enhancement work of the supervisor.

How might we best assess these powerful organizational characteristics? Within supervision, a supervisor can start with some detailed questioning, aimed at defining and describing an incident of concern in the workplace, as perceived by the supervisee. At a more systematic level this can take the form of a structured interview that is administered to a team or to a sample of the members of a large clinical service, where questions probe the exact nature of factors such as unclear management (e.g. guided by the aforementioned research findings). Indeed, interviews later supplemented by direct observation were part of the early research on burnout (Maslach *et al,* 2001). We summarize these findings shortly, under 'formulation', as they helped to clarify the cause-and-effect relationships. This approach is consistent with the first step in the guideline provided by Milne and Reiser (2017, p181):

> *"Clarify the situation: identify what it is about the*
> *supervisee's workplace that is challenging."*

Other staff should play a lead role in assessing workplace challenges. For instance, clinical managers or administrators have a lead role to play auditing important activities defining service standards and arranging for feedback. Questionnaires such as The Manchester Clinical Supervision Scale (Winstanley & White, 2014) have been used extensively to determine how supervisees experience supervision. This guided managers' and supervisors' actions to improve the workplace. To illustrate the use of a targeted questionnaire, Gonsalvez *et al* (2017) developed The Supervision Evaluation and Supervisory Competence Scale (SE-SC) to assess an unusually wide range of supervisor competencies, as rated by their supervisees. This scale measures the supervisees' satisfaction with their supervision, alongside their appraisal of the supervisors' use of specific competencies and their effectiveness. Based on a sample of 142 supervisees in clinical psychology training in Australia, Gonsalvez *et al* (2017) reported that their new questionnaire had good psychometric qualities (e.g. reliability and validity). Six aspects of supervision are subsumed under the 'normative, formative and restorative' functions outlined in Chapter 2 (see Figure 2.1). One of these aspects was termed 'openness, caring and support' and consisted of five questions, whereas a second was called 'restorative' and was assessed by three items (the remaining clusters related to the supervisors' expertise and role-modelling). Examples of the 'openness, caring and support' aspect included 'The supervisor was caring and supportive' and 'The supervisor was accepting of my mistakes and inadequacies'. Examples of the 'restorative' factor included 'The supervisor was sensitive to my emotional and self-care needs' and 'Supervision facilitated emotional ventilation and support as appropriate'. Each of the 31 items is positively phrased and rated by the supervisee on a 7-point scale from 1 (signifying 'not at all, strongly disagree') to 7 ('very much so, strongly agree'). Higher scores indicate greater supervisee satisfaction, higher supervisor competence, and more successful attainment of selected supervision outcomes (e.g. reflection, goal-setting, planning). These items are clearly compatible with some core aspects of supportive supervision, making this a suitable assessment tool to use within a healthcare organization. Furthermore, The Supervision Evaluation and Supervisory Competence Scale (SE-SC) scale is available free of charge (contact Professor Gonsalvez for the latest version and for permission: C.Gonsalvez@westernsydney.edu.au.)

However, the SE-SC scale does not assess or characterize the workplace, so we need a different instrument to measure the context for supervision. Such instruments can be comprehensive, profiling several dimensions of the workplace, or more precisely focused. There are many examples of comprehensive assessment tools for use in the workplace, but only a few that have been used in relation to supervision. One example is the 39-item Work Environment Questionnaire (WEQ), was used in an evaluation of team-based clinical supervision by O'Connell *et al* (2013). The WEQ includes items on workplace stressors (e.g. 'I feel stressed out in my job'; 'I am feeling pressures of time, and there is a risk of failure'), on support from supervisors and peers (e.g. 'I have good relationships with colleagues and co-operate well' and 'I get support from others when I need it'), and on engagement with the work (e.g. 'I feel my job is interesting and stimulating' and 'I have the opportunity to learn new things'). In this research, the WEQ was completed before and after team supervision by 36 nursing and midwifery staff from two wards at a public hospital and two wards at a private hospital in Australia, including a maternity ward and two medical wards. Team supervision involved small groups of team members participating in formally led supervision lasting up to one hour per month, including reflective and confidential discussion of work issues. Team supervision was chosen by O'Connell *et al* (2013) because their literature review indicated that it had been found to increase participants' sense of togetherness, improve communication, and increase shared problem-solving. In this evaluation, team supervision appeared to assist staff to negotiate difficult situations in the workplace, to engage in collective problem-solving on challenging issues, and to improve nurses' sense of empowerment, communication, and their relationships with colleagues.

Perhaps the general workplace assessment instrument with most explicit relevance to supervision has been developed by Saarikoski (2014), namely the Clinical Learning Environment, Supervision and Nurse Teacher Evaluation Scale (CLES+T). This scale is widely used in Europe, most commonly as an audit instrument for measuring the quality of clinical education in nurse training. This 33-item questionnaire assesses the teaching atmosphere, the supervisory relationship, the leadership and management culture on the ward, plus other dimensions, such as the students' perceptions of the quality of care. For example, the management item is 'There were no problems in the information flow related to patients' care'. Each item is rated on a five-point scale of agreement (ranging from 'fully agree' to 'fully disagree'). The CLES+T has good psychometric qualities, has been used internationally, and has become part of the quality assurance system in Finland.

An example of the CLES+T in action has been provided by Gurkova *et al* (2016), who administered it to 503 nursing students in their second or third year of study at six universities in Slovakia. The aim was to describe the student nurses' clinical placements and to compare the findings with those published in other countries. Supervision of these nurses was provided by the ward nurses and ward managers (the 'mentors'), but in practice it was rarely scheduled and 25% of the respondents indicated that their supervisory experiences were unsatisfactory (e.g. because there were no named supervisors or there were relationship difficulties). Students were more satisfied with other CLES+T dimensions (including the leadership style of the ward managers, the premises for nurses on the ward, and the educational atmosphere on the ward) than they were with their supervisory relationship with a mentor. The highest ratings across the CLES+T items came from the 42% of nurses who had received individual supervision from a nursing colleague, especially where the placement was longer than a month, and where the frequency of supervision was greater (managers provided significantly less supervision than their nursing colleagues).

An example of a more precisely focused assessment instrument is the analysis of occupational stress among 69 registered nursing staff, who were working within three units of an academic medical centre in the US (Hall, 2007). The first unit was characterized as having traditional governance, including a conventional organizational structure and a mixed patient population. By contrast, the second unit had a shared governance framework. The third unit had a more specialized, homogeneous in-patient population. Because this study concerned the general shortage of such staff (i.e. there were recruitment and staff turnover problems), Hall (2007) selected instruments that would enable her to understand nurses' job satisfaction and burnout. In terms of the environment, this included a decision-making latitude scale (measuring the amount of job control perceived by the nurses), a scale to assess stressors in the workplace (through ratings of typical scenarios), and a scale measuring the socially supportive behaviours of peers (the co-workers and supervisors). The findings indicated that all the participating nurses felt that job control was relatively low, representing a lack of control over organizational factors. For example, decisions about when and where patients were admitted and how the units were staffed caused the greatest frustration. The lack of control was partly due to such decisions being made by individuals other than the nurses' supervisor. Because of such factors, 10% of the variance in job satisfaction was found to be due to the type of unit in which these nurses worked. To illustrate, Hall (2007) found that the nurses in the traditional governance unit reported significantly more supervisor support than nurses in the other two units. The nurses' perception of greater supervisor support was associated with supervisors seeking their input and being attentive to their concerns. 'Affirmative contact and support' from the supervisor also appeared to influence many of the work-related variables (e.g. more job satisfaction, less work stress, and less staff turnover). 'Affirmative support' refers to the supervisor (a first-line manager to these nurses) offering coaching, praise, counselling, and leadership. Specifically, affirmative supervisors helped the nurse to complete demanding tasks, talked about private and family concerns, praised the nurse's work, helped with co-worker (interpersonal) problems, and assisted with other stressful situations. Support also came from peers and was found to be high across all three units, increasing over time as relationships strengthened. Peer support was strongly correlated with job satisfaction and with a sense of what Hall (2007, p69) called 'collective efficacy'. This is defined as "the individual's assessment of his or her group's ability to perform job-related behaviours".

3. Formulating the workplace

The findings reported by Hall (2007) are consistent with other similar research and indicate how supervisors and peers can address workplace stressors. But to prove successful, any such action must be based on a proper understanding of the workplace, including the perceptions of the individuals who work there. A formulation, drawing on a suitable model, guides and assembles the assessment information into a specific description of a problem, together with a specific local explanation for the problem. In this sense, the study by Gurkova *et al* (2016) is an example of an assessment that defined and described a problem over the implementation of group supervision, adding some analysis of the problem in terms of the low satisfaction of supervisees (with factors such as infrequent supervision and alliance difficulties). However, there was no attempt to develop a formal formulation of the kind that would properly explain these difficulties. Had these authors conducted a formulation they would also have suggested how the problems might best be understood and addressed, ideally adding which outcomes should be measured. In Chapter 4 we gave examples of formulation with individuals (based on coping strategies) and an example based on groups (family therapy).

An example of a more detailed formulation, applied to groups of staff, was provided by Weigl *et al* (2016). They based their approach partly on the 'Job–Demand–Control model' (Karasek & Theorell, 1990); they expected supervisor support to encourage nurses' well-being by buffering them against high work stressors (job demands such as work overload). They anticipated that such support would be especially beneficial for exhausted employees. Additionally, they were guided by the 'Conservation of Resources' model (Hobfoll, 2011), as highly exhausted staff will tend to struggle to manage their resources (e.g. social support), leading to maladaptive coping. Furthermore, this theory predicts that poor coping efforts will worsen the situation (the 'vicious cycle'). To illustrate, Weigl *et al* (2016) noted how a 'downward spiral' might produce burnout, because staff become unable to deal with high job demands or to cope effectively with their own distress. The downward spiral notion was the basis for a formulation of groups of nurses, working in day-care or in-patient settings (see Chapter 4 for more on the coping cycle or spiral). Weigl *et al* (2016) reported results that agreed with this reasoning (although causal conclusions are limited by a correlational study design). For example, those nurses who reported high job demands but who also received supervisor support appeared to be protected (buffered) from burnout. This appeared to be because supervisor support reversed the downward spiral, partly by improving their personal coping strategies.

Formulations can also be based primarily on the workplace itself through approaches such as 'force-field analysis' (Lewin, 1953). Force-field analysis concerns opposing forces or sources of pressure, some 'driving' while other forces are 'restraining' change within a system. This logic is still useful and popular, but now the terms have changed to organizational 'barriers' and 'boosters' (or similar terms). This is indicated by the studies we reviewed in Chapter 3, which we summarized in Table 3.1. The examples we noted included the barriers, such as limited access to supervision, and the boosters of staff support and development (e.g. mentoring like-minded colleagues; supervisor training; preceptorship).

To represent a formulation, such boosters and barriers within an organization need to combine into an understanding of the reasons for problems, such as inaccessible or ineffective supervision. Lewin (1952) did this in his illustration by drawing curved lines, with arrows to represent the opposing forces; we have found it preferable to represent the forces through a 'see-saw' diagram to represent opposing boosters and barriers, as in Figure 5.1. We prefer this approach because this can indicate more precisely the relative force of the different boosters and barriers, and provides a summary of the outcome of the balance of these forces at any particular point in time. These features help to complete a formulation, as they indicate what might best describe a problem, which interventions might best fix it, and it incorporates a simple means of measuring progress. On the right-hand side of the see-saw in Figure 5.1 are the barriers, opposed by the boosters positioned to the left. The boxes represent the weights, creating opposing forces on the see-saw. We have inserted the barriers that were prominent in the reviews by Michie and Williams (2003) and Bhatt and Ramani (2016), mentioned earlier. For boosters we have inserted examples of the factors that typically emerge in analyses of healthcare workplaces, adding some indication of their relative importance or weight. We have illustrated the opposing forces as individual factors (e.g. resilience) and organizational factors (e.g. excessive workload). The weighting given such factors could, for instance, be the percentage of staff, indicating the relative importance of these factors in response to a survey (e.g. 80% of respondents rated 'accessing social support' from peers as a booster). Reflecting the dynamic nature of the situation, slight shifts in the relative weight of the barriers and boosters (or the emergence of new factors) will take the see-saw to a tipping point. The outcome of the balance of these forces is indicated by the position of the see-saw relative to the outcome line on the left of Figure 5.1. In the example in Figure 5.1, the see-saw is mostly forced down by barriers, indicating that the status of the organization (at the time of this imaginary survey) is negative, and hence tending to create the conditions for burnout, etc. The illustration of the tandem bicycle represents the supervisor and supervisee trying to tip the balance downwards, to the positive end of the outcome line, which we have labelled 'greater work engagement'.

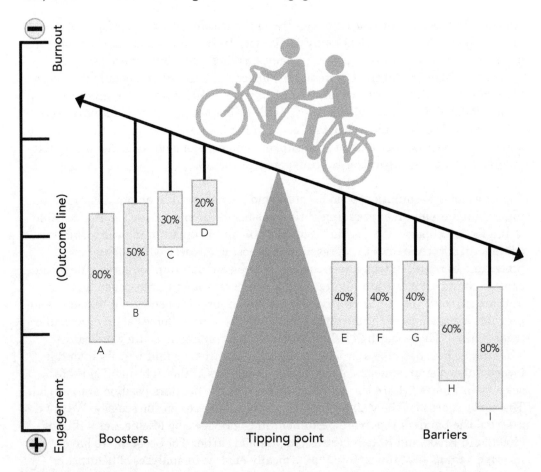

Figure 5.1: An illustration of the balance between individual and organizational factors, related to supportive supervision

Key: A = Accessing social support; B = Resilient personality; C = Effective coping strategies; D = Supervision; E = Work overload; F = Unclear management; G = lack of control over work; H = lack of participation in decision-making; I = inadequate social support

Not included in Figure 5.1 is the context, which we have already seen in this chapter represented by concepts such as the 'social climate' or 'atmosphere' of workplaces. As noted in their review of occupational burnout by Maslach *et al* (2001), context typically includes organizational hierarchies, operating procedures and rules, values, leadership styles, and the available resources. These contextual factors moderate or 'weather' the variables listed in Figure 5.1, in the sense of having a persistent background influence on how things unfold. Maslach *et al* (2001) added that in turn the organizational context is shaped by larger social, cultural, and economic systems. They noted that the commercial context at the time had changed organizations profoundly, through downsizing and mergers, with significant effects on the lives of the staff. Subsequent to their review, in 2007–2008 the economic system experienced an international meltdown in the banking sector, followed by a global economic downturn. There followed heightened uncertainty and the relative weakening of trade unions at an international level, with the consequence that employees today are more insecure about their jobs and are simultaneously expected to give more than ever to their work – more time, effort, and flexibility. It can also be said that, in exchange, staff receive less than before in terms of career opportunities, job security, and so on. This context has therefore shifted the balance in the workplace significantly, creating conditions that act as a booster for burnout and a barrier to job engagement and personal well-being.

The wider context usually impacts on local workplaces, influencing staff and organizations alike. An illustration comes from the research reported from Denmark by Gonge and Buus (2010). They considered how individual and workplace factors influenced participation in clinical supervision by gathering demographic and questionnaire data from 239 psychiatric nurses working either in community mental health centres or in general psychiatric wards. In both settings, supervision was enshrined by the employing organizations policy; all clinical staff were expected to participate (group supervision was the norm). However, this policy was not thoroughly implemented, as over a three-month period only 74% of staff were offered supervision. The frequency of supervision also varied across settings, with roughly twice as many sessions offered within the community centres during this three-month period (an average of 10.5 sessions). Similarly, the duration of supervision was variable (average duration was 90 minutes, with a range from 60–110 minutes), as was the type of supervision that was provided. All supervisors were 'external' (i.e. they were not employed in the units they supervised). Although supervision was mandated by policy, the employing organization gave no directions regarding the nature of supervision, which was therefore left to the discretion of the supervisors, although it appeared that they all emphasised reflection on practice, and some also included teaching.

This kind of disorganized supervision is typical of large organizations. What is atypical in this account is that Gonge and Buus (2010) tried to formulate the disappointing level of supervisee participation using a force-field analysis. Gonge and Buus (2010) reported that 47% of the nurses in the study did not participate at all in the supervision that was offered during the three-month period, all of them being based in the hospital wards. Also, less than 10% of those who did participate had more than one supervision session per month, which was the criterion that was used by the authors for 'regular' supervision. By contrast, all staff based in the community centres participated, and 79% of them had received regular supervision. In addition to working in a community team, the authors found that being offered supervision during the day shift (for the hospital staff), and that being a registered nurse (rather than an auxiliary nurse), boosted participation in clinical supervision, as did social support (from colleagues and supervisors). Indeed, Gonge and Buus (2010) speculated that social support acted as a key mechanism, helping nursing staff to resolve any anxiety or resistance to supervision, such as the concerns felt about the self-disclosure that was expected as part of the reflective process of supervision. The organizational barriers included the unavailability of supervision (staff working evening and night shifts were expected to attend supervision when they were off duty), inconsistent management support, and the demands of the job. Termed 'cognitive demands' by the authors, these demands included monitoring the patients, decision-making, remembering about supervision, and time management (e.g. nurses who attend supervision have less time for other work tasks). The other individual and work-environment factors were not found to have an influence on participation (e.g. education, personality).

However, in keeping with the general literature on the respective roles of personal and organizational factors, the two sources of influence interact significantly. This is illustrated by a subsequent study by Buus *et al* (2017), who interviewed 24 of the Danish mental health nursing staff members who had been observed not to participate in supervision in the three-month period noted above. Interviews were audio-recorded and then analyzed by means of the qualitative method of discourse analysis. The authors found that the staff members' reasoning for not participating in supervision was essentially two points: the first was to accentuate the practical barriers related to participating in supervision, the second was to minimize the benefits that the interviewees had experienced from supervision (and their personal need for supervision). These strategies made the nurse's non-participation appear reasonable and legitimate. Delving more deeply into the nurses' individual motivation to avoid supervision, it appeared that group clinical supervision was perceived as intrusive (through the detailed questioning) and anxiety-provoking (because of prior conflicts, and due to a lack of trust between the group members). Most interviewees felt uncomfortable discussing personal feelings or professional uncertainty with colleagues in the workplace. This was exacerbated by a perceived lack of control over what was happening in supervision because of the challenging questions and comments that occurred, which staff felt could pressure them into making an unwanted disclosure.

At the organizational level, the barriers included unreliable scheduling, cancelling supervision (due to low attendance), or aborting the supervision sessions (e.g. if no one was willing to discuss a work issue). Not surprisingly, managers were regarded as only partially committed because they did not create an environment for people to participate on a reliable, effective basis. These fascinating insights into supervision provide a valuable formulation, describing what is happening (and not happening), in addition to an explanation for the behaviour of staff. This provides a sound basis for taking steps to improve matters, to which we now turn.

4. Intervention options

The studies described so far indicate some possible interventions within the workplace, such as ensuring access to supportive supervision, while reducing the practical and psychological barriers to that supervision (e.g. scheduling supervision, reducing performance anxiety). Because intervention options are so numerous, we will provide a broad summary, including the practical steps that can be taken in supervision to address workplace barriers (see Table 5.1). Similarly, to better manage the high number of relevant studies, we will only draw on a few, clearly relevant systematic reviews. These reviews were selected because they identified effective organizational interventions with healthcare workers, and interventions that were explicitly related to restorative supervision. The included reviews are Awa *et al* (2010), Michie & Williams (2003), Morse *et al* (2012), Rhodes & Eisenberger (2002), Rowe *et al* (2005), and Scott *et al* (2018). The supervision literature rarely even considers tackling organizational problems, and consequently intervention studies are scarce. By 'tackling organizational problems', we refer to interventions that aim to remove or reduce the environmental causes of personal distress, such as high workloads and low job control ('primary prevention'). A rare and welcome exception is the work of Buus *et al* (2016), as just described. Whereas other studies describe organizational interventions, this supervision literature tends to focus solely on helping the supervisee to cope with a stressful workplace ('secondary prevention'), or on rehabilitation efforts to help staff members return to work (e.g. psychotherapy for post-traumatic stress disorder: 'tertiary prevention' (for a summary of these prevention categories, see Bhui *et al,* 2012)). Indeed, this focus on the individual healthcare worker and secondary or tertiary prevention has also dominated the Industrial/Organizational (I/O) psychology literature. This has been attributed to the prevailing assumptions in society about the primacy of individual causality and responsibility, and the pragmatic consideration that it is easier (and cheaper) to treat a few individuals than to treat a whole organization (Maslach *et al,* 2001). The opposite assumption is the 'materialist' one, which is the perspective that the true cause of individuals' distress is environmental, in terms of material factors such as poverty and social disadvantage, and that these represent the context for personal distress at work (Stansfeld & Candy, 2006).

Table 5.1 lists the workplace interventions that the review authors linked to supportive supervision in order of the frequency with which they were mentioned (left-hand column). Thus, in row 1 the most frequently mentioned effective organizational intervention was supervision itself (mentioned in all six reviews). In the second column of Table 5.1 information on the methods that were used is given, as is the underlying mechanism assumed to be responsible for the outcome. When not mentioned by the review authors, these mechanisms were inferred by the present authors, based on their supervision expertise. In the intervention example in row 1, the supervisor is a significant transformative or relational leader (Arnold *et al,* 2007; Cummings *et al,* 2010). The first and most popular intervention in Table 5.1 is supportive supervision, where this has an indirect impact on the workplace. According to Cummings *et al* (2010, p378), relational leaders such as supervisors "can have a indirect impact… by directly working through the workforce and effect the work environment". This is especially likely in contexts where supervision is provided to all clinical professional staff throughout their careers (e.g. the NHS) and not only during initial professional training (e.g. as in the US). In effect, since all NHS clinical staff should receive career-long supervision, supervisors are actually working directly with all clinicians who make up the psychosocial workplace environment (individually and/or in groups). Collaboration by supervisors with the relevant managers (and other service leaders) should make this suitably systemic, and thereby an effective, 'combined' intervention. In the case of leaders who are supervisors, they can be regarded as complementing managers by communicating the employing organization's support to supervisees, and thereby influencing how they undertake their work (Rhoades & Eisenberger, 2002).

The studies in Table 5.1 were selected as they were among the few to address organizational issues through supervision, mostly by introducing an intervention. We also wanted studies that supplemented those already described in Chapter 3, so that we could offer more varied and comprehensive examples of the kinds of interventions that have taken place. Unfortunately, we were unable to locate any studies that could be described as true 'primary prevention' or which were explicitly linked to supervision, so the examples given in Table 5.1 are as close as we could get. For example, Schwartz 'rounds' (in row 1 of Table 5.1) can help all staff to feel supported but they do not directly address the sources of stress in the workplace. However, these 'rounds' do appear to be a popular intervention, at least in the US, and their existence does indicate that the host organization cares about staff well-being. We should also note that the group leader need not necessarily be a supervisor, but overall we thought that these 'rounds' merited a mention (e.g. they are endorsed in recent government documents in the UK).

We should also stress that the interventions, methods and mechanisms are not as neatly or consistently circumscribed within this sample of literature as they are within Table 5.1. This is partly because they exist within an open, dynamic system, which can alter the nature and effects of supervision significantly. For example, supposedly supportive supervision may actually be experienced negatively by supervisees, especially if the leadership style is bureaucratic and punitive ('fault-finding') (Scott *et al,* 2018). Such supervision will not be transformative and indeed may well cause harm to staff and thereby undermine the quality of care to patients. For instance, 'dissonant' leadership is characterised by a commanding style, featuring pace-setting and criticism (Cummings *et al,* 2010). Instead of triggering positive mechanisms such as social support, supervisees in receipt of such leadership may feel criticized and devalued. This contributes to problematic organizational cycles of low staff morale, absenteeism-sickness, burnout, poor quality of care, job resignations, and recruitment difficulties. In this sense, Table 5.1 is illustrative of the typical relationships that have been reported between relational supervisors, effective supervision methods, and outcomes.

Table 5.1 indicates that it is the socially supportive aspect of supervision that is most frequently cited as an effective organizational intervention (cited in all six reviews), followed by efforts to enhance leadership, raise staff morale, and solve workplace problems as a staff group (cited in three of these reviews). Other valuable interventions cited twice involved the use of feedback systems, improved communication, reduced workload and enhancing personal coping strategies. In summary, these reviews portray supportive supervision as both a direct personal and an indirect organizational intervention. Both represent secondary prevention. A rare example is the study by Buus *et al* (2016), who implemented a brief, group-based intervention termed 'meta-supervision' aimed at enabling supervisees to secure effective supervision. Within the group, action learning principles were used to encourage supervisees to collectively develop action plans or projects to overcome barriers to their regular clinical supervision. Barriers deemed to be 'outside' supervision, in the organizational context, primarily inspired projects to create structural changes. Instances included addressing shift work and rosters; workload; interpersonal conflicts on hospital wards; and the role of management. Supervisees were asked to reflect on and write up supervision incidents and then present their reflections to the group. The leader would encourage discussion by the group, paraphrase, and clarify the main issues (the leader in this study was an external consultant). This clarification helped members generate specific and feasible projects facilitated by the leader. Buus *et al* (2016) believe that this interactive process enabled the supervisees to learn from each other, while also validating group members' perceptions. The authors also helpfully provided an illustrative transcript of such a session. An RCT indicated that meta-supervision resulted in a significantly higher uptake of supervision (Gonge & Buus, 2015).

Table 5.1: A broad summary of the main intervention options, related to supportive supervision

Effective workplace interventions related to supportive supervision *(number of mentions)*	Methods *(assumed mechanisms)*	Example review *(illustrative study)*
1. Supportive supervision *(impacting the workplace)* *(6/6)*	Providing and enabling social support *(social support; perceived organizational support)*	Rhoades & Eisenberger (2002) *(Goodrich, 2012: Schwartz groups or 'rounds'; discuss and reflect on the emotional and social challenges of job; not problem-solving; a safe and confidential environment. Rounds are perceived by participants as a source of support, with benefits for patients, team working & the hospital culture)*
2. Boosting morale *(3/6)*	Increasing staff motivation *(collaboration/ social support)* Reducing staff demoralization and interpersonal conflicts *(shared values; organizational commitment)*	Scott et al (2008) *(Singh et al, 2016: Supportive supervision involved creating a non-threatening, empowering environment; supervisee and supervisor learn together and problem-solve to overcome motivational obstacles)*
3. Problem-solving *(3/6)*	Collaborative and constructive discussion of problems; participative action research *(participative decision-making)*	Michie & Williams (2003) *(Buus et al, 2017: brief 'meta-supervision' group, supervisees reflect privately on supervision incidents, write down & present to group; leader encourages group discussion, paraphrases, and clarifies main issues; collectively develop action plans or projects to overcome organizational barriers to their supervision)* →

Effective workplace interventions related to supportive supervision (number of mentions)	Methods (assumed mechanisms)	Example review (illustrative study)
4. Effective leadership (3/6)	Training and strengthening relational leadership (supportive and transformative style); modifying dysfunctional beliefs; reframing the situation; appreciative enquiry (being heard/respected) (fairness/justice at work)	Rhoades & Eisenberger (2002) (Wallbank & Woods, 2012: training restorative supervisors as leaders who help supervisees build constructive relationships with their immediate management team and the wider organization, improving the workplace environment and support within wider team context. Results: increased compassion satisfaction and reduced burnout and job stress)
5. Positive feedback (2/6)	Monitor the quality of care through positive feedback systems; develop the skills necessary to improve feedback (learning through corrective feedback)	Awa et al (2010) (Green et al, 2014: supervisors regularly offer general positive feedback and systematically review clinical outcome feedback with supervisees to ensure adherence to the approach, which may mean skill-development work and to enhance clinical care; feedback specifies the gap between current and expected results and links to guidance; encourage supervisees to be open to learning from feedback; to be proactive, prepared and organized; to seek experiential learning and enhanced self-awareness via reflection. The clinically most effective supervisees had these qualities. Effectiveness linked to colleagues and to the organizations use of a stepped care approach) →

Effective workplace interventions related to supportive supervision *(number of mentions)*	Methods *(assumed mechanisms)*	Example review *(illustrative study)*
6. Clear communication (2/6)	Shared values and goals; agreed standards; well-defined roles (minimize role confusion); communication skill development/ training *(mutual understanding)*	Rowe et al (2005) *(Delvaux et al, 2004: supervision of trainer, including information on the training manual; observation in the pilot phase and role-playing exercises help to ensure shared values, goals and standards. Results: trained oncology nurses felt less stressed and better prepared to provide emotional support to patients and their family; attitudes to cancer and death, to selves and to work improved)*
7. Workload management (2/6)	Joint goal-setting; prioritizing tasks together; achievable work standards *(stress reduction; burnout protection; job satisfaction)*	Awa et al (2010) *(Blomberg et al, 2014: group supervision for new staff to address stress by creating a supportive environment, with confidential discussion, questions about incidents, and promoting learning through shared reflection. Group supervision significantly reduced stress)*
8. Coping strategy enhancement (2/6)	Group supervision to reduce negative thinking about work colleagues (e.g. interpersonal conflict resolution) *(adaptive coping)*	Morse et al (2012) *(Teasdale et al, 2000: group supervision included empathy – understanding supervisee's situation-support, reassurance and advice, reflection on action, new learning, and encouragement to access informal networks for more immediate support and advice; supervision was associated with significantly improved: personal coping at work and perceived support – listening and supportive peers and management)*

5. Case study: Skill difficulties and deficits

Background

Although appointed to a senior grade post as an Occupational Health Advisor (OHA), the supervisee was somewhat inexperienced in occupational health. A female in her early 30s, she had qualified as a general nurse some years before and had confidently moved to her present OHA post to develop specialist skills. The occupational health department provided support services to NHS managers and healthcare staff on a wide range of issues (e.g. sickness-absence; alleged work-related stress and anxiety casework; fitness for work; rehabilitation; and ill-health retirement). Advice to the staff managers on the management of such issues was a major part of the role, partly to ensure compliance with health and safety legislation, and this was where the supervisee's inexperience was most evident. The supervisor was an OHA with senior management experience. Also a nurse by training, she was in her mid-50s, with over 30 years of experience in occupational health. She provided supervision within this busy NHS department (supervision is provided throughout professionals' careers within the NHS).

Critical event

Over some months, the supervisee's inexperience became evident, especially her anxiety regarding her reports. The supervisee sought frequent advice, guidance and reassurance from her supervisor with these cases (in the early stages, all reports were vetted by a senior OH manager and several had been returned, requiring amendment). The supervisor decided to have the supervisee sit in with her during her clinic to try to improve the supervisee's management of her appointment sessions with clients and to help improve her competence and confidence.

Interaction sequence

The first detail that the supervisee noticed was that, before each appointment, the supervisor prepared a standard information sheet for each case. Whereas the supervisee would usually try go through all the information in the client's file while making detailed notes (with limited time to do this thoroughly), in preparing the supervisor relied on essential information: the client's name, the essential core information, and the reason for the referral:

> *"I always complete this standard information sheet before each client, to remind me to clarify key points with them. But my priority is to maintain control of the appointment and obtain the information I require, while establishing a good working relationship."*

The supervisor then greeted the client warmly, explained her role, the reason for the appointment, and summarized what would happen in the 40-minute appointment. The supervisor had already saved about 10 minutes over the supervisee's approach, as the standardization in each case enabled a more concise preparation. Then, during the interview, the supervisor worked hard at gaining the client's trust and cooperation, emphasising that her role was to help the staff member to get the best possible assessment and to enable accurate advice to be given to their manager (while maintaining medical confidentiality). Before being sent, all reports were discussed first with each client, informed signed consent was obtained, and the client was advised that they would receive a copy of the report. The supervisee was also able to see how the supervisor maintained control of the appointment by politely but firmly concentrating on the relevant information and ensuring that, while the client was certainly able to discuss concerns, the appointment was focused and efficient. The whole atmosphere was so different from the supervisee's experience, and encouraged her to try working within a similar structure. This helped to increase her confidence.

Resolution

After sitting-in for most of the day, the supervisee was asked what she noticed.

> *"That was so different. I think I'm so worried about getting all my facts right that I kind of get a bit lost and ignore the person."*

The supervisor reassured her that when she started out, she did the same thing:

> *"It takes a while to feel able to manage the appointment effectively, while ensuring that the essential information is obtained. At the same time, it is important to remember that the client is central to the process."*

The supervisor then asked the supervisee:

> *"Was there any difference in the way that today's clients responded?"*

After a thoughtful pause, the supervisee said:

> *"They were so much more open and trusting. Mine seem to control the appointment more, and time is spent on information that's not really essential or relevant to their case, often going back over history that, although important to them, isn't really what I need to help them. Sometimes they also get defensive and tell me as little as possible to protect themselves."*

"And what then is the consequence for your reports?" asks the supervisor.

"Well, I get much more information that doesn't seem to be relevant and afterwards have a bit of a problem sorting it all out. I always seem to be short of time. You seemed to get to an understanding of the central elements of each case in a supportive but firm way. You don't let the clients control the appointment and you keep it focused on what information you need. The clients accepted this and were more trusting of your role in advising their manager."

"It seems to me," says the supervisor, *"that one consequence is that you can write better reports if you know the essential information you require **before** each appointment. You always need to remain flexible though and allow the clients to discuss their concerns, many of which may be very relevant to your case management and report. However, allowing the client to use the appointment time to go over their full medical history, for example, is not helpful to the client or you (or allowing the appointment to develop into counselling). Referral on for other assistance is one of your options (e.g. to counselling services), but your appointment needs to remain focused. It's not easy, but it does develop with time and a more structured approach should help you with this. Also, by engaging with the clients better, you can obtain their trust and collaboration. You appear to have been unsure of your case preparation and appointment management. Maybe now, by having a structure to work with and by clarifying the requirements and the time available with each client at the start of each appointment, you can get them to help you. They will feel reassured and better able to engage with you in a helpful but focused way."*

The supervisee nods vigorously: *"And hopefully my reports will improve too."*

Discussion

This supervisee was definitely reassured by observing her supervisor for the day. No matter how articulate the supervisors may be, there are aspects of professional practice that the supervisee's have to directly experience and try to understand from their own perspective. Sadly, it is rare for supervisors to allow supervisees such opportunities. If sitting-in is followed by some guided reflection, as here, then the supervisee can have a truly significant learning experience.

Referring to Table 3.1 in Chapter 3, we can see a number of examples of supportive supervision in this case study episode: the supervisor has attempted to develop the supervisee's competence through advice, guidance and demonstration (modelling) and she provided social support through self-disclosure (i.e. acknowledging that she had also struggled early on in her OHA career). She also nicely demonstrated the value of having a collaborative alliance with clients. More relevant to the present chapter, the supervisor is helping the supervisee to recognize and address the requirements of the job, in that workplace. For example, the supervisor modelled the value of concentrating on the action that was required to progress each case within this organizational system. In doing so, the supervisor helped the clients and their managers to resolve such casework. Not least, thanks to direct observation and guided reflection, the supervisor clarified why there was a report-writing problem. There were also examples of the supervisee reacting positively to supervision (see column 3 of Table 3.1 in Chapter 3), including a sense of cooperation, gaining support, and enhanced critical thinking. This suggests that it was an effective supervision session. Longer-term, this kind of supervision may help the supervisee to pay more careful attention to the demands of her workplace and so become more confident, more committed to her job, and more likely to thrive. Although she did not do anything to alter the requirements of her job, she did change her supervisor's behaviour in ways that made supervision more valuable, which had a small impact on her workplace.

6. Summary

In this chapter we have attempted to shift the onus from 'fixing' faulty individuals to considering the organizational origins of personal distress. This represents an appropriate and optimal sharing of responsibilities for developing a healthy workplace (Shanafelt & Noseworthy, 2017). The scarcity of supervision-related interventions at the organizational level (primary prevention) partly reflects this historical emphasis on distressed individuals, but may well also reflect the fact that it is easier and cheaper to change a few distressed individuals than to modify a whole distressing organization (Maslach *et al*, 2001). In so doing, it also implicitly shifts fault or responsibility onto the staff, while excusing the managers from blame. But the material that we have reviewed suggests that responsibility for problems like low staff morale or high levels of burnout should properly be shared by clinicians and managers. According to our model (Chapter 2), personal distress is a function of the individual and the environment, operating in interaction. Neither makes sense alone, but in any case, a supportive workplace will not automatically apportion all responsibility to the worker. This logic is echoed strongly in an analysis of a healthcare disaster in England, as discussed by Tomlinson (2015). And although systematic reviews of the key research literature sometimes stress one more than the other, all agree that effective solutions require a combination of personal and organizational interventions (e.g. Awa *et al*, 2010; Bhui *et al*, 2012; Marine *et al*, 2009; Panagioti *et al*, 2017).

Although the effective solutions that we summarized in Table 5.1 do not include an example of primary prevention, it can be seen that these supervision interventions do at least span the layers within the support model that we developed in Chapter 2 (see Figure 2.2). Specifically, we cited examples of fostering adaptive coping by the supervisee (the intrapersonal system); addressing work challenges through supervision (the interpersonal system); addressing leadership and other workplace factors (e.g. communication; feedback; part of the organizational system); and, lastly, we included in Table 5.1 examples of fostering social support (the contextual system). This represents a valuable range of interventions at the organizational and systems level, options that complement interventions at the personal level (Chapter 4), and which also communicate a commitment to considering a combination of personal and organizational interventions. Complementary primary prevention interventions that managers can lead are many and varied (Shanafelt & Noseworthy, 2017), and supervisors can help by highlighting those that are relevant within their organization (e.g. reducing clerical tasks or increasing the flexibility accorded to staff). In addition, we should recall that many supervisors are also managers, and that some supervisors will become managers, so increasing the likelihood of primary prevention.

There is another reason why supervision can play a vital role in influencing others, which is its potential contribution to creating a healthcare culture that encourages a learning organization thereby minimizing harm and disasters:

> *"Clinical supervision, especially when it is professionally led, learner-centred, educational and supportive... fosters a culture that is educational, self-critical, outward-looking and patient-focused, centred on patient safety and quality care"*
> (Tomlinson, 2015, p7).

In this context, it is appropriate that in this chapter we used a comparable problem-solving cycle (or 'quality enhancement process') (Rowe *et al*, 2005). It is also fitting that we have considered individual and organizational explanations for staff and healthcare problems. From both perspectives, supportive supervision can be regarded as both a direct, personal intervention (see Chapters 3 and 4), and to a much lesser extent as an indirect, organizational intervention (this chapter). That these perspectives yield strikingly similar results strengthens our confidence in the summaries presented in Tables 3.1 and 5.1. This convergence also makes implementation more straightforward. In conclusion, although it is generally poorly organized, we believe that even brief and relatively superficial supervision can make a significant difference to the workplace. As per all chapters, we note the main action implications in Chapter 9.

Chapter 6: Supportive Supervision: Guidelines for Supervisors

1. Introduction

We have already made general suggestions on how to provide supportive supervision in earlier chapters, but these have been in the form of occasional examples, rather than providing a systematic and specific review of all the evidence-based techniques. Therefore, the aim of this chapter is to build on those prior examples by providing a more complete and detailed guide on how exactly to conduct supportive supervision. To ensure that we include all the relevant supervision techniques, we will base our guidance on SAGE, an instrument for measuring competent supervision, as it was explicitly developed to cover the full range of supervision skills (Milne *et al,* 2011b; Reiser *et al,* 2018). In describing these skills, we will focus on the six main supervision competencies that emerged from our review of relevant theory (Chapter 2) and the best available research, which we moderated by reference to expert consensus statements (see Table 3.1 in Chapter 3). Given this comprehensive review of research, theory and expert consensus, we regard these competencies as the evidence-based foundation for supportive supervision.

These six competencies are represented in Table 6.1. This competence list starts with the provision of advice and guidance in order to develop supervisees' personal coping strategies and professional skills. For each of these six supportive supervision competencies we will illustrate two techniques, so that you have enough procedural information to act with confidence and with some flexibility. Please note that our choice of specific techniques tied to competencies in Table 6.1 is intended to be illustrative; there is no empirical justification that dictates the use of specific techniques for each competency. Therefore, you should not restrict your choice of supervisory techniques slavishly to the format of Table 6.1, but instead aim to use your clinical judgement. This means selecting appropriate techniques from this table, based on your full consideration of the particular situation, supervisee, patient, and context.

So that the level of detail in our suggestions is right, we will be following the guideline examples in the CBT supervision manual (Milne & Reiser, 2017), since those guidelines were vetted and approved by over 100 clinical supervisors. We will also continue to provide vignette material to offer illustrations. In order to underline the practical style of this chapter we will adopt a more informal, personal style, by addressing this chapter to you, the supervisor. The next chapter adopts this same practical style for the supervisee, when we consider in turn the competencies and techniques that they can contribute towards making supportive supervision successful. Lastly, we close with some conclusions about providing supportive supervision, including a note on the scope of these techniques, together with the action implications for the other main stakeholders. For the sake of a more balanced and accessible style, another chapter objective is to greatly reduce our earlier reliance on the therapy literature. Instead, we will use the more familiar language of the workplace and broaden our material beyond the healthcare context. A case in point is the business of competence, which requires clarification.

A competence framework for supportive supervision

A confusing variety of technical terms is used to discuss skill in the workplace, such as 'competence', 'techniques', and 'standards'. We will use the simplest and clearest terms, ones that are widely used internationally, and terms that refer to the workplace in general (e.g. drawn from the National Occupational Standards in the UK; and the National Institutes of Health in the US). For our purposes, we define competence as *the ability to perform a skill proficiently, appropriately, and effectively, to the standard that is expected in employment* (based on Rodolfo *et al*, 2005). The competence framework for clinical supervision illustrates these supervision skills (e.g. 'ability to form and maintain a supervisory alliance') (Roth & Pilling, 2008). Within our book, the skills of supportive supervision are the six competencies and 12 techniques described in this chapter. That is, we regard competence in supportive supervision as entailing 'doing the right thing' (applying an appropriate skill). Appropriateness depends on a judgement about which skill is relevant or needed at any one time, in relation to a specific supervisee, drawn from an evidence-based list. Competence also depends on performing the relevant skill with proficiency (to a quality standard: 'doing the right thing right'). Finally, the definition of competence includes performing the skill successfully (performing it effectively, as indicated by the change process and the associated outcomes: 'getting the right result'). These aspects of competence are incorporated into Table 6.1, representing our competence framework for supportive supervision.

Note that the six supportive supervision competencies are expressed in broad terms, such as 'Develop the supervisees' personal coping strategies and professional competencies, by offering advice and guidance'. These competencies are 'the right thing to do' in supportive supervision but leave out the details. Therefore, we need to be more specific if we are to help you to perform these competencies with the necessary proficiency ('doing them right'). More detailed descriptions also help in other ways, such as improving your chances of 'getting the right results', as well as informing supervisor training and guiding evaluation efforts. We will call this more detailed statement the specific supervision *techniques*. In addition to having specificity about what to do (e.g. how to ask a question or give feedback), techniques can highlight how to be most effective ('doing the right thing right'). We will provide this information by noting how the techniques produce change (the psychological mechanism or process of change). To illustrate, in Table 6.1 we indicate that using the technique of questioning should work through the change mechanisms of reflection and awareness-raising in the supervisee. In this example, reflection and self-awareness enable the supervisee to have an enhanced realisation of the strengths and weaknesses of their coping strategies. These are stepping stones towards the major supervision outcomes, such as enhanced well-being, through improved personal coping strategies. The other important reason for focusing on the mechanisms of change is that their activation represents immediate feedback to you on the effectiveness of your supervision (e.g. observing signs that the supervisee is indeed reflecting indicates that you are succeeding in your supervision).

In summary, the competence framework set out in Table 6.1 enables us to describe supportive supervision precisely enough to highlight the key tasks, processes, and outcomes. This should make the techniques easier for you to apply, encourage a flexible approach, and improve your effectiveness. Next, we will use this framework to detail the six competencies, alongside the 12 specific supervision techniques.

The tandem journey continues

Therefore, to return to the tandem analogy that we have used throughout this book, this chapter offers the supervisor a detailed road map, setting out the available routes, the critical objectives, and noting some of the tricky situations. Because of the variable terrain, each stage in the tandem's trip will require different leadership techniques. If executed well, these techniques will produce linked benefits for the supervisee, so that the trip is completed collaboratively, reaching all the developmental milestones efficiently, and with plenty of mutual feedback. Therefore, as a result of drawing on the techniques in this chapter, the supervisor should feel exceptionally well-equipped for the trip, fully fit for purpose, and confident of achieving important progress. In turn, supervisees should experience an exceptionally broad and varied range of practical leadership skills and relationship qualities, helping them to get through some of the more uncomfortable stages, while building their capacity to succeed in the future.

2. The six key competencies of supportive supervision

The six key competencies are listed on the left-hand column in Table 6.1. They are the focus of this chapter. We will describe each in turn, in terms of the two specific supervision techniques that are usually well suited to each competency. These 12 techniques, such as questioning and providing feedback, are of course often equally relevant to other competencies, but for illustrative and practical purposes we have chosen to present them as a useful heuristic in this manner. Also, there are many more techniques that we will not include, due to insufficient evidence for their effectiveness. Therefore, our list of techniques represents the best available and most evidence-based options for supportive supervision, methods that you should judge for suitability in terms of their appropriateness to your supervisee, as a particular individual in a specific context. That is, these 12 techniques should be used in a responsive, flexible manner, depending on considerations such as their acceptability and effectiveness, alongside your proficiency and preferences.

Following this reasoning, we start with the task of helping your supervisee to handle workplace stressors more effectively, partly by becoming more skilled at their job.

Table 6.1: A summary of the 12 techniques of supportive supervision

The main competencies of supportive supervision	Specific supervision techniques and their main functions	Change mechanisms and their main indicators (i.e. the initial 'mini' outcomes for supervisees)
A. Develop the supervisee's personal coping strategies and professional competencies by offering advice and guidance	1. Questioning and facilitating, to gather information and encourage development	Guided reflection, clarification and awareness-raising (e.g. changing assumptions). Enables the supervisee's movement around the experiential learning cycle
	2. Formulating to understand	Personal insight, heightening self-awareness; seeking information; analyzing and explaining problems; identifying development needs; planning improved coping
B. Encourage supervisees to build relationships by accessing and optimizing social support from peers/colleagues; provide social support during supervision protecting/buffering (supervisee from stressors)	3. Collaborating, structuring and managing to develop friendships, organize supervision, and to minimize stressors	Stronger cooperation (active agenda and goal-setting; discussing priorities, tasks, and action planning); requesting and accepting practical support; greater motivation and empowerment; more trust and signs of belonging and group cohesion →

The main competencies of supportive supervision	Specific supervision techniques and their main functions	Change mechanisms and their main indicators (i.e. the initial 'mini' outcomes for supervisees)
	4. Relating to provide emotional support	Increased honesty and openness; feeling better understood, validated and supported; releasing tension (e.g. 'offloading'); engaging in corrective emotional experiences (e.g. seeking belonging, or companionship)
C. Build and strengthen the supervision alliance (e.g. engaging in shared activities; discussing supervisees' feeling reactions to stressors; enhancing rapport; and by focusing on patients and on the caseload management)	*5. Listening* to understand relationship dynamics	Accepting reassurance; signs of personal attachment (e.g. feeling nurtured and safe); reflecting with honesty and openness; problem-solving on workload
	6. Experiencing, to develop the supervision alliance	Recognizing, describing and dealing with uncomfortable feeling reactions; emotional processing ('working through'; 'corrective experiences'); growing rapport and shared activities; experiencing catharsis
D. Challenge thinking errors and clarify associated feelings	*7. Challenging and discussing* to cultivate reasoning and resilience	Expressing concerns about own skills; discussion of reasoning process; shift in understanding to open up possibilities. Enhanced capacity for conceptualizing and critical thinking (greater sense of mastery and resilience)
	8. Experimenting to address issues behaviourally	Engage in trial-and-error learning (e.g. exposure; reality-checking); growing insight and personal comfort; feeling more confident about coping
E. Provide constructive feedback on the supervisees' work performance	*9. Giving feedback, prompting and evaluating* to define gaps, improve competencies, and monitor progress	Open to feedback, seeking guidance on skill gaps; requesting goal-setting and opportunities to experiment and improve competencies; enjoying recognition and sense of personal development →

The main competencies of supportive supervision	Specific supervision techniques and their main functions	Change mechanisms and their main indicators (i.e. the initial 'mini' outcomes for supervisees)
	10. Teaching and training to improve work skills	Engaged in learning episodes (e.g. critical thinking; problem-solving); experiencing developmental struggles; improved competence, capability, and efficiency; increased confidence and reduced intention to leave
F. Address interpersonal problems	*11. Observing* to provide objectivity and perspective	Supervisor's expertise brings perspective and a reality check; open to revising views on causes and cures for interpersonal problems; greater insight and self-awareness
	12. Demonstrating to model interpersonal skills	Grasping ideas and imitating skills; taking responsibility by experimenting with social skills (e.g. greater assertiveness)

Competence A: Develop the supervisee's personal coping strategies and professional competencies by offering advice and guidance

As a supervisor, you will naturally aim to buffer the impact of workplace stressors on your supervisee. But coping with stressors is an inescapable part of professional life, and a requirement for operating successfully in increasingly complex and stressful healthcare environments. So, rather than avoiding stressors, whenever appropriate you should encourage adaptive coping in your supervisee (i.e. the use of logical analysis, positive appraisal, and peer support). By contrast, you should discourage avoidance, resignation, the seeking of alternative rewards (i.e. use of drugs and alcohol to numb feelings of dissatisfaction and help cope with stress), and complaining about or blaming others.

In order to provide you with clear guidance on developing your supervisee's coping strategies, we will next detail how you might utilize two promising techniques. The remainder of the chapter will detail the other 10 supervision techniques that are listed in Table 6.1.

1. Questioning and facilitating

This is the first of the 12 specific supervision techniques in Table 6.1 based on a curious and enquiring stance with the supervisee providing information that enables supervision to be effective when offering advice and guidance. Questioning is not merely a way of gathering information from the supervisee (using closed questions, such as 'Which coping strategy did you use?'), but also a way of gaining a valuable glimpse of how supervisees view their work. With a clearer nunderstanding of how your supervisee perceives things, you are better positioned to offer advice and guidance. For instance, research indicates that novices exaggerate their ability, whereas more competent supervisees will under-estimate their ability. Questioning is a key way to uncover such biases. 'Socratic questioning', for example, is a disciplined process involving a systematic sequence of open-ended questions, posed from a position of assumed ignorance, to encourage reflection on the fundamentals underpinning the supervisee's assumptions or understanding of an important work topic (e.g. leadership). The aim is to clarify what the supervisee already knows to assist them in drawing on past experience to identify helpful coping strategies, and to create the basis for challenging or gaining a new perspective on beliefs, as in questioning their consistency, or evaluating their validity. This process of deep inquiry helps to foster critical thinking in the supervisee, and to draw out a more logical understanding of the matter at hand.

Systematic questioning can arouse curiosity, pinpoint logical errors, and prompt a deeper understanding. In particular, Socratic questioning achieves these results by drawing out what someone already knows in a carefully guided way, transforming existing knowledge rather than by providing instruction. This reconstructive process activates tacit knowledge that enables supervisees to grasp material more thoroughly for themselves, with the benefit of motivating additional reflection and learning. For instance, as a supervisor, you might start with the question: 'How do you prefer to cope in this situation?', then ask why this strategy is preferred, then challenge that understanding with counter-evidence on the strategies that work best. More competent supervisees will be able to go further, and will probably be more thoughtful, open (non-defensive) and creative in their responses. There are several other kinds of questions, each particularly well-suited to achieve a particular result (for a full list, see Table 5.5 in Milne, 2018). The question types include: awareness-raising; comparative; exploratory, critical engagement (e.g. justifying a belief or behaviour); and transformational. The list of the functions that these types of questions can serve includes information-gathering (closed questions) and aiding problem-solving (questions about possible explanations). Questioning works best when done in a gentle, quizzical style, and when combined with appropriate non-verbal forms of communication (e.g. eye-contact to indicate attentiveness; nodding to indicate understanding). When effective, questioning and facilitation may actually cause your supervisee to enter a stage of confusion or 'deskilling', where progress seems to have been lost. This is a desirable phase in the supervisee's development, if kept within manageable limits, because it creates the opportunity for change. Therefore, this kind of perplexity should be acknowledged and normalized.

As summarized in Table 6.1, questions activate change through broadening and guiding the supervisee's reflection process which improves experiential learning (e.g. developing our understanding and action planning). A second mechanism of professional development is heightened self-awareness, which can enhance personal insights and propel the development of coping strategies. The more adaptive coping strategies are those of problem-solving, positive appraisal, seeking social support, and logical analysis. For example, greater self-awareness of coping patterns can contribute to a supervisee gaining a deeper grasp of why certain interpersonal problems keep happening with colleagues, such as a pattern of exaggerating or minimizing problems ('being on the defensive'). As the supervisor, you can encourage reflection on alternative coping strategies, such as positively reappraising the difficult work experiences that have been avoided. Feedback from you can also help, through setting specific and concrete goals for making improvements in terms of coping more effectively with the stressful work situation. This information is best supplemented by you demonstrating how these goals can be achieved (i.e. by you modelling the skill). Your expertise as a supervisor also provides you with valuable perspective, which can help supervisees by providing a reality check (e.g. emphasising that avoidance just does not work), based perhaps on your experience of problem-solving at work.

As this account of questioning indicates, a key underlying aim is to facilitate your supervisee's movement around the experiential learning cycle. This may be through a shift in focus (e.g. moving them on from reflecting to planning), or through the use of different supervision methods. The general supervision style should be supportive and encouraging, akin to gentle counselling (or other 'preliminaries to therapy'). This includes the use of active interventions, but a facilitating effect may also arise through strategic pauses, activating further reflection, or through non-verbal encouragement (indicating that you are giving your attention and following what is being said).

These strategies and associated change mechanisms (increasing reflection, broadening perspectives, and activating more adaptive responses) represent the first indicators of progress in supervision, and development in the supervisee. Sometimes called 'mini-outcomes', they provide the basis for the major, longer-term outcomes, including improved well-being and reduced distress (as listed in Table 3.1 in Chapter 3). As indicated by this example of questioning, we are now specifying in detail how specific supervision techniques link to the early signs of change in the supervisee, contributing to the main outcomes of supportive supervision. In this sense, we are now providing a map that indicates how supervision should proceed (the supervision steps), alongside the developmental milestones that the supervisee should be reaching. We will repeat this mapping process for the remaining 11 techniques.

2. Formulating

Formulation results from the use of information to construct an understanding of what is happening, and to try to explain why it should be occurring now. Having a proper understanding enables you to offer sound advice and useful guidance. Although the explicit use of formulation with supervisees is rarely mentioned in the research literature, it is a core element of CBT supervision. Through questions, observation, and discussion, not to mention empathic listening, you should seek to clarify exactly what is happening to your supervisee at work. This grasp of the situation provides the basis for a shared understanding of the situation. This is especially important in situations that involve strong emotions. For example, your supervisee may be feeling unfairly pressured or even bullied at work. Their understandable anger may prevent you from gaining a proper understanding of what exactly has happened. Your first task is to acknowledge the anger, possibly also validating it as a reasonable reaction to an unacceptable situation. But you also need to clarify what happened, to 'gather the facts' as best you can, so that a relatively objective picture can emerge. This is the assessment aspect of formulation, which may at times be aided by other sources of information (e.g. the perceptions of colleagues; your own observations). Linked to this understanding of the context of a challenge, we also aim to assess the supervisee's capacity to respond, traditionally framed as a 'needs assessment'. As each individual supervisee is different, their reactions will vary, based on underlying specific developmental needs. The next task is to piece this information together into a useful understanding, a personal explanation that may take into account precipitating factors (contributing events), predisposing influences (e.g. the supervisee's personal history of bullying), perpetuating and protective factors (e.g. the supervisee's coping strategies (Carr, 2006)). Formulations should be developed jointly with the supervisee, partly to encourage self-awareness, but also to develop the related coping strategies (problem-solving and logical analysis).

Even if these formulation efforts have little success, the act of attending to the supervisee's concerns in such a thorough way will likely make any advice and guidance that you care to offer more acceptable. Being properly 'heard' increases your supervisees' trust and confidence in you and improves the supervisory alliance. Clearer and deeper understanding may also contribute to greater self-awareness in supervisees, a mental and motivational basis for change. This deepening of personal insight via reflection and joint reformulation of the problem may prove to be the mechanism for change in the supervisee. The formulation should highlight the most promising areas for enhancing the supervisee's coping strategies. As we discussed in Chapter 4, the formulation may also suggest that the main changes need to occur within the organization, not the supervisee (e.g. poor communication or weak leadership). Your role may therefore become that of an advocate or change agent, especially if there is a systemic problem.

Vignette

A supervisee was feeling overwhelmed in her personal life (her father, terminally ill, lived over 200 miles away). As a result, she had barely thought about her agenda for the supervision session and had not located an audio recording to play. In the car on the way in, feeling anxious and self-critical, the supervisee came up with a question about a case that "would do the job" and "cover" her. Before agenda setting, her supervisor made a point of giving her "a bit of space to really check in with you, as I know you have a lot to cope with just now". The supervisee felt able to discuss her sense that she was only just coping, and then disclosed how stressed and underprepared she was feeling, how she had planned to maintain her "game-face" rather than be completely open about her distress and the difficulties of keeping both professional and personal functioning to her preferred standard.

The supervisor allowed sufficient time for the conversation; she was empathic, she helped the supervisee to appreciate that she was in fact coping very well, and did not need to diminish or hide the pressure she was under. When asked to formulate herself, the supervisee could recognize emotional avoidance, perfectionism, and some lack of compassion for herself. Of course her heart was somewhere else, of course her usual relationship with clinical work had altered somewhat. The most restorative element was the supervisor's praise and respect for the supervisee's care for her father. The supervisor endorsed keeping things simple and being "good enough", for now. They reflected on the impact of anticipatory grief, how the supervisee sometimes felt too much and sometimes felt less than usual when working with patients. Together, they problem-solved to reduce pressures of time and caseload, and they explored self-care. In bringing the question about the case, some fruitful, open reflection on practice then began, and the supervisee's flattened sense of competence, professionalism and personal growth was repaired.

Competence B: Encourage supervisees to build relationships by accessing and optimizing social support from peers/colleagues; provide social support during supervision (protecting/buffering supervisees from stressors)

3. Collaborating

Collaboration entails working together, in terms of cooperating on tasks to maximize involvement, ownership, mutual support, and learning. Whereas solo activity can lead to low motivation or destructive rivalries, collaboration should build team spirit and prove more productive than working alone. Other important features are that a collaborative style helps to ensure that your respective needs are considered fully; that it is explicitly empowering, representing training in how to sustain active partnerships with peers; and that it better enables your supervisee to take an appropriate level of responsibility and control. Therefore, collaboration is a more sophisticated approach than simply delegating work to your supervisee, and is inherently more supportive (e.g. through tackling tasks together). Effective collaboration will require you to be careful in judging what your supervisee can manage, and how much help to offer. The art of effective collaboration requires skilfully titrating optimal levels of challenge versus support and adapting to your supervisee's needs, as reflected in their developmental readiness to accept more authority and control. Optimal collaboration assumes that you have achieved just the right balance in providing leadership and managing supervision sessions so that you are neither too passive (in an early stage of supervision, this could be anxiety provoking) nor too active (in a later stage of supervision, this could be stifling, thwarting autonomous efforts by your supervisee).

You can facilitate collaboration by providing and modelling developmentally appropriate structure and leadership, for instance, by careful agenda-setting, through discussing priorities, action planning, and by tackling tasks jointly. An important analogy taken from the literature on developmental learning (Vygotsky, 1978) is that of 'scaffolding' the supervisee's development by organizing an enabling framework. At the outset, when there is a higher need for structure and leadership, this is manifested through establishing a supervision contract, which should include agreeing work objectives, supervision methods, the process of giving and receiving feedback and evaluation arrangements. You manage the contracting process by being organized, as in having available some useful examples or templates of contracts, and by knowing what is expected within your work organization and profession. Such activities provide a clear and consistent structure, which can itself reduce the supervisee's anxiety. As noted previously, scaffolding is also about enabling the supervisee to develop, in the sense of providing 'just enough' support and guidance for your supervisee to succeed in building and maintaining relationships. Other leadership skills are timing and pacing, scheduling tasks or prioritizing topics in a timely way and proceeding at a speed that your supervisee can handle. Obtaining and organizing resources is another facet of managing (e.g. locating and utilizing equipment). The function of managing the supervisee in these ways is to minimize workplace stressors, and to facilitate the supervisee's development and well-being. If your supervision is collaborative, you can expect to see the mini-outcomes of stronger cooperation with you, greater group cohesion with colleagues, and a greater willingness to experiment (e.g. taking some calculated risks; trial-and-error learning). The main mechanism of change is social support, as in the inherent collegiality and emotional support that accompanies collaboration. The mini-outcomes of providing structure and managing your supervisee effectively are greater comfort and confidence in your approach (e.g. a growing commitment to supervision, and to the workplace). The longer-term results are decreased distress and burnout.

4. Relating

Relating within supportive supervision concerns the qualities of your personal interactions with your supervisee, such as genuineness, warmth, empathy, honesty and openness (e.g. feeling free to 'let off steam' by ventilating feelings and sharing emotions). Perhaps the strongest emphasis on relating is to be found in counselling, where these 'core conditions' in a relationship are deemed sufficient to create significant personal change. Note that the boundary that should exist between therapy and supervision is maintained by a clear focus on work, the workplace and work-related performance. We also believe that these core relational conditions are a valuable part of supervision and indeed all human relationships, and so should not be viewed as therapy. That is, relating in this caring and interpersonally effective way does not cross the important boundary between therapy and supervision.

As a result of successful relating, your supervisee is likely to reciprocate, and also engage more effectively with peers and patients. This new level of openness may create some initial difficulties for the supervisee, as it represents a different way of connecting with people (e.g. it could jeopardize avoidance-based coping, such as denying that there are any relationship struggles). Part of being genuine is to discuss such issues freely, which could include you describing some of the difficulties that you have faced ('self-disclosure'). A warm, supportive mode of relating is generally effective, including providing reassurance, encouragement, validation and praise. The key mechanism of relating is emotional support, supplemented by collegiality (i.e. social belonging and acceptance). Relating effectively in such ways as a supervisor should produce improvements in the supervisee's relationships at work, which might include a growing awareness of their need for emotional support, together with an ability to access and use it more effectively. Longer-term, the supervisee should build better relationships, and feel more supported, contributing to enhanced well-being and clinical effectiveness.

Competence C: Build and strengthen the supervision alliance (e.g. engaging in shared activities; discussing supervisees' feeling reactions to stressors; enhancing rapport; focus on patients and on caseload management)

5. Listening

Listening requires active attention to what the supervisee is saying to ensure an accurate understanding and to signal interest. Paying close attention is partly indicated non-verbally, through eye contact, nodding, and through your responsive utterances ('Uh-huh', 'Yes', 'Go on', etc.). It may also involve pauses or brief periods of silence, as you wait for your supervisee to think something through. The supervisor is focused on the supervisee, and not distracted or trying to multitask (e.g. taking phone calls, checking email or text messages, or nipping out). Listening is also indicated verbally, tested by your ability to summarize accurately or to paraphrase what the supervisee has been saying (e.g. 'A number of your concerns seem to revolve around being treated unfairly'). Through this process, you can better understand key relationship dynamics that may be a concern for the supervisee, and you may also be able to observe features of your relationship with the supervisee that offer some illumination of these dynamics. For instance, your supervisee may show some resentment about your perceived lack of support and be reluctant to cooperate with you on a task. Their degree of anger may surprise you and may suggest that there is something else that is causing the supervisee to be uncooperative (e.g. a recent history of feeling badly treated by a manager).

Attentive listening also contributes to your supervision alliance, communicating interest, concern and caring. In the above example, listening in an open and genuine manner may help the supervisee to be more forthcoming and honest. If you respond supportively (e.g. in a non-judgemental way) and help with thinking the issue through, then your supervisee will form a stronger emotional bond, feeling greater personal attachment to you (e.g. feeling nurtured and safe in your alliance; see Chapter 2 for much more on the alliance and how to foster it). The mechanism of change is emotional support, especially feeling accepted, valued and supported by you. Signs of progress include mutual listening, accepting your responses (e.g. reassurance), openness, emotional warmth, and active problem-solving (e.g. on workload management).

6. Experiencing

This technique supplements and enhances listening by deepening the accompanying emotional experience of listening and responding to your supervisee. Experiencing refers to an awareness of the emotional accompaniments to work, including tuning in to the feelings that arise within supervision in an empathic way. For example, you could describe to your supervisee feeling positive about the stronger emotional bond mentioned above and delving deeper into such reactions would be an instance of employing the experiencing technique (e.g. by defining or describing it more fully). Experiencing also means processing feeling reactions, dealing with them productively, rather than trying to ignore them. If you are focusing on the supervisee, then you may try to develop an awareness of their thoughts and feelings about a supervision session to develop greater recognition and understanding of their feeling reactions. To help them process these reactions you can supplement listening and alliance techniques by some awareness-raising questions (e.g. 'What is your most powerful emotion right now?'), leading into a description of the key event that triggered the emotion (e.g. clarifying the role that your supervisee felt that they played in the incident). Note that this is approach-based coping, in place of the more common denial or 'warding-off' or ventilation of negative feelings (e.g. blaming or complaining). Next you might consider other ways of thinking or feeling about the incident or reenact some important aspect through a role-play. Further expression of feelings should be encouraged (and accepted, if valid), leading into the resolution phase in which a clearer and more comfortable feeling reaction is achieved (e.g. self-compassion), some sense or meaning is developed to better grasp what happened, and some constructive planning is done to minimize these reactions in future. These steps are based on the assimilation and resolution approaches (Stiles *et al,* 1990; Greenberg & Malcolm, 2002).

The mechanisms of experiencing are awareness-raising, insight, catharsis (releasing pent-up emotions), and the processing of feeling reactions ('working-through' them, with methods such as the assimilation and resolution approaches). Signs that your supervision is proving effective in fostering experiencing in your supervisee include their increasing emotional engagement in clarifying and processing reactions, and a growing rapport between you. Experiencing deepens the sense of meaningful work being accomplished in supervision and can be extremely motivating and rewarding. In these ways you can build and strengthen your supervision alliance.

Competence D: Challenging thinking errors and clarifying associated feelings

7. Challenging

Supervisees in training are naturally prone to making errors of judgement and becoming upset, which is part and parcel of being a novice. Indeed, thinking errors, mistaken actions, and negative feelings continue throughout our careers, as part and parcel of professional life. Although a supportive and empathic reaction may be a common response, supervisors can also help by spending time gently challenging supervisees' negative thinking patterns. By challenging, we mean discussions that encourage your supervisee to become more aware of their assumptions and thinking biases, and to develop their reasoning powers (e.g. through Socratic questioning and re-evaluations of problematic thinking patterns). Challenging is intended to develop the supervisee's problem-solving capability (Fraser & Greenhalgh, 2001). An example is provided in the vignette that ends this section. But challenging is also appropriate in relation to routine work activities, and even when there are no obvious thinking errors, in order to enhance your supervisee's capacity for conceptualizing key issues and for engaging in critical, reflective thinking (which can be thought of as them imitating your challenging style). Getting into the habit of critically reflecting on our work is a vital professional skill, aiding our reasoning powers, skill development, and emotional resilience.

Challenging can undoubtedly be a personally threatening technique, and so you should be prepared to help your supervisee to cope effectively with it (e.g. through some self-disclosure). Encouraging such coping empowers your supervisee to handle criticism or disagreement more comfortably, ideally through improving their understanding of the accompanying feelings and how best to manage them (e.g. the imposter syndrome: see the vignette below).

8. Experimenting

Experimenting refers to a behavioural approach, where thinking errors and associated feelings are addressed through action-focused, trial-and-error learning experiences ('learning from experience'). The 'experimenting' technique involves testing out beliefs through action-based experiments, as opposed to disputing faulty thinking via verbal or emotional means (e.g. through the supervision techniques of challenging or experiencing). Therefore, it equates to the behavioural aspect of CBT and includes the same kinds of activities selected to help the supervisee to test out dysfunctional thoughts or feelings. A well-known instance of experimenting within CBT involves conducting behavioural experiments to test out assumptions, rules or beliefs about what is likely to happen. For example, supervisees can often be reluctant to be appropriately directive, and so instead they may structure therapy sessions more informally, with the rationalization that patients might otherwise get angry or feel invalidated. Rather than challenging this belief system or attempting a purely didactic approach to this problematic belief, the supervisor will probably be more effective by giving supervisees a chance to test out their belief system through setting up a behavioural experiment that serves to test out their assumptions. Behavioural experiments are aimed to test out faulty assumptions and can provide powerful 'expectancy violation effects', where the supervisee is surprised by the outcome and so learns something new that was not expected (i.e. that violates their sense of what 'should' have happened). This creates an extremely potent form of experiential learning. In order to be most effective, behavioural experiments need to be carefully set up and clearly designed to test out specific underlying assumptions ("The patient will get mad at me and feel invalidated"). Typically, we would ask the supervisee to write down in advance what they expect to happen (their prediction), and to assign a rating of how confident they feel that this will occur and to identify other possible predicted outcomes and what will count as countering evidence that does not support their prediction. Countering evidence must be observable and behavioural and not, for example, a subjective feeling or reaction as to how the patient is feeling. After the experiment is conducted, the supervisee is asked to write down the outcome and what they learned from their experience. This is then discussed in supervision and additional behavioural experiments may be agreed on to strengthen the new learning or to develop a fresh test of the prediction if the outcome of the previous experiment was ambiguous or subject to multiple interpretations. A vignette in the next chapter gives an example of this method.

Experimentation may include examining the reactions of colleagues to the supervisor's involvement in joint-working. For example, your supervisee may think that peers are scornful and treat them as a failure, but gathering some evidence may weaken or disconfirm that perception (e.g. evidence from careful observation, or from requesting specific feedback). Other kinds of shared activity may also prove helpful, as in reviewing perfectionistic standards in the light of the supervisor's goals (see the 'imposter' vignette). To succeed, a behavioural experiment needs to be targeted to the learning needs of the supervisee and their stage of development. The supervisor needs to be sensitive to the anxiety that is often encountered when conducting such activities, and thus should conduct the activity empathically. Through such careful experimenting, your supervisee should become more aware of their thinking errors, developing insight into their patterns and feeling reactions, and gradually become more comfortable and confident when challenging uncomfortable ideas or emotions. Experimenting also helps to build competence, so can contribute to growing feelings of mastery.

Vignette 2

A trainee had a secret fear that he was an 'imposter', a fraud who was not really worthy of supervision. This came to light in a discussion about why he was seemingly dissatisfied with everything that had been achieved since the last session. Although there had been one slip-up, most of the supervisee's work in this fortnight was actually to a high standard. Something wasn't right! It turned out that this supervisee believed that he was inferior to his peers and will be 'found out' one of these days. The supervisor thanked him for explaining, and started by pointing out that the 'imposter syndrome' was actually a common experience, even affecting high-achieving individuals, who report intense feelings of professional fraudulence. The supervisor also disclosed that she had had similar feelings at some stressful times, but had got into the habit of challenging this negative way of thinking. The supervisee wanted to know more, so she explained that she always began with the facts: what was the evidence for being an imposter? She would then get a piece of paper, writing her 'imposter thoughts' down the left-hand side, and then would challenge these thoughts with the counter-evidence. The supervisee asked if they could do that for his 'imposter thoughts', particularly the belief that any success he had was down to luck, as this that kept depressing him. The supervisor obliged, asking some questions to clarify some typical recent work tasks that had been completed successfully. She then invited the supervisee to take the sheet away and complete the evidence column for their next supervision session. This would be a detailed account of the work he had done in relation to each success (the methods, procedures, techniques, etc.). In order to challenge the negative thinking, she added that she would also complete the sheet, by noting what she would have done in these situations. When they later compared their respective approaches to these work tasks, the supervisee was surprised to be unable to spot any major differences, leading to the conclusion that he had been acting competently, and exaggerating the role of luck. The supervisor closed by asking whether he still felt dissatisfied with this work, in order to improve his understanding of the link between his exaggerated imposter thoughts and his negative feelings.

Competence E: Provide constructive feedback on the supervisees' work performance

9. Giving feedback

Feedback is an essential and powerful element in skill development and professional growth (Tracey *et al,* 2014). Perhaps more than any other technique, feedback draws on your ability to advise and guide your supervisee, based on your expertise. In theory, feedback is circulating information about outcomes around a system, especially to the source or control unit, so as to strengthen or modify actions and effectiveness. In practice it involves providing knowledge of results to supervisees (e.g. clinical outcomes) and other kinds of informational feedback or reinforcement, because of the supervisee's actions. This process usually takes the form of your evaluation of the supervisee's performance, leading to your providing information that helps the supervisee to do better next time ('formative' feedback). The most fundamental feedback is information that specifies the key skill gaps, pinpointing the difference between the supervisee's current and desired skill levels (Hattie & Timperley, 2007). For example, at the start of their training supervisees will typically struggle to demonstrate the basic clinical competencies. With effective supervision, plus the other elements of professional training, supervisees should be able to demonstrate competence by the end of training. This leads to the successful completion of their training, and usually to a degree or an award (i.e. to summative feedback).

The novice's proficiency gap highlights the current level of performance as a baseline, alongside the standard that is required (i.e. goal-setting). Supervision should address that competence gap systematically, which can be done most effectively by a combination of goal-setting, advice, and modelling. Advice will usually take the form of teaching, in order to explain the nature of a skill (e.g. why it has to be performed in a particular way). This is then best followed by some action to ensure that an adequate understanding has been achieved (e.g. an educational role-play: 'Show me how you would do that'). A vital action in feedback is modelling a skill, either before or after the supervisee attempts to perform the skill. As the supervisor, you should demonstrate how to perform the skill with sufficient competence to meet the required standard, while being clear that this is what is required from your supervisee to close the performance gap ('Here's how I would do it'; see the 'demonstrating' technique below). This represents the second essential kind of information within effective feedback: indicating how a competence gap can be closed. At times, feedback may indicate that there is no gap, as a competence has been fully demonstrated, which is usually accompanied by praise (in summative feedback it may also be accompanied by a 'pass' mark, or progression to the next stage of training).

In our experience, feedback to supervisees in training is surprisingly rare, and the inclusion of modelling is even less common. Specifically, until we required it explicitly, after three months of a six-month placement, the majority of trainees within one of our university programmes did not know how their supervisor thought they were doing; there had been no proper feedback. Despite the strong theoretical and research support for feedback, this scarcity of feedback appears to be a common situation in routine professional practice (i.e. supervision as part of career-long, continuing professional development). Feedback is more frequent within research contexts, where it is usually found to play a valuable role (Milne & Reiser, 2017). Given that feedback is such a powerful and straightforward technique, you need to make sure that feedback is a common occurrence within your supervision (including mutual feedback). We understood that the reason that feedback was so rare in the example above was that both parties avoided it, as something threatening and out of keeping with a warm and supportive collegial relationship or with 'the cult of the positive'. The idea that 'feedback is not for friends' needs to be countered by the frequent, routine, and low-key use of mutual feedback. It is a truism that 'there is no learning without feedback', and so it should be a routine and non-threatening feature in all your supervision sessions, and this will gradually develop in supervisees the capacity to monitor and adjust their own performance.

Feedback is as relevant to supportive supervision as it is to the other supervision functions. This means that it is equally powerful in relation to developing the supervisees' personal coping strategies, social support resources, and so on. However, feedback will only work if it is presented in a professional manner (e.g. is constructive and respectful), and when it includes manageable amounts of generally positive information (e.g. using praise and validation to guide supervisees' coping efforts). Precision, timeliness, and objectivity are essential, as is a collaborative approach to tackling gaps. Sometimes it is also important to explain the need for feedback, as a core feature of ongoing professional development. In providing feedback, it can be particularly helpful to distinguish between the success of the supervisee's action (outcome feedback), the execution of the skill (performance feedback), and feedback on the way that the supervisee tackled the task (process feedback). This is especially true when the outcomes depend significantly on factors beyond the supervisee's control, when greater emphasis should be given to performance or process feedback. For example, a supervisor could praise the supervisee for persisting in the face of a setback, and for calmly and patiently trying different methods. The least helpful approach is personal feedback (concerning the style, manner, or other personal qualities of the supervisee, e.g. 'You seemed unsure about what to do next'). One of the six guidelines in the CBT supervision manual is devoted to feedback, with two video clips offering detailed demonstrations (Milne & Reiser, 2017).

Feedback on your supervision should also be sought from the supervisee to gain potentially helpful information, to improve as a supervisor, to model receptiveness to feedback, and to empower the supervisee. Feedback in both directions can usefully employ a variety of information sources, such as patient satisfaction data via questionnaires, clinical outcome monitoring, skill ratings, and direct observation.

The indicators that your feedback is working include more disclosure of challenging or difficult clinical situations and other signs that your supervisee is open to feedback, such as in providing you with relevant information (e.g. a draft clinical report), or seeking your guidance on how to close any identified skill gaps; requesting some goal-setting (targets or objectives, within a development plan); creating opportunities to experiment and improve competencies; enjoying recognition and sense of personal development.

10. Teaching and training

Teaching and training are defined as systematic and protracted educational methods of instruction and practice, designed to bring a supervisee to a desired competence standard. The intended outcomes are to encourage supervisees to learn the knowledge, skills, attitudes, and other attributes that result in their improved workplace performance (based on Goldstein & Ford, 2001). By contrast, teaching is identified with education (schools, universities) and can be distinguished by its greater emphasis on theory and the use of symbolic academic methods (i.e. reliant on language and thinking, e.g. lectures, seminars, and research projects). It also features in-depth questioning, protracted discussion and the systematic challenging of ideas or knowledge. The main objective of teaching in healthcare is to develop capability – improving the supervisee's thinking capacity so that they can solve problems and create new knowledge (Fraser & Greenhalgh, 2001). In this sense, some of the supervision techniques already discussed are examples of teaching (e.g. 'questioning', 'formulating' and 'challenging'). In practice, the supervisor mainly teaches by providing information or resources to the supervisee which help them to grasp theories, facts, figures, ideas, methods, articles (sometimes termed 'information transmission'). This is done in a didactic fashion, as in traditional classroom teaching. 'Symbolic' (i.e. verbal) learning should be emphasised and is intended to improve the supervisee's ability to comprehend the relevant knowledge base.

By contrast, training is identified with the workplace, exemplified historically by the apprenticeship system that provided industry with skilled workers. It is more practical in style and purpose than teaching, and usually follows well-established, top-down educational systems (e.g. competence frameworks and standards set by professional bodies at a national level). Training draws on suitably practical methods of instruction, such as the supervision techniques of 'demonstrating', 'experimenting', 'observing', and giving corrective 'feedback'. As these examples indicate, the supervisor helps supervisees to learn by engaging them in an appropriate experiential activity. The training methods are behavioural and problem-based, including: modelling, demonstrating, watching videos, simulation, behavioural rehearsal, and educational role play. The methods should be used sensitively and be appropriate to the learning needs of the supervisee (especially to their readiness, their stage of development), and also should build on their strengths.

Competence F: Address interpersonal problems

11. Observing

Observation means gaining a first-hand awareness of your supervisee at work, obtaining some 'raw data' on what is actually happening in real time. This can be done through co-working, through audio or video recordings, or through simulations and behavioural rehearsals (e.g. educational role-plays). Sometimes the observations can also come from others who are involved in healthcare (e.g. patients, co-workers or administrative staff), and at other times some work produces 'permanent products' that represent another type of observation (e.g. clinical reports and other hard evidence bearing on the competence of interventions, such as complications or recovery rates). Observations of this kind are partly a means of checking the inevitable biases that accompany the supervisees' own perceptions ('self-report'). It is only natural that supervisees, like supervisors and everyone else, have some automatic perceptual biases, ones that are typically self-serving (e.g. protecting us against criticism, or boosting low self-esteem). But these biases do create a barrier to fully understanding what is happening, and for that reason alone experts advise that observation be used routinely (APA, 2015; Roth & Pilling, 2008). Your understanding of the observed work should be discussed with your supervisee, and ideally you will be able to pinpoint specific moments on a recording viewed jointly, to maximize the supervisee's learning and involvement. Such observation leads naturally to your advice and guidance, hopefully complementing self-report. Although your observation will itself contains biases, supervision that is based on observation leads to better supervision results, better intervention adherence, and improved clinical outcomes (APA, 2015; Milne & Reiser, 2017).

It can be time-consuming to observe your supervisee, unless it is incorporated alongside routine joint work. For this and other reasons, observation is actually rare (e.g. observation can sometimes be intrusive and cause 'reactivity' in patients, rendering it invalid). This is a great shame, as time given to observation is very likely to be handsomely repaid, as it affords a unique perspective, complementing the supervisee's self-report. For example, novices naturally lack the ability to judge their own competence (i.e. they are unskilled, but unaware of it) (Dunning *et al*, 2003). This means that your relative expertise can better inform supervision, and that your feedback will be more likely to pinpoint gaps between actual and desired practice. Observation also brings a new and different perspective, which can help to make sense of puzzling phenomena (e.g. interpersonal strife) and can serve as a reality check for the supervisee (a rude awakening, leading to change). In such ways you can help your supervisee to develop greater self-awareness, insights that can illuminate interpersonal difficulties. One of the video recordings in the CBT supervision manual, on 'providing specific negative feedback' (Milne & Reiser, 2017), presents an example of a reality check, in which an experienced therapist receives some belated and disturbing feedback on her work from an observer. Although this depicts an awkward moment in supervision, it encourages insight and heralds improvement.

12. Demonstrating

Demonstrating is also based on observation, but this time the supervisee watches how you believe a skill should be performed, modelling their behaviour on your example ('role-modelling'). Another link is to feedback, where we stressed the vital role of modelling in showing your supervisee exactly how a performance gap can be closed, creating the basis for observational learning. Learning through observing how others carry out a task is core to apprenticeships, and indeed to much of social life in general. Since we are focusing on interpersonal problems in this section, we should start with the supervision alliance, which is your prime opportunity to address any such problems with your supervisee. Alliance 'ruptures' are setbacks or breakdowns in the collaborative bond between you and your supervisee and demonstrating how to resolve the rupture is a powerful and valuable method (including self-disclosure on your own past experiences). It is one of the recommendations within the original work on alliance ruptures by Safran *et al* (2007), and is detailed in our supervision manual (Milne & Reiser, 2017). The suggestions we provide in the manual are linked to an emotionally charged video clip depicting an alliance rupture (Clip 3). According to these sources, modelling is part of a package of methods that can help repair ruptures, starting with some clarification of the trigger or cause of the rupture, leading into some perspective-taking and non-blaming mutual clarifications. Role-modelling is especially valuable in clarifying subtle professional skills (e.g. ethical practice; respect for patients; professional demeanour). The power of role modelling is boosted by telling your supervisee what exactly you are trying to portray, and why it matters.

Of course, interpersonal problems are also likely to occur in your supervisee's dealings with colleagues or patients in the workplace. As these may be out of your awareness, or even concealed from you, the importance of observation and modelling becomes even more valuable in detecting and addressing any difficulties. By providing regular and varied role-modelling, you also provide your supervisee with opportunities to resolve some difficulties without the need for any further help, which is often a far more attractive and comfortable way forward for all concerned (incidental learning). Put more positively, role-modelling contributes in a profound way to the development of your supervisee's professional identity. Summarizing this process, Goodyear (2014) noted how learners like supervisee will typically internalize the attitudes and perspectives of those on whom they model themselves. This is indicated by the way that we ask ourselves how our model would handle a trying situation ('What would my supervisor do here?'). This can be an enduring guide to our behaviour, as indicated by a quote that Goodyear (2014, p86) reported from an informant in a qualitative study, who was a supervisor from 20 years ago: *"I have been running around in my mind words, phrases, quotes that I periodically pull back to ... and sometimes I say to myself, how would John handle this situation?"*

Role-modelling through demonstrating professional skills, attitudes and ways of thinking is therefore of profound value and can help your supervisee to better understand their role, and to gain confidence in their work from seeing you succeed. This applies strongly to interpersonal difficulties, where you can display, discuss and encourage your supervisee to develop their key social skills in managing workplace relationships (e.g. experimenting with assertiveness).

Summary

This chapter has centred on a detailed discussion of 12 specific supervision techniques that underpin the six main competencies of supportive supervision. Our aim was to provide enough detail to enable you to use them successfully. To help to ensure effective practice, we also specified the mechanisms (processes of change). Table 6.1 provides a summary. One reason for highlighting these support mechanisms was to encourage some flexibility, in that various techniques may trigger the mechanism (from elsewhere in the list or through additional techniques). You will no doubt have some favourites or find that certain techniques or strategies fit more comfortably with your personal style or circumstances. In this sense, we are adopting a 'tight-loose' strategy: being tightly focused on the mechanisms, but looser about how they are applied. A second reason for highlighting these support mechanisms was to enable you to receive optimal feedback. Inviting your supervisee to comment on your use of supportive techniques is a useful and recommended device, but noting how your supervisee **responds** to these supervision techniques will probably provide the most valid and valuable feedback on your effectiveness. As such, this represents the best form of corrective feedback, and the firmest basis for making any adjustments to your supervision.

Are these techniques evidence-based? Although firmly grounded on the evidence-based SAGE manual that guides the systematic observation of clinical supervision (Milne *et al*, 2011; Reiser *et al*, 2018; see the Appendix on page 239 or www.pavpub.com/supportive-clinical-supervision-resources/), the material in this chapter has been slightly redrafted to emphasize supportive supervision, and so is not yet suitable for use as a formal measurement tool within research. In particular, we grouped the 23 SAGE items to fit with the six supervision competencies that emerged from Chapter 3, judging for illustrative purposes which items were most important to each competence. For example, we considered that *collaborating* was essential to supportive supervision (technique 3 in Table 6.1), while *structuring* and *managing* were secondary in importance. Similar judgements were made throughout Table 6.1, so that we achieved the best possible fit between SAGE and supportive supervision. There is strong endorsement for the competencies and techniques outlined above, from successive reviews based on over 50 research studies (Milne & James, 2000; Milne *et al*, 2008).

Chapter 7: How Supervisees Can Make the Most of Their Supervision

1. Introduction

Ironically, the role of supervisees in supervision is a sorely neglected topic. Most of the literature on supervision focuses exclusively on the supervisor, which is a myopic perspective that implies that the supervisee is of little significance. Worse, when the literature on supervisees is mentioned, it typically concerns various 'games' that they are thought to play to avoid engaging in supervision (Kadushin, 1968; McIntosh *et al*, 2006; Muller *et al*, 2019). To illustrate the extent of the neglect, we know of only one clinical supervision text that aims to enhance the supervisee's ability to benefit from supervision (Falender & Shafranske, 2012), a few papers that encourage supervisees to play an active role (e.g. Parker *et al*, 2017), only a handful of studies that focus on empowering the supervisee as a supervisee, and only one evidence-based guideline (Milne & Reiser, 2017). By contrast, relevant theory, expert consensus statements, and the available research all suggest that the supervisee plays an essential role in successful supervision. For example, expert consensus statements that pinpoint best practices for supervisors suggest that effective supervision always involves close collaboration, mutual establishment of responsibilities, and tailoring interventions to the developmental level of the supervisee (APA, 2015; Roth & Pilling, 2008). This guidance reflects the nature of supervision as a transactional, two-way interpersonal process, is consistent with general systems theory (see Chapter 2), and is also compatible with widely held views within the supervision literature (e.g. the importance of the 'co-construction' of supervision (Watkins and Milne, 2014)).

Perhaps the clearest illustration can be found in the development of the supervisory alliance, "a supervisor – supervisee construction that develops over time and is built through sustained interaction" (Watkins, 2014a, p44). This collaborative approach also agrees with theories of 'active' or 'experiential' learning (Kolb, 2014; Prince, 2004): "The core elements of active learning are student activity and engagement in the learning process" (Prince, 2004, p223). To emphasize the importance of supervisee engagement and empowerment, we address this chapter to the supervisee. In addition, we should complement this experiential emphasis with attention to your educational development as a supervisee through utilizing the more academic methods of supervision to build your capability (e.g. discussing; questioning; challenging (Fraster and Greenhalgh, 2001)). This is vital in order to empower you to better self-regulate and self-manage your own professional development, such as improving your emotional well-being and learning expertise (Milne & Reiser, 2017).

It also follows that, in asking more of you as a supervisee, the necessary emotional support and practical guidance is provided, so as to enable you to succeed. Logical examples are training workshops in supervision, where supervisees can learn how best to strengthen the supervision that they receive, alongside other continuing professional development and support arrangements (e.g. peer mentoring). To illustrate, Bearman *et al* (2019) provided a workshop to 23 trainee clinical psychologists on CBT supervision. The evidence base for the workshop content and methods included research on the CBT supervision provided within CBT clinical trials (Roth *et al,* 2010), resources used within the Improving Access to Psychological Therapies (IAPT) supervision initiative to support CBT (Turpin & Wheeler, 2011), and the supervisory competencies recommended by the APA (2015). Experiential methods were emphasized within the eight-hour workshop, including modeling, educational role-plays, and observation-based feedback. The effectiveness of the workshop was indicated by significant improvements at the post-workshop assessment in comparison with the pre-workshop assessment in the supervisees' knowledge and self-rated supervision competencies. Although the emphasis was on preparing these trainees to become supervisors after graduation, the material and learning exercises were also relevant to being a competent supervisee (e.g. collaborative goal-setting; using outcome data to make clinical decisions; seeking feedback). There was a restorative element within this workshop, concerning CBT practices that could support supervisees in making behaviour changes (Socratic questioning, motivational interviewing, sequential problem-solving). This is an exceptionally well-detailed account of supervisor training, and it also includes a justification for providing such training. The pre-workshop results suggested that merely being supervised was insufficient preparation for becoming a supervisor. Another rare example of attending to the supervisee is the clarification of the competencies needed to empower them to make the most of their supervision, such as self-evaluation (Kangos *et al,* 2018). This clarification was based on the supervision guidelines provided by the APA (2006).

The same supervision guidelines were also valuable in operationalizing an instrument for observing interactions reliably within supervision in Columbia, as described by Novoa-Gomez *et al* (2019). This study indicated the relative frequency with which supervisees' initiated a range of interactions with their supervisors (there were nine supervisor-supervisee dyads, providing 15 hours of tape recordings). The largest percentage of the observed interactions initiated by these nine supervisees was discussion of their clinical assessments (up to 35% of the interactions), followed by formulation and intervention skills. In stark contrast supervisees rarely initiated discussion of restorative topics that might contribute to their personal well-being. The categories of self-evaluation (e.g. assessing one's own limitations), interpersonal difficulties (e.g. alliance ruptures in supervision or clinical work), self-disclosure or emotional expression were observed less than 5% of the time. This portrays supervisees as primarily focused on their clinical work, and providing few prompts to their supervisors to engage in vital topics such as strengthening alliances or dealing with emotions. The supervisors also neglected these restorative themes. Novoa-Gomez *et al* (2019) concluded that the very limited attention to relational skills in their observations of supervision (e.g. empathy and appropriate affective experiences) jeopardized clinical work and did not properly address the well-being of the supervisee, thereby omitting an important intervention which they termed 'remoralization'.

Evidence from these studies indicates the need for this chapter, namely the need to focus on you, the supervisee, in a constructive way. Having already considered in earlier chapters how the supervisor might best contribute to this collaborative process, we now ask how you in turn can best play your role in making the most of your supervision experience? Our concerns remain the same ones that emerged from our reviews of relevant theory and research (Chapters 2 and 3), but this time we consider these issues from your perspective as a supervisee. Therefore, our main questions mirror the supervision methods that appeared in Table 3.1 (Chapter 3): What can supervisees do to manage their painful feelings and distress? How can they improve their adaptive coping efforts in the workplace? Is energy invested in enhancing their alliance with the supervisor worthwhile, or does it make more sense to seek social support from peers? To emphasize the contrasting perspectives of the supervisor and supervisee, we next develop the supervision methods listed in Table 3.1 (see Chapter 3) by presenting them from the perspective of the supervisee (see Table 7.1). Our aim remains that of empowering supervisees in their work through identifying evidence-based methods that they can use to improve their well-being, professional capability, and interpersonal effectiveness. As you review these methods, note that we continue to build on our original support model (Chapter 2), especially emphasizing the critical role that is played by your personal coping strategies, your engagement in social support, and your experiential learning.

To return to the tandem analogy that we have been using throughout this book, while the supervisor remains the leader and retains ultimate responsibility for steering a suitable course, as the supervisee you also assume some responsibility for getting to the destination in an appropriate way. This includes contributing equally to the general effort required to reach the destination (i.e. being personally fit for the trip), being in sound health (i.e. able to play a full role), through being a team player (i.e. contributing interpersonally), and through engaging in activities that maximize social support. Riding a tandem cycle to a destination successfully depends on all of these contributions by the supervisee. The investment you make in taking on these additional roles is repaid with interest by your deepened, ongoing personal and professional development, preparation for a lifetime of professional engagement, job satisfaction, and an increased sense of well-being. The supervisor also benefits significantly from your collaboration and professionalism, and receives important dividends related to satisfaction and pride that you have grown into an independent and effective colleague.

Given the scarcity of research directly concerned with the supervisees' role, and especially the dearth of studies that focus on the supervisees' role in restorative supervision, our evidence-based strategy will be fully extended in this chapter. Although we will, of course, detail the few available empirical studies, we will have to rely more than usual on relevant theory, expert consensus, and on extrapolating from neighbouring literatures (especially research on therapy). As before, we aim to be explicit about when we are extrapolating, and to be suitably cautious in drawing conclusions. We hope that this chapter can help to inform future research on the role of the supervisee, so that firmer evidence-based guidelines can be presented in subsequent texts.

2. Be ready for your work

To play your role in supervision as a supervisee, you first need to be fit and well. This includes having the necessary physical energy and motivation for the supervision process, and the emotional resilience to meet the demands of the job. It also means having the 'right attitude', as in viewing your personal well-being as primarily your responsibility (i.e. it's not acceptable to turn up for supervision or work in an impaired state). Your well-being will probably affect your clinical work, as indicated by a meta-analysis (Beutler *et al*, 2004), by a longitudinal study by Nissen-Lie *et al* (2013), and by a cross-sectional survey (Delgado *et al*, 2019). Nissen-Lie *et al* (2013) reported that therapists' personal distress impaired the therapeutic working alliance. Patients were actually more aware of this association than their therapists. By contrast, therapists who had been trained in mindfulness were judged by their patients to be more effective (Ivanovic *et al*, 2015).

Getting into the optimal personal state, one in which you are 'ready for your work', depends on your utilizing suitable psychological coping strategies and managing your motivation effectively. Your supervisor can help you to review and develop these 'self-help' techniques, where they are relevant to your performance and well-being at work. When not relevant to work (i.e. your personal life), then they are best addressed by seeking other kinds of help that is distinct from your supervision (e.g. consulting a physician or a therapist). These coping strategies are also vital in relation to your being professionally able and interpersonally effective, as it is primarily through your adaptive coping efforts that you meet the stresses and demands of your work. Therefore, we will next expand on what we have said about coping strategies in Chapters 2 and 4, extending that general introduction to describe in detail the most suitable ways of being personally ready for work. Later in this chapter we will resume our discussion of coping strategies to consider specific techniques that you can utilize to also be professionally able and interpersonally effective.

In Chapter 2 we developed the 'support model' as a framework for understanding supportive supervision. This model included the supervisee's personal functioning as an intrapersonal system that was nested within other, related systems (interpersonal, organizational and contextual: see Figure 2.1). Then, in Chapter 4, we detailed the main aspects of personal functioning, prioritizing the role played by our personal coping strategies. To recap, these strategies are ways of thinking, feeling or behaving in order to deal with stressors at work. Table 4.2 listed the effective 'approach-based' strategies (e.g. engaging in a logical analysis of the stressor) and the maladaptive 'avoidance-based' strategies (e.g. emotional discharge). This table also included popular examples of each of these common coping strategies, based on a survey of counsellors (e.g. they reported achieving 'emotional discharge' by describing their work frustrations to colleagues). In this chapter we next summarize evidence-based, psychological ways in which you can be ready for your work. These methods are summarized in Table 7.1. We start with altering the way that we suggest that you look at stressors, termed cognitive reappraisal or mental reframing.

Table 7.1: A summary of the main ways that supervisees can make the most of their supervision		
The main ways for supervisees to make the most of their supervision	Examples of supervisee self-help techniques	Examples of the associated positive outcomes for the supervisee
1. Be ready for your work (especially by improving your personal coping strategies, so as to be fully motivated and healthy)	a. Reappraisal (e.g. 'reframing') and emotional processing b. Enhance use of personal coping strategies	■ Improved mental health performance, job satisfaction (Bond & Bunce, 2000); enhanced resilience (Stacey *et al*, 2019) ■ Reduced psychological distress, improved self-care (Bennett-Levy, 2019) →

The main ways for supervisees to make the most of their supervision	Examples of supervisee self-help techniques	Examples of the associated positive outcomes for the supervisee
	c. Reflection (including 'Self-practice/self -reflection': SP/SR) d. Contemplation (mindfulness and acceptance-based methods)	■ Enhanced self-reflection (Bennett-Levy et al, 2001; Bennett-Levy et al, 2014) ■ Lower levels of burnout, improved self-care and physical health (Kaeding et al, 2017)
2. Be professionally able (especially by developing competencies to better perform your work duties)	e. Build and strengthen the supervision alliance (e.g. seek advice and guidance to aid competence development)	■ Improved clinical effectiveness (Green et al, 2014) ■ Better supervisory relationship (Beinart, 2014) ■ Facilitated learning (Goodyear, 2014)
3. Be interpersonally effective (the social dimension, achieved through enhancing your supervision alliance and by boosting your social support)	f. Enhance your social support (e.g. optimize social support from colleagues, ensuring reciprocity; address interpersonal problems and discuss feeling reactions, to regulate your negative emotions)	■ Higher levels of perceived support and improved mental health (Lakey & Orehek, 2011) ■ Gain social support, with benefits for patients, team working, and the hospital culture (Goodrich, 2012) ■ Successful emotional processing and joint problem-solving discussions (Kennedy-Moore & Watson, 2001)

a. Reappraisal, reframing and emotional processing

Choosing how best to cope with a stressor starts with your appraisal of that stressor – is it a threat or a challenge? Can you handle it? A survey of 249 female professionals in social work, nursing and psychology indicated that perceiving stressors as challenging but controllable was correlated with reduced burnout (Ben-Zur & Michael, 2007). This is a common finding, indicating the central role played by appraisal in the coping process (Gomes et al, 2016; Stacey et al, 2019). We outlined the stages of appraisal in Chapter 2, noting that reappraisal is an evaluative cognitive phase that follows the initial appraisal of a stressor (Lazarus & Folkman, 1984). During reappraisal your aim is to identify and more objectively reframe your own unhelpful reactions, beliefs and assumptions about stressful events. Note that in reappraisal the facts of the situation are to be accepted and processed, rather than denying or avoiding them. For instance, you may have overly negative, pessimistic or unhelpful thoughts about an event, such as being criticized for an action that you took. This self-critical initial appraisal can result in equally negative emotional reactions, ones that can make you unfit for work (e.g. doubting your competence to deal with a particular incident, leading to avoidance). A more helpful reappraisal can lead to a more realistic, balanced and objective view of stressful events, effective problem-solving and better coping strategies that increase your sense of personal well-being, competence and capability. Reappraisal leads to more adaptive coping, and so contributes to your fitness for the workplace. For example, Buus *et al* (2013) ran staff groups to help supervisees to reflect on their access to supervision, shifting their appraisals about the barriers so that the staff felt empowered to improve its availability and quality.

The methods that we group under reappraisal vary from these brief and simple self-help methods just described (e.g. the reframing of barriers), to more structured and effortful techniques, such as CBT-based reappraisal, to which we now turn. After an example drawn from therapy, we will describe a method with a greater educational emphasis (Self-Practice/Self-Reflection), followed by a discussion of mindfulness and acceptance-based techniques of relevance to being fit for your work. Later in this chapter we will turn to the best available psychological methods for being professionally able and interpersonally effective (for a summary of these techniques, see Table 7.1).

Cognitive Behavioural Therapy (CBT)-based reappraisal methods

An example of using CBT methods to help reappraise negative reactions related to a client is provided in the vignette that follows, labelled 'Addressing perfectionism and performance anxiety'. We further discuss this vignette in the section on mindfulness and acceptance-based strategies, and develop some alternative approaches to help the therapist come to terms with such negative emotions.

Vignette: Addressing perfectionism and performance anxiety

A mid-career CBT therapist tends to take on very challenging clients with chronic mental health conditions that are often resistant to treatment. She is currently working with a patient who has not responded well to CBT, and has chronic lifelong depression and dysphoria. Specifically, the patient has a pattern of minimizing therapy efforts and progress, feeling hopeless and pessimistic, and often complains that therapy is not working. Consistent with this presentation, the therapist receives a message that this patient left her CBT homework folder in the restroom (toilet) at the clinic.

The therapist finds herself developing strong negative emotional reactions to this patient. In order to cope, she uses a CBT worksheet that prompts her to identify and rate the intensity of her negative thoughts and feelings. This is a common CBT technique, one that links unhelpful ways of thinking with negative emotions (see Table 7.2).

Table 7.2: CBT worksheet, recording a therapist's distressing thoughts and feelings	
Distressing thoughts	% Belief
This means that I have not been an effective therapist	80%
I don't feel like I am doing a good job	80%
I feel really pessimistic about helping this patient	100%
This patient is not taking me/therapy seriously	80%
I am trying really hard with this patient and it doesn't seem to be working	80%
I am not a 'good enough' therapist	60%
Negative emotions	Intensity 0–100%
Sad, depressed, down	50%
Inadequate, incompetent	60%
Pessimistic	60%
Frustrated	40%
Irritated, upset	40%

After reviewing her thoughts and feelings in this way, the therapist determined that there were underlying beliefs related to perfectionism, including overly high standards and unrealistic beliefs about patient progress. To appraise the situation more objectively, she next tries to come up with a more balanced way of understanding the current situation, one that would allow her to continue to work effectively with this patient. Therefore, after reflecting on her negative thoughts and feelings, she writes down a 'reappraisal script'. This represents a more helpful and balanced way of viewing the situation, and she plans to take this script with her to the next session with this patient to remind herself of her reappraisal. Here is the script:

"I tend to work with very challenging patients and sometimes progress is slow and I can be vulnerable to feeling that I am not doing a 'good enough' job. But realistically therapy does not always progress in straightforward ways, and many of my patients have failed to benefit from prior courses of therapy. I need to give myself a break and not be too hard on myself when I start to feel I am having setbacks. I am having a

problem with excessively high standards. Furthermore, leaving CBT homework in the bathroom does not necessarily mean that my patient is devaluing me or therapy. These are the types of behavioural and interpersonal problems she experiences in her life and why she came to therapy in the first place and I shouldn't take it personally."

CBT-based interventions for perfectionism and other sources of distress have employed similar 'cognitive restructuring' techniques with some success (e.g. Chand *et al*, 2018; Salyers *et al*, 2011). The essence lies in recognizing unhelpful thinking patterns, such as believing that one has to always do everything to a high standard or something terrible will happen; feeling like an imposter; fear of failure. Intervention techniques include providing education about how our thoughts and feelings operate, disputing negative thinking, assertiveness training, and stress management methods (e.g. progressive muscular relaxation).

Summary and action implications

Therefore, the essence of reappraisal lies in being self-aware, so that you can recognize and rectify how you are automatically thinking about something that happened (e.g. a critical remark that someone made). You may realize that the criticism is upsetting you, which paves the way to realizing that you may have automatically started to react to it by denying the criticism, as you judge it unfair, and by getting angry. This will typically all occur privately, in your head and your gut, seconds after the criticism, although it could also be processed out loud (e.g. by letting your critic know how you are feeling, or arguing that the criticism is unfair). Either way, the scene is set for reappraisal, which leads into the way that you cope with the stressor. Reappraisal is likely to trigger more adaptive approach-based strategies or reduce the likelihood of utilizing maladaptive or avoidant coping strategies (see Table 2.2 in Chapter 2). For example, if on reflection you take the view that the criticism was actually a fair point (perhaps after discussing what happened with a friend) and reframe it as something from which you can learn, then you are engaging in the process of positively reframing what happened. You are consciously shifting to a different mental perspective, a fresh viewpoint on the stressor and adopting a problem-solving perspective. This is a constructive vantage-point, one that can help to lead you into adaptive coping strategies, such as becoming more objective, or engaging in problem-solving activity (i.e. considering ways to avoid such criticism in the future; joining a peer-support group, as per Buus *et al*, 2013). This will tend to enhance your coping skills, encourage your resilience, and nurture your well-being.

b. Personal coping strategies

Reframing or reappraisal of upsetting events often triggers adaptive coping, but how will you decide which strategies will work best for you? In general, active or 'approach-based' coping strategies are the most effective (see Chapter 4 for a general review, and

Walklet & Percy (2014) for a specific study of adaptive coping among healthcare staff). What is meant by approach-based coping? It is the opposite of 'avoidance-based' coping (e.g. denial, or hoping that a problem will simply disappear), and consists of taking positive action to resolve concerns. To illustrate, an audit of the strategies reported by a naturalistic sample of 59 supervisees who successfully completed their training placements highlighted the value of collaborating actively with the supervisor, being organized, and engaging in mutual feedback (Milne & Gracie, 2001). More compelling data on some of the same coping strategies were provided by Green *et al* (2014) in a study of relative therapist effectiveness. Their longitudinal clinical outcome data, derived from over 1,000 patients, indicated some statistically significant differences in the relative effectiveness of the 21 participating therapists, further illuminated by qualitative methods. In relation to their supervision, the most effective practitioners were more proactive, for example they planned how best to use supervision, asked their supervisors more about clinical procedures, and they were also more open to the use of experiential learning methods in supervision (e.g. suggesting educational role-plays to address difficulties that they were experiencing). This willingness to deal with some of the emotional aspects of being a supervisee is a promising way to begin processing difficult feelings, starting a process of 'working through' or problem 'assimilation'. One of the recommendations to supervisors within our guideline, partly developed through expert consensus, is to 'encourage emotional processing and personal growth' (Milne & Reiser, 2017). This guideline was also partly based on the few available studies, such as Bertsch *et al* (2014), who surveyed 81 counselling supervisees about the methods that they thought worked best in relation to problematic experiences. Exploring feelings, improving relevant skills and boosting self-confidence were the main methods, which improved the supervisees' self-awareness, alliances, and skills. A blow-by-blow case study of this assimilation process can be found in James *et al* (2004), which clearly illuminates how the supervisee was able to reduce her anxiety by exploring her feelings within supervision. When a sample of 16 'wise' supervisors were interviewed about such emotional difficulties, their expert consensus was to help their supervisees to name their emotions, and to acknowledge, explore, and validate these feelings (Grant *et al*, 2012). In addition to accessing help from others, you should develop your capacity for 'self-care'. One way in which this happens naturally is through the learning process of 'internalising' your supervisor; through a period of supervision, we start to view our work through the eyes of our supervisor, which may well include incorporating some of their personal coping strategies. A second way to develop self-care is through cultivating methods that enhance your clinical effectiveness, such as improving your working alliances, or using outcome information (Barnett & Cooper, 2009; Pereira & Barkham, 2015).

An extensive complementary list of ways in which you might play a full and satisfying role as a supervisee was provided by Chow *et al* (2015), in that their regression analysis of how therapists coped with the challenges of developing their clinical expertise can also serve as a blueprint for making the most of supervision. Specifically, they asked 69 therapists, all members of a research practice network drawn from diverse professions and varied organizations within the UK (representing a sample of 4,580 clients), to rate the time spent, relevance, and effort entailed in 25 different professional development activities, in relation to improving themselves as therapists. These items were based on a systematic review of the literature, and on advice from a leading expert. Five of these items were non-work activities that might help them to be ready for their work. These items were 'tending to self-care activities and emotional needs', 'socializing', 'resting', 'exercising', and 'other' (which included meditation, spiritual practices, and reading novels). The 20 items concerned with coping at work included five items on supervision, preparatory reading (journals, case studies, and textbooks), viewing tape recordings of therapy, attending educational events, discussing and formulating cases with peers or mentors, plus the mental rehearsal of procedures, reflection and planning (written and spoken). This list is mostly educational in nature, and so is designed to foster the kind of emotional self-regulation that we stressed in the introduction to this chapter. A similarly valuable list was provided by Parker *et al* (2017).

Consistent with the literature on expertise development, in their 'therapist effects' study Chow *et al* (2015) found that the amount of time that these therapists spent on these professional development activities was a significant predictor of their client outcomes. The top 25% of the participating therapists (i.e. those with the best clinical outcomes) spent significantly more time engaged in professional development activities (approximately three hours per week longer). In particular, the most effective therapists reported that they had made an exceptional effort when reviewing therapy recordings, compared to the rest of the cohort. However, aside from this correlation, there was little indication that any particular development activity was especially helpful, suggesting that what matters is the amount of time and effort that is dedicated to the deliberate practice of relevant skills. Also consistent with the expertise literature, the participating therapist's ratings of the relevance and effort entailed in using these activities were high. For example, supervision received higher than average ratings on these dimensions, suggesting that it created the ideal conditions for professional development. Interestingly, other demographic variables, such as years of experience and highest qualification or profession, did not account for any significant variance in client outcomes.

Although the 20-item list presented by Chow *et al* (2015) is highly detailed, note that it still does not embrace all of the supervisee self-help coping strategies reported from naturalistic studies by Milne & Gracie (2001) and Green *et al* (2014). Nor do these summaries include maladaptive coping strategies, such as avoidance and venting negative emotions (Walklet & Percy, 2014). This limited coverage of the full spectrum of coping strategies is hardly surprising, as even a brief study of the range of possibilities suggests that the theoretical scope of coping strategies is huge, reflecting the full spectrum of human diversity, versatility and resilience. This is indicated by Table 4.2 in Chapter 4, including the illustrative strategies listed there (from a survey of counsellors by Lawson, 2007). Other especially promising coping strategies for supervisees that enjoy empirical support are described below and overlap with the strategies in Table 4.2 and in Chow *et al* (2015), such as seeking social support.

Summary and action implications

Our personal coping strategies enable us to handle work stressors and find ways to thrive, most commonly through taking positive action to resolve concerns or to seize opportunities (Folkman & Nathan, 2010). A full review of coping strategies was provided in Chapter 4 and highlighted the importance of adapting rather than avoiding workplace stressors (see Table 4.2 for a summary). Major options that tend to be effective are positively appraising stressors, logical analysis of difficulties, problem-solving efforts, alongside seeking advice and assistance. Respectively, this means that in practice you should aim to cope through such means as perceiving the stressors as opportunities rather than the threats, maintaining objectivity, reflecting carefully on issues that are challenging and accessing (and reciprocating) social support.

c. Reflection

Reflection on one's practice has long been recognized as core to successful clinical work, a necessary condition for experiential learning in general (Kolb, 2014), and a specific method for the development of clinicians (Schon, 1991) and supervisees (Buus *et al*, 2013). SAGE, our instrument for observing the supervisees' role in supervision (Reiser *et al*, 2018), includes reflection as one of five ways of engaging in experiential learning during supervision. According to the SAGE manual, reflection is when supervisees *"...summarize relevant events and offer their personal understanding... They actively and explicitly draw on their personal experiences, understanding and history to make sense of these events. Supervisees reflecting effectively show signs of integrating material; assimilating things into a reasoned understanding; and of developing their own understanding"*.

An earlier version of SAGE defined reflection as: *"Working (thinking and listening) with the information in (supervision), for example giving background information, thinking things through, and asking questions."*

This earlier tool, 'Teachers' PETS', was used to code the relative frequency of reflection by three supervisees within an intensive, n=1 (small n) observational study (Milne & Westerman, 2001). The data indicated that reflection occurred far more frequently than any of the other forms of supervisee participation that were observed using PETS (i.e. experimenting, experiencing, conceptualizing, and planning). Throughout the study period, reflection took place on over 90% of observations, based on sampling what the supervisee was doing every 30 seconds, within the hour-long supervision sessions (the longitudinal sample consisted of 30 successive sessions over a 13-month period). A contingency table, summarizing the associations between the supervisees' reflection and supervision, indicated that the most frequent link was between reflection and the supervisor engaging in listening, supporting, and questioning the supervisees. More recent studies with SAGE as our observational tool have generated similar data, indicating the dominant role that reflection plays in supervision (e.g. Milne *et al,* 2011). Supervisees can enhance their reflective skills in various ways, as we next discuss.

The use of reflection in peer groups may be especially helpful in expressing emotions related to challenging work and in sharing thoughts on adaptive coping strategies (Buus *et al,* 2013; O'Neill *et al,* 2018; Wallbank, 2013). Recent interest in the emotional resilience of health practitioners has further strengthened the status of reflection (McCann *et al,* 2013). For example, a review of research indicated that reflective ability was essential to resilience (Grant & Kinman, 2014). These authors detailed research studies indicating that students with the best reflective skills were more resilient, better at problem-solving and interpersonal interactions, and reported higher levels of psychological well-being. In a second example, Stacey *et al* (2017) reported favourable reactions to resilience-based supervision that included 'reflective discussion'.

 A particularly sophisticated approach to reflection is 'Self-Practice, Self-Reflection' (SP/SR) (Bennett-Levy, 2001). SP/SR is a psychological technique that can be used repeatedly, on an individual basis or in groups, in order to reflect on and deepen your understanding of suitable aspects of your clinical work and is linked to experiential learning exercises. Additionally, SP/SR has been found to benefit personal and/or professional development (Bennett-Levy, 2019). SP/SR is an approach which encourages therapists to use CBT methods to reappraise their negative thoughts about difficult patients, and to help them to process any negative reactions. For example, Kaeding *et al* (2017) found that maladaptive thinking patterns, especially relating to 'unrelenting standards' (perfectionism), were associated with higher levels of burnout in a group of counseling and psychology trainees. 'Unrelenting standards' were defined as an inability to set healthy limits on one's work demands, and a relentless striving for higher standards (Kaeding *et al,* 2017).

One of the benefits of the SP/SR approach is that it takes a strengths-based view of professional development, utilizing experiential exercises to build up more adaptive ways of thinking and feeling – ones that are consistent with the need to develop your professional identity. The specific methods of SP/SR are detailed in a useful workbook (Bennett-Levy *et al,* 2014), which encourages the use of experiential methods such as behavioural experiments (i.e. testing out your assumptions and beliefs in work situations), the use of imagery, and other methods designed to modify deeply held beliefs. The workbook also guides the reader in the use of cognitive methods, such as education and restructuring (i.e. reappraisal and reframing dysfunctional thoughts). Using these strategies individually, in pairs, and in group formats, trainees within an evaluation study reported better understanding of CBT methods, and viewed SP/SR as both personally and professionally useful (Bennett-Levy, 2019). In a review, Bennett-Levy (2019) has noted several positive effects of SP/SR related to therapists' personal development and well-being, including reduced psychological distress, better understanding of problems, enhanced coping strategies, and improved emotional processing of problems. Although Bennett-Levy (2019) limits his review to the role of SP/SR in relation to personal therapy, in our view it is also applicable in relation to the workplace (e.g. for processing distressing workplace situations, and for resolving emotional problems). This is borne out by the general success of CBT in relieving emotional problems, indicated by a substantial body of research (Butler *et al*, 2006). Theoretically, SP/SR is also consistent with the coping model, as described above and in Chapter 2.

Practical implications

Bennett-Levy *et al* (2014) present a self-help workbook intended to serve as a 12-week course for improving supervisees' coping strategies by helping them reflect on their difficulties. Note that the workbook primarily serves as a guide for group facilitators and supervisors, but may also serve as an individually paced self-help guide. The practical implications of the SP/SR method are illustrated within the 'deskilling' vignette that follows at the end of the chapter.

Summary

Reflection on your clinical work is essential for your development as a clinician and represents a major way of playing your part within supervision. A specific reflection method that may improve your reflective skills is SP/SR, as this provides a robust and thoroughly elaborated set of methods for altering problematic ways of thinking and behaving, and more importantly for constructing a more adaptive set of beliefs in regard to facing distressing issues in the workplace and supervision. The techniques within the Bennet-Levy *et al* (2014) workbook are based on empirically supported principles that have been demonstrated to be effective in the workplace. It is the most detailed and comprehensive system specifically designed to assist supervisees in reflecting on their work and thereby identifying and modifying their problematic attitudes, beliefs and behaviours.

d. Contemplation-based strategies

In the prior sections we illustrated approaches to coping with negative emotions and distressing thoughts primarily using reappraisal (reframing) and reflection-based strategies. In this section we develop an alternative framework for addressing your negative emotions and identify additional strategies that you can use for coping with the uncomfortable feelings associated with your work, such as the deskilling experience. Contemplation-based strategies include mindfulness meditation and acceptance and commitment therapy (ACT) (Hayes *et al*, 2009; Bond *et al*, 2011).

An illustrative evaluation of mindfulness meditation was reported by Shapiro *et al* (2007), who enrolled 22 supervisees into a 'mindfulness-based stress reduction' programme (MBSR) that took place over eight weeks and lasted two hours per week. This programme was designed to develop mindfulness-based meditation, which encouraged awareness of the moment-by-moment private events occurring within the supervisees' realm of experience (i.e. sensory experiences, thoughts, feelings, somatic sensations, and behaviours). It was assumed that MBSR would bring greater awareness to these experiences in the 'here and now', and encourage disengagement from negative self-related thoughts and emotions (i.e. ones that can have a detrimental effect on well-being). There were five different mindfulness techniques, an example being the 'body scan'. This involves a progressive movement of attention through one's own body, from the toes to the head, while being aware of the physical sensations in each body part. A strength of this study was that the MBSR programme was itself measured (a rare manipulation check), using a self-rating questionnaire, The Mindful Attention Awareness Scale (MAAS) (Brown & Ryan, 2003). This scale has 15 items intended to assess the frequency with which an individual is openly aware of present events and experiences. Example items of the scale include "I could be experiencing some emotion and not be conscious of it until sometime later" and "It seems I am 'running on automatic' without much awareness of what I'm doing". Higher scores indicate higher mindfulness. The MAAS has demonstrated good reliability and validity. As a second evaluation of the actual implementation of the programme, the MBSR participants completed daily practice diaries at the end of each day throughout the eight-week intervention to record how many minutes they had spent on each of the five different mindfulness techniques. The findings from these two intervention checks indicated that MBSR participation had indeed increased levels of mindfulness, although the average participant practiced for an average of eight minutes per day. The programme outcomes were also measured by self-report tools. The data indicated that, compared to the 32 control group members, the supervisees who used mindfulness meditation reported significantly better results by the end of the eight-week period, including lower perceived stress, less negative feelings (e.g. anxiety), and a significant increases in positive affect and self-compassion. The authors concluded that MBSR can enhance the ability to regulate emotional states, increasing participants' ability to enhance their well-being.

Among the weaknesses in the study by Shapiro *et al* (2007) were that the groups were not randomly allocated, and there was a complete reliance on self-report instruments (as is unfortunately typical of the whole field of clinical supervision). From the perspective of this chapter, it is also unfortunate that there was no information to indicate whether the participating 'therapists in training' were also supervisees, but we assume that they were probably not (in the US, most students do not have any clinical or counselling practicum/placement in their first year of graduate work). Therefore, this is another instance where we have extrapolated from a neighbouring literature, in order to include what we judge to be relevant material which we could not find within the studies of restorative supervision.

Ideally, future studies would include at least one more rigorous, objective measure, such as direct observation or permanent products, involving supervisees who are explicitly receiving supportive supervision. For instance, Levinson *et al* (2014) developed a reliable and valid breath-counting approach as a measure of mindfulness (i.e. skill in counting one's breaths accurately correlated with less mind-wandering and greater disinterest in passing thoughts).

A second contemplation-based method is 'acceptance and commitment therapy' (ACT) (Hayes *et al*, 2009; Bond *et al*, 2011), an approach that, like mindfulness meditation, views efforts to control unwanted thoughts and feelings as the root cause of psychological distress. Therefore, unlike reframing and reflection, the goal of ACT is not to dispute or alter the meaning of distressing thoughts and emotions, but to accept difficult internal experiences as a given (acceptance) and work towards meaningful personal goals (commitment). We illustrate ACT techniques in the 'deskilling' vignette that follows at the end of this chapter.

Practical implications

At the end of the chapter, we illustrate the phenomenon of deskilling, a feeling that skills and capabilities previously assumed to be intact are now experienced as no longer reliable, and this is often accompanied by a deep sense of confusion, perplexity and self-doubt, as is the case with this a late-career psychologist undertaking advanced training. We use this case example to examine negative emotional reactions to training and supervision and to review helpful strategies related to mindfulness and acceptance-based approaches, especially ACT. In the ACT strategies that are identified in the vignette, there is no attempt to challenge or dispute the problematic belief ("I am an incompetent therapist").

Summary

Contemplation-based self-help strategies provide you with sophisticated tools for reflecting on how you react to your emotions at work and afford ways of distancing and stepping back from distressing thoughts, feelings and beliefs (e.g. worrying about not being good enough). The small amount of evidence that exists indicates that these strategies yield definite benefits of direct relevance to your psychological well-being (e.g. improved resilience; see Table 7.1). By contrast, attempts to avoid these emotional responses using emotion-focused coping strategies (like the use of drugs and alcohol, suppression of feelings, and social withdrawal) are likely to lead to a vicious cycle of anxiety-avoidance – one that simply amplifies and perpetuates negative emotions, and which may also have other unwanted negative interpersonal effects, including diminishing the usefulness of supervision. The opposite strategy, however counterintuitive, is far more helpful as it normalizes these emotions, reappraising them as essential and accepting them as necessary to professional learning and personal development.

The self-help strategies in this section can provide a valuable 'first-line' way for you to address some of the anxiety-provoking experiences associated with supervision and the workplace. But these strategies are not a substitute for therapy and if distress persists, then seeking out professional help is recommended. Your supervisor should be able to help you to apply these strategies effectively and, if necessary, can guide you to professional help.

3. Be professionally able

e. Build and strengthen the supervision alliance

In this section we explore how you, the supervisee, might take proactive steps to improve the supervisory alliance. Reviews of supervision have identified the supervisory alliance as an important factor in achieving positive outcomes from supervision (Beinart, 2014). Some have even argued that it has a primary role and "has increasingly come to be seen as the very heart and soul of supervision itself..." (Watkins, 2014, p151). We should note that others (Goodyear, 2014; Milne & Reiser, 2017) have viewed the supervisory alliance as a necessary but not sufficient moderating factor, one that facilitates other learning processes in supervision. Most of the literature solely considers the role of the supervisor in creating an optimal supervisory alliance, but in reality such an alliance is co-created and depends upon the interaction between supervisor and supervisee. Survey-based and qualitative research on the alliance by Beinart (2014) and her colleagues in Oxford have indicated that it consists of five interrelated factors: a 'safe base', the supervisor's commitment, the trainee's contribution, external influences (including organizational issues; past history of supervision), and the supervisor's emotional investment.

While much of the related research focuses on the supervisor's behaviour, it is intriguing to consider other possibilities. For example, supervisees can also work to proactively improve the alliance and other aspects of the supervisory relationship by anticipating likely problems and emotional reactions. They can even work towards connecting with the supervisor, rather than being withdrawn or on the defensive. Indeed, Beinart (2014) describes how the supervisee can contribute to the 'safe base' through engaging emotionally (open, honest, enthusiastic and responsive) and can also be open about any difficulties. She also details how the supervisee can contribute to the alliance, as follows: "Take responsibility and work hard, make a useful contribution (e.g. manage a caseload), be organized and considerate of others" (p267). This rare but welcome affirmation from Beinart (2014) probably underestimates the potential for supervisees to positively or negatively impact the supervision processes and outcomes. Pereira and Barkham (2015) have provided a case study of an exceptionally resilient clinician, partly because of her skilful development of working alliances.

Practical implications

It follows from the supervision research that, as a supervisee, you play a full and active part in supervision, taking your share of the responsibility for addressing problems proactively and collaboratively. Falender and Shafranske (2012) have identified a broader range of positive proactive strategies that you can use to help improve the supervisory alliance, including managing expectations, preparation, collaborative work on goals, conveying openness to feedback, and explaining your emotional reactions (e.g. anxiety and discomfort). Other aspects of supervision where you can play a valuable role include negotiating the supervision contract (e.g. clarifying your expectations (Zorga, 2002)), being prepared for every supervision session with your own agenda (e.g. specific clinical issues), and developing clarity about what you want to get out of supervision; agreeing how you will tackle any conflict or disagreement, supervisory strains and ruptures (Falender & Shafranske, 2012 p.173); and discussing difficult aspects of your work, including mistakes, cultural differences, the handling of emotional reactions in supervision, understanding how you will be evaluated, and any other expectations about supervision (in terms of rules, roles and responsibilities (Thomas, 2007)). Such actions on your part will usually be repaid in enhanced learning and support, and can greatly improve the supervision experience overall.

Summary

As a supervisee you should be prepared to experience a number of difficult emotions, and accept the likelihood that there will be challenging moments in supervision, including potential disruptions or ruptures in the supervisory alliance. Given the power imbalance, and the multiple roles of supervisors (gatekeeper, mentor, counsellor, teacher), this is nearly inevitable. So, the question becomes, how can supervisees be best prepared? The best preparation involves taking a collaborative and proactive approach, anticipating the likelihood of problems arising due to the inherently challenging nature of supervision and training, and hence being ready to address problems 'up front' by developing a strong supervisory alliance (Parker *et al*, 2017).

4. Be interpersonally effective

f. Enhance your social support

Establishing and developing a successful supervision alliance is a prime example of being effective interpersonally. In this section, we go on to review strategies related to developing and maintaining social support, considering how you can best access and reciprocate social support as a supervisee. This builds on the material that we discussed in Chapters 4 and 5 by taking the supervisees' perspective, and by emphasizing the evidence-based practical actions that you might take. A systematic review of burnout and stress management interventions for mental health professionals indicated that social support and peer support are among the most frequently reported coping strategies (Edwards *et al*, 2003). To illustrate, in Chapter 5, Table 5.1 presented a summary of six systematic reviews of most relevance to improving the workplace through supportive supervision (e.g. Rhoades & Eisenberger, 2002), together with an illustrative research study. All six reviews provided evidence to justify a social support intervention, which was by far the most popular approach. One of the illustrative studies we cited was Goodrich (2012) who described and evaluated Schwartz groups or 'rounds'. To recap, these rounds encouraged staff to discuss and reflect on the emotional and social challenges of their jobs in an interpersonally safe environment. Goodrich (2012) reported that the rounds were perceived by participants as a source of support, carrying benefits also for patients, team-working and the hospital culture. Drawing on the review by Edwards *et al* (2003), and other related studies, our guideline recommended that supervisors encourage their supervisees to make use of social support from their supervisors and their peers (Milne & Reiser, 2017). In the context of supportive supervision and healthcare professionals, what do we mean by 'social support', what evidence is there that it helps, and how might you best access it?

Social support can be defined as the perception of companionship and emotional, informational, or practical assistance from significant others, such as family members, friends, or co-workers (Thoits, 2010). Being largely informal, social support depends on reciprocity; to be useful and available, it is essential that there is a balance between giving and receiving social support. Individuals who take more than they give (in quantity or quality) will tend to be excluded or avoided, a stepping stone to burnout or depression. An example that will be familiar to most is when a colleague expresses their distressing emotions (e.g. anger) repeatedly, and without any willingness to consider how they can move on from blaming others. But when a better balance is established then the social support mechanisms can work, as when the reasonable 'ventilation' or 'emotional discharge' about the source of the anger is followed by feelings that are more sensitively communicated, which leads to some constructive emotional processing and joint problem-solving discussions (Kennedy-Moore & Watson, 2001).

Informal social support takes myriad forms (e.g. see the classic High Street surveys by Cowen, 1982), but results in a few fundamental benefits for people, such as a sense of attachment and acceptance. The more formal social support that should occur in supervision does not depend on reciprocity, as providing support is part of the job. Also, the range of supportive actions in supervision are more restricted (e.g. it would be inappropriate for a supervisor to lend their supervisee money). Table 7.3 offers a summary of the links between the different forms and functions of social support.

Table 7.3: The various forms and fundamental functions of social support

Forms of social support	Functions of social support
Informational support	Guidance (e.g. feeling helped through advice, information, problem-solving and goal-setting)
Emotional support	Personal attachment (e.g. feeling nurtured, supported and safe)
	Acceptance (e.g. feeling welcome and accepted; the opposite of criticism or rejection)
Practical support	Practical assistance (e.g. borrowing equipment or receiving a helping hand)
Social companionship	Social belonging (e.g. feeling part of a group; integrated; mutual trust and ease)
	Recognition (e.g. feeling socially validated; having a sense of worth based on personal qualities)

As noted in earlier chapters, systematic reviews of social support indicate that the forms of social support listed in Table 7.3 have a significant effect on improving physical and mental health outcomes, partly by protecting or 'buffering' us against stressors, sometimes by assisting our coping efforts, and generally by helping us to stay fit and well through feeling supported. These positive benefits are highly applicable to the healthcare workplace and supportive supervision in particular can be regarded as a major organizational vehicle for social support. For instance, social support has an important role in mediating the effects of work-related stressors and reducing the likelihood of health-related conditions, depersonalization, burnout and loss of a sense of personal accomplishment (Adriaenssens *et al*, 2014; Johnson

& Hall, 1988; Pereira *et al,* 2011; Stansfield & Candy, 2006; Woodhead *et al,* 2016). More recent thinking suggests how social support works, through emotionally coloured conversations. Relational regulation theory suggests that informal, ordinary conversations and shared activities may serve to help us regulate our emotions, rather than explicitly talking about stressors and how we might cope with them (Lakey & Orehek, 2011; Lakey *et al,* 2014, p405). But just like our personal coping strategies, social support can also be unhelpful at times ('anti-social support'). To illustrate, Carver *et al* (1989) described emotional support as a 'double-edged sword', in that it may either foster increased problem-solving efforts or may result in an unhelpful ventilation of feelings, increasing avoidant coping strategies, such as denial and social disengagement. Recent research on social support has built on these early foundations and we will next detail some of the most valuable examples to address the question of how might you best access and reciprocate social support.

Informational support example

Group-based supervision is a popular format, intrinsically incorporating social support, and is commonly offered to aid stress management within healthcare. Buus *et al* (2011) interviewed 22 mental health nurses in Denmark about their experiences of a supervision group. From their replies, it appeared that supervision provided informational support that included gaining a fresh perspective, which helped to solve or at least relieve the work problems that were presented. Some nurses felt that the group's discussions were invigorating, as a new perspective could be created through mutual reflection and the exchange of experiences or through the supervisor's teaching. One interviewee described how the group had to keep quiet while they spoke about a work problem: "Afterwards, they were asked: 'How do you see it?'. It was very interesting; in particular, one person who said something where I thought: 'My goodness. I had not thought about it that way' and that gave me something. I simply had not thought of it that way. I was not even deadlocked, but it was someone else, a different angle. I just remember thinking: 'This is clever'" (p98). From the researchers' perspective the group supervision worked by encouraging personal insights through guided reflection by the supervisor and through the insights offered by other group members. There was also some associated emotional support, as the authors believed that there was some emotional relief and enhanced self-esteem when the other participants listened to and acknowledged the problem.

Practical support example

Hall (2007) studied support in three nursing care units in the US, reporting that nurses who perceived themselves as receiving high levels of supervisor support also reported multiple benefits (e.g. more job satisfaction, less work stress, less turnover, and fewer somatic complaints). Peer support was also beneficial and may have been enhanced by supervisor support, including what Hall (2007) termed 'collective efficacy'. This refers to the mutual dependence between the nurses in

terms of getting the work done jointly through 'pitching in' physically on unit tasks. Other types of practical support may also have occurred, as the questionnaire that was used had items on supporting peers through lending money (or something that was needed), teaching one another how to do something, and providing a room. Hall (2007) speculated that the nurses' working relationships with one another become stronger over time, increasing the practical co-worker support.

Emotional support example

In a qualitative report, Edmonds *et al* (2015) described the effects of group supervision within a multidisciplinary palliative care team in the US (including clinical social workers, pharmacists, and physicians). Such teams are at high risk of compassion fatigue and burnout. The group was started after team members noticed strong emotional reactions to certain patients, including feelings of avoidance, urges to become over-involved, or desires to be the 'saviour'. They recognized that such feelings could compromise the quality of their care and contribute to compassion fatigue and ultimately burnout. The groups were largely peer-led, with participants taking turns to present a clinical case that was associated with a strong emotional response. The other participants clarified the presenter's feelings and provided emotional and other forms of support. For instance, one physician described discomfort over her attempts at helping a patient to manage his abdominal pain. *"I felt as if there was very little that I had done for this patient; he had resisted all my efforts to address his total pain and hadn't responded well to traditional pain management. I just couldn't connect with this guy and it's been bothering me since"* (p275). The other group members responded by reassuring the physician that progress had actually been noted, and by heightening awareness of the associated emotions and biases. Relevant biases were that the physician assumed responsibility for making clinical progress and for 'fixing' patients, when this patient was actually experienced as challenging by other team members.

Social companionship example

As the group supervision above illustrates, peers are a significant source of social support. Although formal supervision can afford a sense of professional companionship (e.g. providing a role model, or validation of group membership), a potent source of social companionship comes from peers and other informal sources. Results of an online survey of 146 beginning trainee therapists indicated that, when feeling stuck or when they have made a clinical mistake, they most often consulted their supervisors. The supervisor was followed in popularity by consulting with other trainees in their programme, their own psychotherapist, and with their significant others. Their aim was to get reassurance and suggestions, which they found helpful (Farber & Hazanov, 2014).

Practical implications

Social support in the workplace may occur within formal, structured activities (clinical supervision, practicum groups, case consultation groups, study groups, mentoring) or it may be absolutely informal in nature, consisting of spontaneous, informal conversations and shared activities with peers, co-workers, staff or administrators. Social support may involve conversations that ask for help with stressful problems and so directly focus on developing coping strategies; or it may entail engaging in quite informal activities in relationships with others that provide distraction and enjoyment. Our review of social support suggests that these actions are likely to increase the likelihood of receiving and maintaining social support:

- The value of social support lies, at least in part, in helping with our cognitive and emotional processing of difficult experiences. Talking to others and explaining the problem can provide 'distancing' and provide some perspective in relation to some of the raw emotions that we experience. In turn, this 'calming' process can be quite useful in terms of problem-solving.

- Social support that results in useful information gathering, taking different perspectives, processing thoughts and feelings, and problem-solving is more likely to be helpful than emotional support consisting of ventilation of negative emotions or expressing distress.

- As a result, try to avoid seeking social support during very high levels of arousal, as this potentially limits your ability to process thoughts and feelings and may result in your expressing high levels of negative affect that can be distressing or off-putting to others (e.g. threatening or overwhelming supporters by your complaints or constant expressions of distress).

- On the other hand, the skilful communication of distress or negative emotions can be helpful, especially if accompanied by a recognition that this may be stressful for the supporter and an indication that you are seeking help for your coping strategies from the supporter.

5. Case study: The 'deskilling' phenomenon in an experienced therapist

A late-career 'expert' in CBT, with over 20 years of clinical experience, opted to undertake specialized training in CBT for people with a psychosis. This training involved submitting recordings of his therapy sessions for review by a supervisor (including a formal rating of competence) and feedback. After initially sending in a 'safe' tape for review, he next began sending in 'problem sessions', i.e. ones with quite complex and challenging patients. Then, somewhat unexpectedly, after sending in a recording of a difficult session, this late-career CBT expert began to experience feelings of anxiety, including a sense of deskilling that occurred in the midst of a session. This was accompanied by a temporary sense of demoralization, in which he began to doubt his CBT skills and competence. This was startling and shocking, given his experience, which included extensive training and credentialing through the prestigious Beck Institute, and over 10 years of teaching and supervising CBT at the graduate level.

He began to have negative automatic thoughts related to his competence: "I'm blowing it"; "I'm lost"; "I am waffling around and not really getting anywhere"; "This is probably the worst session ever". He completed the session with a sense of demoralization and anxiety, especially because he had agreed in advance to send this recording in for review by his supervisor. There was a sense of being trapped; there was 'no turning back', just a feeling of impending doom involving potentially catastrophic outcomes to his reputation (this recording would be reviewed by a well-established consultant, well known to peers).

Reappraisal-based coping strategies

In an effort to regain some perspective on this 'deskilling' tape, he carefully listened to it and noted down specific instances on the tape that matched CBT competency items on the rating scale, and simultaneously tried to gain some perspective on his feelings of incompetence and anxiety over impending humiliation. In doing so, he noticed with relief that he was seemingly demonstrating many of the required competencies, which helped to ease his feeling that something disastrous had occurred in this session. Nonetheless, he remained concerned, wondering if his self-assessment was inaccurate, perhaps due to a self-serving, positive bias.

To boost his coping efforts, he also began a journal in advance of the next supervision meeting, taking the time to write down many of his personal feelings about the 'deskilling' session in a raw and unguarded way, as a way of processing his feelings and documenting his self-appraisal. He paid particular attention to the stream of negative thoughts about his competence that he had experienced in the session and the associated painful emotions, trying to identify the distressing thoughts in detail and write them down in an objective fashion (i.e. as a mindful observer of his own thoughts). He planned to share this material with his supervisor, as a way of coming to terms with these negative feelings.

Self-Practice/Self-Reflection (SP/SR) based strategies

Because he also considered these concerns about competence to be an 'old repetitive theme' in his life, and one that surfaced periodically under stress, he determined that it would be useful to incorporate some strategies from the Bennett-Levy et al (2014) Self-Practice Self-Reflection workbook. He chose worksheets from the second section, which focused on constructing and enacting 'new ways of being'. The rationale was that this approach could help him begin to develop and construct a new alternative and more adaptive schema, ones that would support his ongoing training efforts. The worksheets focused on a two-stage process: 1. Constructing a new and more adaptive way of being; and 2: Strategies to enact the more adaptive framework in his daily life (through a series of ongoing behavioural experiments).

When he reviewed his negative automatic thoughts during the 'deskilling' therapy session, they included "I'm blowing it"; "I'm lost"; "I am waffling around and not really getting anywhere"; and "This is probably the worst session ever". Through this reflection process he recognized that the central theme involved concerns that related to his competence. The core theme was: "I am not a competent therapist." He recalled that in prior supervision sessions, even though his supervisor had rated the recording as very competent, he still had misgivings and could not entirely 'take in' the feedback. Fitting in with these negative automatic thoughts, it seemed to the therapist that an old schema (belief system) appeared to be activated and was operating in a way that made it hard for him to accept and really 'digest' positive feedback. From the point of view of this old belief system, positive feedback did not 'fit', hence there must be an error (perhaps the supervisor was incompetent or had inflated the rating out of pity to spare his feelings). The therapist realized that this negative, self-devaluing perspective was a result of this old belief system. From his knowledge of psychology, he recognized that his selective attention, emotional reasoning, and selective abstraction could maintain this belief system indefinitely. It was time to take some decisive action. Using the SP/SR worksheets (Bennett-Levy *et al,* 2014), he worked on constructing a new set of beliefs about his competence, using mental imagery and recalling positive feedback to prime himself for the next supervision session. The goal was to be able to listen to and properly hear his supervisor's feedback on the deskilling tape without the old belief system interfering. As part of a behavioural experiment, he would then record this new 'evidence' systematically and work to test out his old beliefs. Over time, in theory this process should enable him to construct a new set of more helpful, adaptive beliefs, such as:

- I am actually quite competent as a therapist, but one who takes on very challenging and difficult patients.
- Naturally, challenging patients do not always make smooth progress, and severe setbacks should be expected over the course of therapy.
- I also have high standards, and sometimes I too quickly take these setbacks as evidence of my incompetence.
- What's more, I choose to treat quite complex clients, people that many other therapists will refuse to treat. Therefore, it's unfair to draw direct comparisons between my clinical outcomes and the ones claimed by other therapists.

Supervisory alliance-based strategies

Nevertheless, he approached his next supervision session with considerable anxiety, driven by a sense that it was going to involve some very humbling and challenging feedback, ratings of his competence that would possibly also reflect badly on his self-esteem and even his clinical work with patients. In the supervision session, he immediately engaged in an honest discussion of his negative feelings about his performance in the recorded session during which he had felt 'deskilled'. There followed a fuller elaboration of his negative emotional reactions and a comparison between his reactions and the supervisor's impressions, including their respective ratings of the session. The therapist was pleasantly surprised to find that his supervisor had rated the session quite highly and particularly liked his use of guided discovery (as it seemed to be really genuine and not overly directed). What the therapist had viewed as 'fumbling', his supervisor viewed as genuine curiosity and careful listening to the patient to develop a full understanding. There was then a detailed discussion of the discrepant ratings. It seemed that the supervisor had focused on the many positive aspects of the session and was actually quite enthusiastic overall about the formulation of the patient's problems, the focus on key cognitions and behaviours, and the therapist's use of the CBT technique of 'guided discovery'.

Acceptance-based strategies

After this uplifting supervision session, the therapist reflected on some of the overly negative self-ratings. He became even more sure that, in seeking out specialized training in CBT, he had inadvertently activated his long-held beliefs about being incompetent. Now he asked himself: How helpful was it to dwell on these feelings and to what extent did ruminating about incompetence actually improve his approach to therapy? It was clear that change was needed. One potential strategy for altering his beliefs about incompetence was to 'accept' that these types of thoughts might often be present, activated by particularly stressful or challenging clients or training situations. If this were true, then the best approach might be to recognize that concerns about competence were a 'normal' part of the process, a natural human reaction. A further way that the therapist reframed his reactions to the deskilling session was to realize that the discomfort and painful feelings could quite accurately be viewed as the price of his continuing commitment to learning, a natural part of the deskilling process when acquiring significant new skills. After all, if he attempted to avoid all uncomfortable or difficult feelings, the likely outcome would be stagnation and 'failure to thrive' in terms of further professional development. This brought to his mind the literature on the development of expertise, which suggests that therapists often reach a competence plateau within a few short years of qualification.

When the therapist absorbed these various perspectives, he felt that the prize of continuing professional development was worth the price of the unpleasant feelings that came with the deskilling experience. After all, this was consistent with some of his other deeply held beliefs and highly valued personal goals (e.g. becoming a better psychotherapist; utilizing CBT approaches to anxiety management). He also recognized that he would have to maintain his new approach to deskilling. Acceptance and commitment therapy in particular offered several helpful strategies to raise awareness of stressful internal conflicts. He made these reminders to himself:

1. Identify the Costs of Avoidance: Make a list of all the things you do to avoid feeling incompetent (including limiting professional development opportunities and distracting himself from painful thoughts).

2. Defusion practice: Keep a card stating "I'm an incompetent therapist" in his jacket pocket during the next therapy session. Use it as a way of defusing the power of that belief through demonstrating that he could behave competently even with that belief 'showing up' in the session. The goal is to 'delink' the negative thoughts and unhelpful beliefs from his actual behaviour. This would help to defuse the situation.

3. Develop an Action Plan: The therapist realized that he must be willing to have these uncomfortable thoughts about his incompetence without expending excessive energy on struggling with them, or in trying to control them. Instead, his plan was to focus on his deeply held beliefs and highly valued personal goals. This meant continuing to send in recordings of his therapy sessions and being willing to select further 'difficult sessions', even if they activate this sense of incompetence.

Social support-based strategies

In addition to sharing some of these challenging feelings with close family members, he also contacted several of his closer professional colleagues from within a peer-based consultation group and discussed this sense of deskilling and feeling challenged as a clinician – at times using a little self-deprecating humour. Many of his colleagues expressed positive support for his undertaking this type of advanced training and sympathized with the sense of deskilling that occurred. Some of his colleagues were themselves undertaking advanced training that had required similar challenging types of deliberate practice, so there was some heartfelt validation of the accompanying feelings. For example, these valued peers agreed that 'staying in one's comfort zone' was not really the optimal learning strategy.

6. Summary

As a supervisee, it is essential that you play a full and collaborative role in making your supervision a success. This conclusion follows clearly from the material in this chapter, including relevant theory, expert consensus statements, and the best available research. Although earlier reviews of the role of the supervisee have used different terms and approaches (Falender & Shafranske, 2012; Milne & Gracie, 2001), the common denominator is self-regulation. That is, rather than relying on the supervisor, successful supervisees get the best out of themselves, enhancing their supervision (Green *et al*, 2014). They aspire to personal effectiveness through effortful engagement in making supervision as valuable as possible (Parker *et al*, 2017). In essence, they utilize their personal coping strategies to be in a position to apply their learning expertise (Bransford & Schwartz, 2009), enabling them to commit to personal and professional development. This is the opposite of the 'game-playing' manoeuvres that some have ascribed to supervisees as a way of avoiding supervision (McIntosh *et al*, 2006; Muller *et al*, 2019).

Thankfully, playing your part in the 'co-construction' of supervision is made readily possible by a handful of effective, evidence-based self-help techniques. In Table 7.1 we listed six such techniques, alongside some of the main outcomes that you should aim to achieve. Most of these techniques are straightforward, familiar and not too time-consuming, and can be applied at work during stressful episodes and at home to re-group or prepare. These self-help strategies and techniques address the questions that we posed at the outset. They represent the best ways for you to exercise self-help, in terms of managing and processing your painful negative feelings and distress; of improving your adaptive coping efforts in the workplace; and of engaging more effectively in social support. If successful, you stand to replace the threat of burnout with personal well-being.

Seeking out social support is a universal way to try and deal with workplace stressors or difficulties in coping. Social support in the workplace can take many forms, but there are four main types (e.g. emotional support) and these serve a small number of functions (e.g. personal validation; see Table 7.3). As long as your attempts to gain social support are appropriate (e.g. acceptable or customary in your context), then there are many possible approaches to obtaining social support based on personal preferences or a result of circumstances (e.g. who to approach for support). The vital thing is to ensure that you find ways of achieving these functions in relation to your needs at the time (e.g. getting a sense of belonging following an experience of rejection). It is also essential to reciprocate, as this is the 'give and take' currency of informal social support (as formal supporters, supervisors do not require full reciprocity). We should also acknowledge the importance of the other potential sources for formal social support in the workplace, not to mention the immense value in developing and maintaining your informal support networks, including your family and friends.

Chapter 8: Supporting Supervisors Through Training and Support Arrangements

1. Introduction

There is good reason to believe that supervisors who are themselves supported in their work are better able to support their supervisees, who in turn are then more supportive to their patients, with attendant clinical benefits. This 'support cascade' is suggested by the support model that we put forward in Chapter 2, in that the same factors that influence the well-being of supervisees also affect their supervisors. Major examples noted were receiving social support, stress prevention, and improving personal coping strategies. The converse also appears to be true, in that a dysfunctional organization can create a 'distress cascade' (Mor Barak *et al*, 2009), including a situation where supervisors themselves experience burnout (Erera, 2008). For this reason, we closed Chapter 2 by recommending that supervisors should seek training and ongoing support to enable them to maintain their own well-being and to develop how they can best provide supportive supervision. Research examples were provided in subsequent chapters. We now detail how best to support and develop supervisors in relation to facilitating their well-being and their restorative role in clinical supervision. Our fundamental question is: How can we best support clinical supervisors?

There is no definitive or readily available answer to this question, as the literature is almost exclusively concerned with training supervisors to perform their 'formative' educational function. Indeed, the supervision literature contains scant attention to supporting clinical supervision in general. For instance, Dorsey *et al* (2017) observed that the majority of programmes for promoting evidence-based mental health treatments in community settings had ignored support for supervisors, even though supervisors are widely recognized as vital to treatment success (e.g. Callahan *et al*, 2009; Roth *et al*, 2010). Within the supervision literature, organizational systems have 'rarely been investigated or discussed' (Holloway, 2014, p612). It was to rectify this neglect that we organized a special issue of a research journal (*The Cognitive Behaviour Therapist*) to gather opinions and examples of how supervisors can be appropriately supported. Ten papers were included and they illuminated many of the options (Newman & Kaplan, 2016). We will draw on those papers in this chapter, starting with the 'support our supervisors' (SOS) model that we developed especially for that journal issue (Milne & Reiser, 2016). This model argued that, for supervisors to be properly developed, guided and supported, it was necessary for their employing organizations to provide them with the same kind of normative, formative and restorative support that they normally provide to their supervisees. Here we extend that reasoning, in order to construct a suitable rationale for supporting and developing the 'restorative' or supportive function of supervision. In addition, we will build on the earlier thinking in this book, especially the summary of relevant theory and empirical research in Table 3.1, which detailed how supervisors could support their supervisees. In particular, because of the strong fundamental similarities between supervisors and supervisees (such as the need for social support and coping strategy enhancement), we propose to mirror Table 3.1 as the basis for this chapter. However, we will also refine this reflexive approach by once more considering the most relevant theories, the most relevant studies, plus expert consensus statements and guidance. This will give us greater confidence in detailing the key, evidence-based ways to support supervisors who are working restoratively.

Based on these forms of evidence, we have organized this chapter so that it provides a clear and practical summary of the main options for supporting supervisors through normative, formative and restorative methods. This reflects the blueprint set out in Chapter 1, where we planned to outline the best options for ensuring supervisors' continuing professional development (CPD, including supervisor training and feedback); the most promising support arrangements, (emphasising the role of peer support); and the other important organizational aids (e.g. enabling policies and management procedures). Guided by this evidence-base, Table 8.1 sets out these three broad options for supporting supervisors, the related support methods (e.g. training in supervision), plus some typical outcomes with illustrative research evidence. These methods all share the potential to improve supervisors' well-being and to reduce any symptoms of burnout that they may have (e.g. by heightening their sense of personal accomplishment). Additionally, they allow supervisors to experience supportive supervision for themselves, which may afford insights and also boost their ability (like 'Self-Practice/Self-Reflection'; see Chapter 7). Not least, these arrangements show an organization to be 'caring for the carers'.

Therefore, to resume the 'tandem model' analogy that we have used throughout this book, this chapter represents a well-earned pause on the long and undulating supervision road, a time for the supervisor to consider how best to manage the personal demands of the journey. It is a moment for the supervisor to stop and reflect on what can be done to ease the relentless effort, and especially to consider the kind of support that would be most helpful.

Table 8.1: A summary of the main evidence-based ways that supervisors can be supported and developed in relation to their restorative function

Options for helping supervisors	Methods	Outcomes for supervisors (example of evidence)
Formative approach (facilitating supervisors' adaptation through guided learning, including opportunities for continuing professional development)	Aid adaptation to the demands of the role through **training** and related **educational activities** (e.g. workshops on supervision; guidelines; journal clubs; work shadowing; preceptorship). Maintaining training effects through support arrangements; better comprehending the nature of the work through **consultancy** or **mentoring** (expert advice and guidance).	Develop supervisors' competence and capability in providing supportive supervision (Rees *et al*, 2019). Transferring competencies from training to the workplace (Beckman *et al*, 2017); improved clinical effectiveness (Funderburk *et al*, 2018); fewer thinking errors or problematic feelings.
Restorative approach (ensuring that supervisors have adequate personal coping strategies and social resources, including peer support)	Consultancy or mentoring can also boost supervisors' personal coping strategies (e.g. developing an attitude of self-care/compassion; skills in self-regulation, such as managing distressing emotions). Social resources include **peer support groups** and **manager support** (e.g. engaging in shared activities, such as quality circles or peer review groups).	Encouraging supervisors to develop their personal coping strategies and to access peer support; better understanding and self-control (e.g. heightened self-awareness and self-acceptance); and related skills in self-regulation (Tsutsumi, 2011).
Normative approach (managing the workplace to reduce stressors and improve organizational support arrangements)	**Supervision-of-supervision** and workplace **management**, help by creating a healthier workplace (e.g. adequate resourcing and information, such as time for supervision; organizational leadership, including supervision strategies, policies and procedures; action research, audits and feedback).	Building relationships and addressing interpersonal problems; buffering supervisors from workplace stressors; monitoring and adjusting workload; providing constructive feedback on the supervisors' work performance; validation, social support (companionship) (Schoenwald, 2016).

2. Formative methods for supporting supervisors

Formative methods of supporting supervisors focus on the use of training and educational methods in order to foster adaptations through the process of learning, as in enhancing knowledge, skills, and attitudes. While the most common method of providing formative training involves workshop-based training, other methods are more educational in nature but are equally relevant and relatively underutilized in most healthcare professions (including utilization of research and guidelines; journal clubs; work shadowing; consultancy, mentoring and preceptorships). There are important differences between training and education, but these are complementary approaches to adapting to the workplace through the learning process (Milne, 2018). The main use of training lies in developing supervision competencies (e.g. skills in providing feedback), whereas education is best-suited to developing capability (e.g. problem-solving skills (Fraser and Greenhalgh, 2001)). We will detail examples of both forms of learning in this chapter, but the great bulk of research has concerned supervisor training, which is where we start.

Training is usually defined as a systematic instructional process that helps trainees to develop skills, knowledge, and attitudes that directly promote work-related competencies (Goldstein & Ford, 2001). Supervisor training has belatedly become established internationally (Watkins & Wang, 2014). In the UK, post-graduate training for supervisors is mandatory and it generally involves an introductory workshop with subsequent periodic follow-up, in the form of continuing professional development (CPD) (Milne and Reiser, 2017). In Australia, the CPD requirements for all registered psychologists are even more robust. For example, supervisors require accreditation, which is a mandatory process of formal approval as a supervisor, initially based on passing a supervision training programme (followed by career-long mandatory refresher training (Watkins and Wang, 2014)), making it the best-developed system for developing supervisors in the world. Training as a supervisor is supplemented by other CPD arrangements that emphasize an individualized approach to setting learning goals and encouraging career-long reflection (Psychology Board of Australia, 2015: https://www.psychologyboard.gov.au/Registration/Continuing-Professional-Development.aspx).

The most comprehensive and systematic approach to training supervisors has probably occurred within the Improving Access to Psychological Therapy (IAPT) initiative, an English mental health programme that will be reviewed in detail below. In the US, continuing education (CE) requirements for mental health professionals generally include a requirement for a fixed number of hours of workshop-based training in supervision. Such CPD constitutes a massive financial investment for healthcare organizations. The costs of continuing medical education for physicians alone in the US have been estimated to exceed $2.8bn in 2018 (ACCME, 2018). Despite this investment, workshops are typically delivered in a one-off fashion, with no follow-up or ongoing consultation. Typically, standards for determining the amount, quality or suitability of the content of workshops vary widely between professions and even from region to region, resulting in a patchwork of inconsistent practices and regulations. In general, many workshops for healthcare workers are not based upon empirically supported or even educationally sound methods. To illustrate this unsatisfactory state of affairs, a report prepared for the US Institute of Medicine concluded:

> *"The evidence is also strong, however, that continuing education is too often disconnected from theories of how adults learn and from the actual delivery of patient care. As a result, CE in its present form fails to deliver the most useful and important information to health professionals, leaving them unable to adopt evidence-based approaches efficiently to best improve patient outcomes and population health"* (Warden *et al*, 2010, p47–48).

In particular, CE tends to rely on didactic teaching techniques (e.g. lectures and reading assignments), which generally have the least benefit (Bloom, 2005; Bluestone *et al,* 2013).

In summary, workshops are the predominant method of providing post-graduate clinical training, including supervisory training, and a great deal of resources are consumed in providing these workshops. Sadly, there is scant empirical evidence to support the effectiveness of these traditional, didactic practices, in terms of improving clinical competencies or supervision skills, or of positively impacting healthcare services or patients through supervision (Watkins & Wang, 2014). Is there a better way? In particular, what is the evidence-based way to design a more efficient system of supervisor training?

In general, there is now compelling theoretical and empirical grounds for adopting more experiential approaches to training (Kolb, 2014; Rees *et al,* 2019). These approaches utilize educational techniques that engage the learner in active mental processing, for example, case studies, clinical simulations, and other interactive strategies (Bluestone *et al,* 2013). Active behavioural engagement during training is generally effective, such as interactive techniques that include multiple exposures to activities over protracted periods (e.g. regular performance feedback (Davis & Galbraith, 2009; Warden *et al,* 2010)). The theoretical and empirical bases for the superiority of such experiential methods is supported by expert consensus statements, guidelines, and recommendations (e.g. Warden, 2010). Combining these sources of evidence with the broader educational and expertise literature, we can conclude that training can be an efficient form of CPD (e.g. Lee & Anderson, 2013; Marinopoulos *et al,* 2007; Prince & Felder, 2006; Rakovshik & McManus, 2010; Rousmaniere *et al,* 2017; Snowdon *et al,* 2020). But it must be done systematically. This means that it addresses the learners' educational needs, incorporates multiple methods of active learning within work-simulations, such as opportunities to observe demonstrations and to practise new skills, and when there is adequate time to digest and incorporate knowledge, linked to corrective feedback. Sometimes termed 'active learning' or 'discovery learning', these kinds of experiential methods encourage learners to explore concepts and rehearse skills, helping them to reconstruct their knowledge over time within their workplaces, based on problem-solving activities.

From these general findings on training, it does indeed seem that there is a 'better way', entailing less didactic and greater experiential emphases. We should now turn to the development of supervisors as a specific kind of CPD/CE. In the next section we ask how this might best be accomplished.

What is the evidence-based way to design supportive supervision training?

These general findings, theories and expert recommendations are entirely consistent with our own most recent supervisor training review (Milne & Reiser, 2017), which also drew on the supervisor training literature to consider how training should be tailored for the restorative function. Based on this review, we summarized the 'gold standards' for efficient clinical supervisor training. We considered that it should:

1. Be based on an educational and organizational needs assessment, including consideration of any 'barriers' and 'boosters' to supervision within the workplace; needs assessment process to include collaboration with stakeholders in order to develop training materials, providing a clear rationale and set of challenging learning goals to motivate and orient supervisors.

2. Address supervision-specific theories and methods, part of treating supervision as a discrete professional competency.

3. Utilize a combination of didactic and experiential methods:

   a. Use experiential training methods such as demonstrating, observing and providing corrective feedback to develop procedural knowledge and competency.

   b. Use educational methods including teaching, discussion and reflection to develop declarative knowledge and metacognitive capabilities that provide a more generalizable capability (e.g. durable problem-solving abilities).

4. Engage learners with demonstrations (live or video-based), incorporating behavioural rehearsal and opportunities for immediate feedback on skills.

5. Make provision for follow-up training, such as group or individual consultation, oriented to assisting new supervisors in implementing supervision.

6. Continually evaluate the workshop's effectiveness by getting feedback about the training and its transfer to routine supervision, and employ this feedback to improve future workshops.

However, these gold standards were developed in relation to all three functions of supervision: formative, restorative and normative (Milne & Reiser, 2017). Although these supervisor training methods are embedded in England's IAPT programme, it does not explicitly address restorative supervision (e.g. the competencies cultivated within training are all formative). Similarly, our systematic review of supervisor training (Milne *et al*, 2011c), based on a sample of 11 controlled, naturalistic and successful studies, included no restorative examples. The same bias towards formative workshop content and goals can be found in similar reviews, with only the supervision alliance as a token potentially restorative topic (e.g. Watkins & Wang, 2014). Although some RCT studies of staff training have appeared more recently, including supervision, these are also formative in focus and do not involve supervisor training (e.g. Beckman *et al*, 2017). The few studies of supervisor training that we were able to locate with at least a partial restorative focus had weak research designs (e.g. Browning & Pront, 2015; Clipper & Cherry, 2017; Gilleatt *et al*, 2014; White & Winstanley, 2009), although they are highly relevant to this book and produced some promising findings (e.g. a significant effect on outcomes such as 'My [supervisor] helped me develop collegial working relationships and promote a positive work environment in my new department' (Browning and Pront, 2015)).

Therefore, in the absence of an established evidence base, we turn again to our integrative approach in order to develop a sound rationale for training in supportive supervision, such as extrapolating from closely neighbouring literatures. How well do these general standards apply to the more specific training of supervisors in supportive supervision? What changes would need to be incorporated in the content and delivery of workshops to most effectively assist supervisors in developing the restorative domain of their work? Supportive supervision workshops should surely themselves include an element of support and self-care to foster insight and to boost well-being among supervisors. In addition, experiential learning theory (Kolb, 2014) would suggest that training in supportive supervision should primarily activate the 'experiencing' mode of learning, with correspondingly less emphasis on 'conceptualizing'. This emphasis on addressing 'experiencing' is reflected in our earlier definition (see Chapter 2):

"Supportive supervision addresses supervisees' emotional experience of their workplace, and their personal functioning in that context. It is a formal, case-focused, and intensive relational process... (including a strong supervisory alliance)... problem formulation, coping strategy enhancement, facilitating peer support, and empathic debriefing..."

This definition is one way of thinking about the necessary changes to the content of training in supportive supervision.

Another way of considering the changes that would be needed in the content and delivery of workshops on supportive supervision is to study the most relevant research. Unfortunately, the two approaches that we were able to locate have not been subjected to rigorous outcome evaluation, and hence we need to be cautious about drawing overall conclusions as to their effectiveness in promoting the well-being of supervisors or their supervisees. However, these examples nonetheless provide potentially valuable information. Therefore, we review these two approaches to providing training in supportive supervision, taking into account the next-best empirical foundation – our earlier reviews of successful supportive supervision methods. For instance, the material in Tables 3.1 and 6.1 represent the relevant research evidence, pointing to the effectiveness of certain techniques with supervisees (e.g. developing their coping strategies; processing feeling reactions). Because the methods and their mechanisms are fundamentally shared with supervisors, we assume that this kind of evidence should also be considered with due caution (e.g. that coping strategy enhancement work and heightening self-awareness are probably equally appropriate ways of supporting and guiding supervisees and supervisors). We moderate this analogy with the few specific studies, guidelines and competencies that we were able to locate. This leads into a summary of the training and educational approaches, where we integrate all the reviewed information into an evidence-based approach. We also spell out this approach by providing a detailed and practical plan for training supervisors in supportive supervision. This is based on a power-point slideshow (see the Appendix on page 239 or www.pavpub.com/supportive-clinical-supervision-resources/) that includes information on specific theories and methods (the didactic element), followed by our suggestions on suitably experiential learning exercises (including video demonstrations).

An example of training in supportive supervision: The Proctor model

Even though Brigit Proctor is cited multiple times as a model for fashioning supervision within a balanced formative, normative and restorative framework, her early model for clinical supervision (Proctor, 1986) highlighted the supportive function of supervision and prized it over the normative and formative functions. This emphasis was maintained in her later chapter *Training for the supervision alliance*, in which Proctor (2010, p25) noted that:

"Clinical supervision will be a major opportunity for professional and, hopefully, personal refreshment so the restorative task in these stressful times should, I think, be placed first. If supervision is not experienced as restorative, the other tasks will not be well done."

Proctor proposed a supervisor training course that emphasized a 'non-hierarchical' working alliance between supervisor and supervisee, instead focusing on establishing a collaborative, cooperative relationship as a counterpoint to the culture of many work settings. It is refreshing to see that her 'supervision alliance' training model (Proctor, 2010, pp24–25) reflects profoundly restorative values, namely that:

"practitioners are usually keen to work well, and to be self-monitoring, if they are brought to professional maturity in a learning environment which sufficiently values, supports and challenges them... learners require a trusting and safe environment if they are to share their experience and practice honestly with themselves or others."

The format of the supervision alliance training model (Proctor, 2010) is flexible and appears to be easily adapted to either a group workshop or individual consultation with supervisors. For instance, the programme is geared to the developmental capabilities of the participating supervisors and includes an initial focus on jointly developing a supervision contract with a goal of 'creating a culture of participation, safety, and challenge' (p29). The training is rich in experiential components, including audio-visual examples and demonstrations of supervision skills, self-awareness exercises designed to promote self-reflection and self-management, and other experiential exercises incorporating modelling and feedback.

In summary, Proctor's training model (1986; 2010) provides a thorough, educationally well-grounded experiential approach to developing skills in supportive supervision, consistent with the above gold standards. Unfortunately, descriptions of the model do not offer sufficient operational detail to enable formal studies to be conducted, which also hampers large-scale implementation. We only know of two evaluations of the effectiveness of Proctor's training model. Firstly, Gilleat *et al* (2014) studied the effects of a one-day workshop with a group of occupational therapists, social workers, and nurses. The evaluation design was a comparison between data obtained before and after the workshop, and contained no objective assessments of skill development (e.g. questionnaires were used to assess the suitability of the model, plus self-rated improvements in skills and confidence). However, these obtained reactions to the workshop were positive. Secondly, White and Winstanley (2009) provided a systematic, experiential four-day workshop for 22 nurses in Australia, preparatory to their RCT evaluation of supervision, which was based on Proctor's training model, but the workshop evaluation was a simple satisfaction survey.

We provide a related example below, in the section on 'restorative' methods of support, because it emphasises support to the participating supervisors (Wallbank & Woods, 2012). First, we turn to educational approaches to supporting and developing restorative supervision.

Educational approaches to developing restorative supervision

In addition to training, the summary of formative methods for supporting supervisors that we presented in Table 8.1 noted 'educational activities' and we listed research (its consumption, production and utilization: e.g. reading textbooks); studying guidelines; participating in journal clubs; work shadowing; and preceptorship. These are the most frequently cited examples but they are far from common, being less used than training as a form of support (whether in the research literature or in practice). In an ideal world, some of these educational activities would be combined with training, as part of a systematic, multiple-method ('blended') approach to staff development.

Probably the most common such combination is training that incorporates guidelines on supervision (sometimes as part of a guidance manual) and examples were provided in Chapter 3, when we described the sample of key research studies (e.g. Milne & Westerman, 2001; Wallbank & Woods, 2012). Guidelines are concise statements that seek to educate and inform, suggesting or recommending specific professional behaviours (APA, 2015). They summarize the best available research evidence, moderated by expert consensus, often disseminated by health authorities or professional bodies. To illustrate, in collaboration with The British Association for Behavioural and Cognitive Psychotherapy, we developed and disseminated six supervision guidelines (Milne & Reiser, 2017), including one on the training of supervisors and a second on supporting supervisees. All of these guidelines included recommendations to supervisors, linked explicitly to the available evidence. For example, two of the five recommendations in the guideline on supporting supervisees were: 'encourage emotional processing and personal growth' and 'strengthen the supervisee's coping strategies'. Because of their importance, you will find further descriptions and evaluations of guidelines throughout this book. For those who want more, literature reviews are reported in Milne and Reiser (2017) and in Milne (2016). A larger-scale example of guidelines in the form of recommended competencies can be found in the IAPT programme for supervisor training, the contents of which should be based around the Roth and Pilling supervision competencies framework (http://www.ucl. ac.uk/clinical-psychology/CORE/supervision_ framework.htm; Richards, 2009). We return to this impressive programme below, but as it is entirely formative in its emphasis, we will only pick out those features that are relevant to supportive supervision (e.g. the training methods; the organizational context). Similarly, Australian guidelines for supervisors and their trainers barely touch on the restorative function (e.g. Health Workforce Australia, 2013).

As this brief summary indicates, research plays a core role in guidelines; the authors 'consume' research by getting to grips with a topic such as 'emotional processing', then review relevant studies. The study findings were 'utilized' in drafting the guideline and this was also true in relation to the development of the IAPT competencies, in that a group of supervision experts drew on their knowledge base (including research and relevant theories) to define these competencies. Research on guidelines sometimes also contributes to the 'production' of research, for instance when guidelines are evaluated. A rare example was provided by Milne (2010), who published a national evaluation of a supervision manual that included four guidelines (more below). Those who train supervisors (workshop leaders) should also be consuming and utilizing supervision and related research, and again some go on to publish their training findings (e.g. Newman-Taylor *et al*, 2012). Unfortunately, such evaluations are rare (Watkins & Wang, 2014), limiting our ability to create an effective system for educating and training supervisors. Evaluation is an essential element within a pro-active organizational strategy for ensuring the successful implementation of supervision, providing corrective feedback on progress to the programme leaders and other key stakeholders. A stepwise succession of outcomes should be assessed to help pinpoint problems (see Figure 3.1 in Milne & Reiser, 2017). Examples of system-wide evaluation are yet more scarce, such as 'participatory action research', but some thoughtful analyses and systematic studies do exist and are hugely informative (e.g. Lynch & Happel, 2008; Reid *et al*, 2003; Schoenwald *et al*, 2013). They indicate that educating supervisors within an organization is best viewed as a system change, 'organizational development', or innovation challenge. To illustrate, a review of the implementation of supervision manuals and guidelines in organizations concluded that:

> "...*supervision only improves when there is a suitable innovation effort in place, including an action-research, 'bottom-up' ethos and supervision-of-supervision. Paradoxically, from the present sample of studies it was the smaller-scale, 'local' implementation projects that appeared to succeed in improving supervision, seemingly because of their attention to innovation factors*" (Milne, 2016, p10).

Such findings are themselves an education for those involved in implementing supervision programmes.

Innovation based on suitable evaluation and feedback methods can transform an organization, supporting supervisors in multiple ways. An inspirational example is provided in Lynch & Happell (2008, p69) by an interviewee commenting on the supervision programme: *"The conversations around the place are fantastic. People are talking about mental health nurses as a profession again. They are talking about the joy of being a nurse. They're talking about the differences that they can make and – yes, the place is just a lot healthier. And we have got people who are receiving supervision who would just say that this is the greatest thing since sliced bread. They just love it... They are all just so focused."*

Participating in journal clubs and work shadowing are two of the other examples listed in Table 8.1 under 'educational activities', but there is little sign that these are used in supervisor development. Of course, supervisees may often shadow their supervisor and discuss what is observed, but this concerns the work that they undertake, rather than supervision itself. By contrast, preceptorship is a major educational experience for supervisees in professions such as nursing. Preceptors are more experienced healthcare staff who help new graduates to adapt to their initial professional roles and workplaces. They are an important source of procedural knowledge, an important source of supportive supervision, and are "an essential component of education" (Ke *et al*, 2017, p2). As we have already mentioned preceptors in various parts of this book, we will say little more here. For instance, in Chapter 3 we summarized a study by Kristofferzon *et al* (2013), who reported that their sample of 107 Swedish nursing students rated most highly the supportive function of the preceptors. Wisely, these preceptors also encouraged critical thinking, reflection, and the discussion of clinical experiences, core educational activities.

Consultancy (formative function)

Consultancy is typically provided by someone with relevant expertise who is external to the supervisor's organization, and who primarily encourages reflection and problem-solving on issues raised by the supervisor, with the aim of providing inspiration and guidance, intended to benefit consultees and their patients (Kilburg & Diedrich, 2007). The problem-solving analysis includes the stages of relationship building, problem identification, problem analysis and action-planning, concluding with plan implementation and evaluation (Kratochwill, 2008). A more extensive account of the role is provided by Nadeem *et al* (2013), who detail additional tasks, such as adapting interventions and sustainability planning. Some of these activities overlap with preceptorship, and indeed may be performed for different reasons. Therefore, we will discuss consultancy and mentoring in this section with respect to their formative function, entailing the development of professional competence and capability, such as enabling decision-making, and then we will return to consultancy in the restorative section, as it can also serve that supportive purpose.

As a term, consultancy is often used interchangeably with supervision, but consultancy is advisory, a source of optional advice and guidance. The supervisor who consults is entitled to take or leave this input. By contrast, a supervisor who supervises another supervisor (i.e. 'supervision-of-supervision': more below), who we shall call the 'meta-supervisor', has formal (organizational) authority over that supervisor. That is, in supervision-of-supervision, a meta-supervisor (i.e. the senior supervisor) must have the authority to observe and direct the work of the junior supervisor. There is also the risk of fuzzy definitions with the related term of 'meta-supervision', which is sometimes used interchangeably with supervision-of-supervision and consultancy, when it appears that they are referring to consultancy, as defined above (e.g. Buus *et al,* 2016; Newman and Kaplan, 2016). We are wise not to blur these overlapping roles, as in 'peer supervision', because it carries major risks concerning safe and effective clinical practice (Martin *et al,* 2017).

Consultancy provides vital sustenance to supervisors and has become recognized as a necessary supportive element in implementing evidence-based practice in healthcare (Funderburk *et al,* 2018). For example, follow-up consultation has been demonstrated repeatedly to help workshop participants consolidate and maintain their competence gains once back in their workplaces (Beckman *et al,* 2017; Beidas & Kendall, 2010; Schwalbe *et al,* 2014), and is a standard element within the most impressive supervisor development programmes (e.g. Reid *et al,* 2003; Schoenwald, *et al,* 2009). To illustrate, Funderburk *et al* (2018) compared phone versus video-based consultancy, reporting superior clinical outcomes for the latter. The clinical intervention was behavioural parent training as a treatment for early childhood disruptive behaviour problems. The video consultation was live and used audio-visual technology over the internet. This technology allowed a remote consultant in another state to:

a. directly observe live parent–child interaction in the clinic

b. listen to the therapist coaching the parent

c. communicate directly and provide skill coaching to the therapist during the session; and

d. model skills for the therapist.

They concluded that video-based consultation led to "a small but potentially meaningful impact on downstream client outcomes" (p738), thanks to good transfer of training ('transportability'), which itself holds for large-scale implementation (i.e. multi-agency 'scaling up'). Similar positive findings from an RCT have been reported in relation to consultation that included the supervisors (Martino *et al,* 2016). The consultation included two days of workshop training, monthly feedback based on audio-recorded supervision sessions, and expert advice via monthly on-site or phone consultations throughout the study. This package had a significantly larger effect on the supervisees' competence in therapy then supervision as usual (but no differential effect on adherence). Worryingly, it should be noted that their findings suggested that supervision-as-usual "may be virtually no supervision at all" (Martino *et al,* 2016, p16).

Mentoring

Mentoring is similar to consultancy in affording healthcare professionals emotional support and a 'thinking space' based on support and guidance within the workplace from a colleague with greater experience or expertise. Mentoring may also differ in being obligatory for new recruits in some professions or countries, where the mentor acts as a role model, counsellor, and source of emotional support (Johnson, 2007). Again, there are overlaps apparent in relation to supervision, but the relationship should be different, in that the mentor is more like having a guardian, buddy, or work partner. That is, someone with closely similar work experiences, and therefore well placed to offer inspiration, empathy and compassionate support. Lennox *et al* (2008) provide a historical overview, indicating various styles of mentoring, and urge that confusion with overlapping roles be addressed. Chena *et al* (2018) described an instrument for measuring mentoring that could afford exceptional clarity, The Mentors' Behaviour Scale in Nursing. This concerns mentors' behaviour in clinical teaching of pre-registered students, and includes facilitating learning (e.g. teaching and guiding), professional development (e.g. role modelling) and psychosocial support (which includes the establishment of relationships, emotional support and encouragement). Mentoring has been arranged to good effect as a support strategy between supervision peers in physiotherapy, based on a range of meeting formats, to reflect jointly on supervision issues (Thomson *et al*, 2016). However, only a satisfaction evaluation was undertaken. Therefore, in the absence of something specifically addressing supportive supervision and backed by firm evidence, we can only assume that such mentoring activities could also be helpful to supportive supervisors (e.g. a more experienced supervisor in an organization mentoring novice supervisors).

Summary

We started this section by asking: What is the evidence-based way to design supportive clinical supervision training? Our answer is to ensure that educational activities address the relevant content areas (e.g. see Tables 3.1 and 6.1) through a blend of needs-led, contextually-appropriate, evidence-based, experiential methods, all guided by corrective feedback (e.g. action research). These should include a definite emphasis on emotional 'experiencing' to boost supervisors' insight and to offer them support. In the Appendix, we translate these fine words into action by setting out how we would lead a workshop on supportive supervision. This blueprint is based on similar workshops that we have led in person and which have been well-received by supervisors. However, we should close by stressing that, while the general evidence-base on staff training is robust, little explicit research evidence exists on supporting restorative supervision through educational activities. The few rigorous studies focus on supervisees/therapists, although seem applicable to supervisors (e.g. an RCT evaluating a one-day-day educational event designed to reduce job ditress (Poulsen *et al*, 2015)). Therefore, we urge trainers to be guided by careful evaluations of their own work; and we encourage supervisors, meta-supervisors and consultants to exercise caution in applying our suggestions.

As per the rest of this book, in this section we have again adopted our distinctively integrative and constructive approach to the available evidence, including extrapolation from neighbouring literatures. But we have also drawn analogies between the different functions of supervision. We were inspired and comforted in this perspective by the father of restorative supervision, Albert Kadushin, who suggested:

> *"Supportive supervision is often implemented not as a separate, explicitly identifiable activity, but rather as a part of the work of educational (formative) and administrative (normative) supervision... The functions of educational and administrative supervision can be performed in a way that communicates respect for, interest in, and acceptance of the supervisee. If administrative supervision cannot alleviate burnout by reducing ambiguity and role conflict, the supportive and educational supervision may help."* (Kadushin, 1976, p182).

In this integrative, functional spirit we next revisit consultancy support for supervisors, this time identifying its restorative role. We supplement consultancy with peer support arrangements and other social support options, again based on the summary in Table 8.1.

3. Restorative methods for supporting supervisors

Consultancy may also serve a restorative function implicitly, by the supportive style in which it is done (Kadushin, 1976). More explicitly, a consultant may supplement reflective or problem-solving strategies with attention to personal issues that affect work. Perhaps by encouraging the supervisor to seek more feedback, or may encourage a supervisor to improve their self-care by facilitating emotional expression to lower tension ('ventilation'), as in acknowledging 'the loneliness of leadership' (Kilburg & Diedrich, 2007). Consultancy is not the only restorative method for supporting supervisors, and we will also describe two popular supplements (formal peer support and peer support groups). Informal social support is core to these activities and vital to well-being but we will not describe that again here, as it is already addressed thoroughly in earlier chapters.

Consultancy (restorative)

Restorative consultancy shares the methods and goals of formative consultation (i.e. encouraging reflection and problem-solving, providing inspiration and guidance, seeking to benefit consultees and their patients). It adds greater attention to consultees' emotional experiences at work, encouraging self-awareness and other adjustments (e.g. the use of more appropriate coping strategies). A restorative aim was part of the post-training consultancy provided to supervisors in the large-scale programme reported by White and Winstanley (2009). They ensured that their group of 22 supervisors received 'support and advice' throughout the research period, including monthly help from one of three experienced clinical supervisors ('coordinators'), plus opportunities to reconvene with the small group of colleagues with whom they had trained. These supervisors maintained diary records of this research period, which indicated major institutional barriers:

> *"implementation of (clinical supervision) was disrupted by… unsupportive managerial cultures, low staffing ratios… increasingly demanding clinical workloads, frequent turnover of key individuals and a time-poor workforce"* (p901).

We return to this issue below, in relation to workplace management. In the case of the outcomes reported for the purely restorative supervision programme (Wallbank & Woods, 2012), consultancy was reported to aid supervisors in improving their self-care, emotional self-regulation, stress inoculation and capacity for reflective practice. Our earlier reviews of research regarding what works in supportive supervision suggested that consultancy can achieve these important outcomes by including the methods listed, such as discussing feeling reactions to stressful incidents (see Table 3.1, Chapter 3; Table 6.1, Chapter 6).

Within the above section on formative consultancy, we described a study by Funderburk *et al* (2018), a rare and welcome illustration of consultancy for supervisors, focused primarily on ensuring treatment fidelity. Although some restorative aspects of supervision were measured (e.g. a 'collaborative, affirming, supervisee-centred' style), this did not explicitly extend to consultation, nor were any such data presented. We are unaware of a study that focused instead on restorative consultation for supervisors, although in one of our own n=1 studies the supervisor (RR) received fortnightly feedback on his supervision based on the direct observation instrument SAGE (Milne & Reiser, 2014). This included qualitative feedback (written and verbal), provided by email and phone, which at least provided a restorative element (e.g. affirmation and praise for the approaches used; encouragement; guidance on possible improvements). The supervisor also felt able to express to the consultant (DM) his anxieties about the direct observation of his work and the associated consultation sessions, particularly coming after 20 years of unsupervised supervisory practice. He reported feeling at times "profoundly intimidated", then "humbled" when the initial feedback was somewhat critical, which "required hardiness and a willingness to persevere… despite frustrating moments" (p412).

This kind of consultation has been used repeatedly in our work, unfortunately, with a similar tendency to prize formative consultancy for formative supervision. An exception was consultancy partly intended to address a pattern of collusion between the supervisor and supervisee (Milne *et al*, 2009). As with the above example (Milne & Reiser, 2014), consultancy was intended to mirror supervision i.e. modelling the expression of affect and role-playing enhanced ways of supervising (in this sense, the supervision manual is also effectively a supportive consultancy manual). A final consultancy session was arranged to give the supervisor the opportunity to reflect on her perceptions of any collusion, structured by a six-stage SP/SR procedure for reflecting on therapeutic relationship difficulties (Bennett-Levy & Thwaites, 2007). Following this process, the consultant asked a series of questions to facilitate the supervisor's reflections on collusion with one of her supervisees, aided by selected segments of audio recordings from her supervision sessions. The tone of the consultation was empathic and exploratory, based on a shared collegial recognition of the difficulties of managing alliance problems such as collusion. The supervisor drew attention to some ways in which the supervisee was unhelpful or avoidant, such as only offering general objectives for the session. She reflected that in such situations she had terminated the collaborative agenda-setting effort prematurely, partly in response to the supervisee's negative reactions, which included looking confused and repeating himself. The consultant then tried to facilitate the supervisor's personal reflections, leading to a shared understanding, an educational role-play between the supervisor and the consultant to rehearse a better way of managing collusion, concluding with an action-plan.

Summary

It is unusual to find an explicit restorative emphasis in reports of consulting with supervisors. It appears that, while a restorative element is valued, it only plays a background or facilitating role in relation to either normative issues (e.g. improving access to supervision (Buus *et al*, 2016)) or formative concerns (e.g. the development of CBT supervision skills (Newman, 2013)). The latter is a rare account of consultancy for supervisors, and there are several references to a restorative style, such as 'giving a great deal of positive reinforcement' and being 'as warm and enthusiastic as possible'. This interpretation is consistent with the helpful transcript provided by Newman (2013), which deals in part with relationship issues and includes a moment when consultant and supervisor both laugh together. The following vignette illustrates this important but implicit role for supportive work within consultancy.

Vignette 1: Example of supportive consultancy with supervisors in a small group format

Several follow-up, video-based group consultation sessions were scheduled with supervisors in a public community mental health clinic and hospital system in the US (duration: 90 minutes each). This followed an initial full-day supervisor training workshop, based on the Milne and Reiser (2017) manual. During the second consultancy session, the group reviewed the guideline for 'feedback and evaluation', having just watched an accompanying video. The video shows a mid-career supervisee visibly angry and upset after getting feedback about her level of CBT competence. This challenging feedback was based on a critical review of one of her tapes by a younger male supervisor. She indicates that no one has ever given her this type of explicit feedback before based on an objective scale for rating CBT competence), making it especially difficult to digest. The ensuing group discussion focused on the importance of providing regular formative feedback and how supervisors are often reluctant to give specific detailed feedback, despite feedback being a key component of effective supervision.

One of the supervisors in the group had a visceral reaction during this discussion and then recounted a situation that had occurred in his training where he had received a very negative evaluation at the end of his internship training. This was also upsetting for him and similarly had come completely without warning. He was utterly unaware that his supervisor had identified some problems (he had never previously received any feedback and so naturally assumed that all was well). This surprising feedback episode resulted in a very difficult, time-consuming, and pressured effort to address the perceived problems at a very late stage of his training. In the group, this supervisor indicated that he still feels distressed and emotional recalling this event and that he had made a personal pledge to work hard with his supervisees to give ongoing formative feedback, so as to avoid any repeat of shocking surprises. In response, the consultant validated the difficult emotional experience of recalling this supervisory event and praised the supervisor's value system (doing a better job on behalf of his supervisees). The consultant then used summarizing, formulating, and teaching (referring to the literature of unethical and harmful supervision) before closing by establishing a consensus on the need for supervisor training.

Peer consultation

We prefer the term 'peer consultation' to 'peer supervision' for the same reasons we gave earlier, when introducing formative consultation, but with a similar reservation, as the term 'peer consultation' can also be viewed as self-contradictory. We think, however, that in consultation it is perfectly possible for a peer (at least a colleague from the same profession) to have relatively greater experience or expertise in relation to a particular topic. And as the relationship is optional and advisory, we can see no comparable concerns to that of 'peer supervision'.

The main difference between 'consultation' and 'peer consultation' is that peers will work in the same profession, clinical service, or specialty, and will tend to lack the degree of expertise or experience of the external consultant. Peer consultation is also structured more informally (e.g. no accountability relationship; no organizational hierarchy; no evaluation; no mandatory participation). It also typically occurs in small groups with a rotating Chairperson, addressing the pressing clinical concerns raised by participants. According to the definition used by The Psychology Board of Australia, peer consultation is a form of CPD that should also aid professional development and support: CPD is specifically linked to preventing burnout and boosting job satisfaction (Psychology Board of Australia, 2015, p4). The Board's annual CPD requirements for psychologists in Australia include 10 hours of peer consultation activities (Psychology Board of Australia, 2015; https://www.psychologyboard.gov.au/Registration/Continuing-Professional-Development.aspx)

According to this Board, peer consultation is a very broad category of activities, including individual supervision, mentoring or consultation (with a peer, supervisor, manager, or other professional person) and peer support groups. In addition, this peer consultation can address any area of the psychologists' work, including supervision. Therefore, peer consultation in Australian psychology can include a peer-based version of supervision-of-supervision, if sought by the consultee. The Board addresses the relative lack of expertise among peers by encouraging consultation with others that have identified expertise that is relevant to an individual's CPD goals (e.g. academics and researchers, psychiatrists, or management consultants).

Although the general absence of experts limits the scope of peer consultation (e.g. probably less teaching and expert guidance than in external consultation), it is particularly well suited to playing a valued supportive role, due to factors such as the shared experiences and ready empathy. Bernard and Goodyear (2014) and Borders (2012) have reviewed the participation rates from surveys of clinicians, concluding that peer consultation was one of the most popular forms of support and guidance, with 30–50% of several professional groups participating. This is especially so in countries or professions (unlike Australian psychologists) where no supervision is required following the completion of initial professional training. The most important restorative elements reported by survey participants were countering isolation and burnout, receiving support in relation to work stressors, and exploring problematic feelings towards patients. A potentially valuable account of the functioning of supervision groups can be found in Vec *et al* (2014). Again, most accounts concern consultation among clinicians about patients, but in principle they could discuss a supervision matter, or peer consultation groups on supervision could be formed. We know from our own experience that peer consultation groups for supervisors have happened in relation to some university training programmes in the UK, and that peer discussion is a significant part of clinical supervision workshops. Shiels *et al* (2016) reported similar contacts (e.g. meetings and online links), based on interviewing clinical supervisors associated with a related clinical psychology programme in England. However, although enjoying strong anecdotal approval, we know of no formal evaluation of such restorative groups, which appears to be typical of peer groups in general (Bernard & Goodyear, 2014; Borders, 2012).

The second author (RR) belongs to a CBT-focused peer consultation group that meets twice monthly, consisting of psychologists, clinical social workers and marriage and family counsellors. As a testament to the supportive and restorative value of the group, five core members have attended regularly for over 15 years. Hence, the group clearly provides great value in terms of a 'safe base' for CBT practice, with surprisingly strong group cohesion. This experience is quite consistent with Milne's (2009) account of peer consultation as providing social support, validation, a sense of belonging and interpersonal connectedness. But one of the drawbacks of peer consultation is that, without clear leadership and a focus on normative and formative functions, these consultations groups can be very supportive but lack adequate challenge. In point of fact, within this CBT-focused peer consultation group the use of more formal, empirically supported methods for providing consultation (routine use of recordings, explicit case formulation work and feedback) have lapsed in favour of more general case review followed by suggestions.

How can some of the relative disadvantages of peer-based consultation be minimized? Martin *et al* (2017) warn that peer supervision cannot replace clinical supervision, but have suggested several strategies for compensating for the lack of formal leadership, accountability and authority in such groups. Some strategies that might help compensate for the inherent weaknesses of the peer consultation model include taking a more structured approach, possibly involving rotation of leadership, developing a mutually agreed set of goals for consultation, and some light-touch evaluation. We would also recommend considering a more systematic, evidence-based and experiential approach. This might approximate to formative supervision methods, such as incorporating direct observation, including the formulation of distressing work, and at least occasionally utilizing active experiential methods (including demonstration, role play and feedback). This could be extended to incorporate periodic literature reviews of highly relevant topics to keep up to date on empirically supported methods. However, it seems from surveys that these kinds of methods have rarely been employed in peer consultation groups (Borders, 2012). This may be about to change, at least in Australia, where direct observation is encouraged (or another method to achieve the necessary "critically reflective focus" (Psychology Board of Australia, 2010, p2)). As Borders (2012) concluded, although a more systematic, evidence-based approach may require dealing with some discomfort and vulnerability, these methods seem vital for peer consultation to achieve a "rigorous evaluation of ...professional activities" (Australian Psychological Society, 2008, p2).

Vignette 2: Peer support and consultation within a challenging working environment

A group of CBT supervisors were training psychiatric residents within a psychodynamically oriented training program. Residents were obligated to take a training course in CBT in order to fulfil a national credentialing requirement to demonstrate competency in CBT and hence were not necessarily volunteers for the training programme. In fact, residents were currently being supervised and trained mainly within a psychodynamic training environment. One of the CBT supervisors felt frustrated with the lack of organizational support for training and consultation with residents. This manifested itself in initial meetings with residents who were highly sceptical of CBT and a great deal of time was taken up discussing residents' negative attitudes towards CBT and concerns that CBT was a superficial, formulaic and technical approach that might actually not address significant patient problems and even be potentially harmful. Secondly, residents regularly had other duties that conflicted with their supervision time. Finally, CBT supervisors were asked to make judgments about competence in CBT within a rather confined training period. One supervisor contacted other CBT supervisors within the CBT supervision group and an ongoing peer support and consultation group was scheduled. Over several meetings the group led by a senior CBT supervisor addressed topics related to institutional barriers to CBT and how best to provide effective CBT supervision within the current organizational context, which was deemed to be rather impervious to change due to the highly embedded training culture. The senior CBT supervisor shared his personal sense of frustration with the demands of the position and the constraints and limitations that he had experienced. In particular, a group email sent to CBT supervisors asking about evidence-based strategies used in supervision (role play, live observation, case formulation, and behavioural rehearsal) had generated a rather negative response from a higher level institutional manager, who suggested that this email had a negative tone and that supervisors were all highly experienced clinicians who were quite capable of making their own decisions about how to conduct supervision. The group meeting mainly provided support through ventilation of feelings and validating supervisors' concerns within a context of increasing social support and a sense of joint working together on issues of concern. The main feeling was a shared sense of frustration about the tension between trying to do an effective job and these institutional limitations. This approach resulted in a sense of relief, in that supervisors felt valued and supported, and that they felt they were being effective, despite ongoing limitations of the workplace and within an organizational context that did not fully support CBT training. The sense of relief was specifically the result of recognizing limitations and unspoken 'rules' that minimized the value placed on training, while brainstorming together as to how to be most effective within the current context, given the limitations and barriers.

Peer support

Of course, peer support may be a significant implicit bonus of peer consultation, but the review by Borders (2012) contained only two studies in which mutual support was an explicit goal.

More likely, social support occurs informally in peer groups that are primarily formative. Also, Borders' (2012) review concerned clinical supervision in general, with little or no attention to restorative matters. Thankfully, there is at least one example of supervisor training that is unique in being focused entirely on restorative supervision, and which includes peer support. This is the approach of Sonya Wallbank, who developed a programme that has been disseminated to over 3,500 healthcare professionals working in obstetrics and gynaecology in the UK and Australia. We have placed this example in this 'restorative' section because the training in restorative supervision specifically targets high levels of stress and burnout experienced by professionals in emotionally demanding environments, including the participating supervisors.

"The emphasis of the model is on the resilience of the professional, improving their own health and well-being, and supporting their capacity to think and make complex clinical decisions" (Wallbank & Woods, 2012, p22).

The effectiveness of this approach to restorative supervision has been evaluated favourably within a small RCT study, involving 30 midwives and doctors working in obstetrics and gynaecology (e.g. highly significant group differences were obtained in burnout and compassion satisfaction (Wallbank, 2010)). However, the training of the restorative supervisors has only been evaluated through a self-report questionnaire, administered before and after the training (Wallbank & Woods, 2012: see Chapter 3 for more on the methodology and findings).

In the pilot phase the supervisor training programme was targeted at midwives but was later expanded to include health visitors, nurses, and other healthcare professionals in workplaces with significant emotional demands. The training is structured as an initial day-long workshop, supplemented by a manual to support continued learning. The second phase of the training programme is for the workshop participants to receive six sessions of restorative supervision. It seems that participants are then supported to become supervisors ('leaders'), a role sustained by individual or group supervision (Wallbank, 2013), in order to cascade the model successfully (initially to no more than four of their colleagues). This makes the training model potentially sustainable and cost-effective within commissioning organizations (Wallbank and Woods, 2012). It appears that this receipt of supportive supervision is partly intended to demonstrate how to provide supervision (modelling supervision to help participants to acquire the necessary skills), in addition to experiencing it first-hand, partly to benefit personally. We have placed this example here as we understand that it is peers in supervisor training who provide the support.

Wallbank and Wonnacott (2016, p4) identified the following key goals of restorative supervision:

- Providing a safe space that enables the professional to be open about their true sense of self

- Providing a supportive and challenging supervisory environment

- Improving the capacity of the individual to remain resilient in the face of challenging case work through their ability to recognize personal triggers

- Enhancing the ability of professionals to relationship build with fellow professionals to avoid isolation and reduce difficult collegiate behaviours

- Encouraging the professional to focus on the events and/or situations they can change so they experience less helplessness

- Improve the ability of the professional to communicate issues so they can be escalated effectively.

One of the major advantages of Wallbank's model for supportive supervision is the provision of ongoing post-training supervision (Wallbank, 2013) and another is the reflexive way that the training reflects the supervision (e.g. both address resilience and well-being through the same methods). However, it appears that the supervisor training evaluation has been limited to one self-report questionnaire, administered before and after training, a research design that is usually uninterpretable. Therefore, until such data are forthcoming, we need to be cautious in our assessment of this otherwise highly impressive and important training programme.

Summary

Restorative consultancy shares the methods and goals of formative consultation, adding greater attention to consultees' emotional experiences of their work and encouraging the use of appropriate personal coping strategies. Although reports indicate that a restorative element is valued in consulting with supervisors, it only appears to play a background role as it is overshadowed by formative and normative issues. The outcomes of restorative consultancy can be boosted by peer consultation and peer support groups. Peer consultation is one of the most popular forms of support and guidance in healthcare, and has latterly become a required form of CPD in Australian psychology. Other reported benefits are countering isolation and burnout, receiving support in relation to work stressors, and exploring problematic feelings towards patients. However, although there is a sound theoretical rationale for these supportive methods and clear approval from professional and health bodies, research findings are only affirmative in relation to the basic processes (consultancy, social support). The vignette below illustrates how a consultant managed a supervisor's difficult emotional experience over negative feedback (using several techniques, including validation and praise).

4. Normative methods for supporting supervisors

Normative supervision is a managerial or administrative role, typically enacted by overseeing the supervisees' successful integration with organizational expectations, while ensuring that they have the necessary resources to perform their duties to the required standard. Such integration applies equally to the supervisor, who may appreciate support and guidance at certain times, such as when commencing the role of supervisor. In Table 8.1 we noted that supervision-of-supervision and workplace management actions might help to ensure adherence to supervision policies and procedures, could provide corrective feedback (e.g. from audits), enhance the quality of care, and should ensure that there are adequate resources to perform the required duties (such as time and financial support for training in supervision). These examples are consistent with the original definition of normative supervision (Kadushin, 1976), with Proctor's (1992) account, and with the EBP model (see Figure 1.1), including the employing organization's context. By context, we refer to governmental or professional policies that may be dictated nationally and linked to funding for the services in which supervision-of-supervision occurs (e.g. standards for supervision). There are many ways in which organizations might best manage supervision but we will focus on supervision-of-supervision, since this emerged as the main method from our review of research (Chapter 3). But first a note on workplace management actions, to set the scene and to supplement what we have already said about leadership in Chapter 4.

Management of supervisors

Leadership within organizations should ensure support for supervision arrangements, creating a culture where supervision can prosper, including the roles of administrators, service managers, and line managers, possibly supplemented by tutors from linked training programmes. As we will see in the section below on the IAPT programme, when clinical outcome targets, productivity standards and caseloads are high, clinical leadership can make all the difference, helping staff to feel energized, engaged, and resilient (Clark, 2018). Conversely, supervision "…cannot compensate for inadequate facilities, for poor management, or for unmotivated staff" (White & Winstanley, 2009, p901). This kind of systemic reasoning is articulated in our 'support model' (see Chapter 2), buttressed by reviews of research (e.g. Beidas & Kendall, 2010; Milne *et al*, 2008). Despite the compelling evidence, we also noted that only a minority of clinical supervision models factored in organizational systems and we could only locate one restorative example. This is the '4x4x4' model (Wonnacott, 2016), which extends Proctor's model (1991) by adding 'mediation' with partner organizations to the restorative, formative, and normative functions. As we noted, the 4x4x4 model alerts us to potential problems, such as the provision of clinical supervision by line managers. This can be problematic because normative issues tend to dominate supervision, and also because supervisees may be reluctant to reveal their support needs to their boss, as such needs may be perceived as a personal failing or weakness. The same concerns apply to supervision-of-supervision. The 4x4x4 model also attends to the emotionally challenging aspects of the work, helping professionals to process and reflect on their experiences, so developing their capacity to think and make decisions for themselves (Wallbank & Woods, 2012, p21):

"Traditional models of supervision tend to emphasise the content of the work being undertaken, rather than the professional delivering the care. This often means a managerial approach is taken through the use of checklists and targets... and the professional suspends their own autonomous decision-making."

Like most other experts, Wallbank and Woods (2012, pp.20-21) suggest separating the normative and restorative aspects of supervision:

"...access to clinical supervision that remained separate to administrative or managerial supervision was rated as significant to community staff... Too often within services the emphasis of clinical supervision is on the content of the work... rather than on building the resilience and autonomy of the professional."

The same points could be made in relation to supervisors, but we should recognize that a healthy organization can also use normative approaches to help supervisors. A major illustration is the IAPT programme in England, which is primarily concerned with case management within an evidence-based clinical system. As we have described IAPT earlier in this book, we will now simply draw out the main normative features that may influence supervisors:

- Training in supervision: in addition to systematic clinical training, the IAPT approach standardizes supervisor development. All supervisors must complete one of the IAPT five-to-seven-day-long training programmes, which are evidence-based in their content and methods, and can include guidelines on supervision.

- Competence framework: training addresses the Roth and Pilling (2007) supervision competencies framework, which provides supervisors with a clear role statement.

- Evaluation: post-training, the supervisors' competencies are assessed and evaluated (staff, peer, supervisee, or self-assessment). This may be achieved through supervisors bringing in tapes of their work with supervisees. For example, Newman-Taylor *et al* (2012) examined the impact of a five-day training course for 28 IAPT supervisors, using a questionnaire based on the Roth and Pilling (2007) supervisory competencies. Such evaluations can provide valuable feedback for supervisors, guiding their competence development and providing encouragement.

- Contextual factors and organizational support are also recognized as important, including protected time for supervision, and an emphasis on supervisees playing a full part in making a success of supervision.

However, the demands of the IAPT programme are exceptional, and the focus on standards and targets can negatively affect staff morale and increase distress and burnout. Surveys of IAPT therapists (Steel *et al,* 2013; Walklet & Percy, 2014) found high levels of emotional exhaustion and noted that this was predicted by high volume workloads, administrative demands, 'target-oriented work', stressful emotional involvement, and a lack of autonomy. A third study (Westwood *et al,* 2017) indicated that supervision was a related protective factor, reducing emotional exhaustion, disengagement, and burnout among IAPT practitioners. To our knowledge there has not yet been a similar analysis of how supervisors cope with the related demands that they face, but effective leadership from managers is likely a protective factor. A review of the 12 best-performing IAPT sites suggested that they were differentiated by clinical leadership that was supportive of staff and:

> *"helped create an innovation environment in which the… leaders supported staff in this enterprise by enabling them to attend multiple continuing professional development events. Staff also received personal feedback on the outcomes that they achieved with their patients, benchmarked against the service's average"* (Clark, 2018, p16).

Although these comments do not specify supervisors, we assume that supervision would be fully supported by such leaders, given that it is explicitly prized within IAPT. One such support mechanism is supervision-of-supervision, and here we give this arrangement a normative slant. In practice, supervision-of-supervision should also include restorative and formative aspects, just like supervision.

Supervision-of-supervision

Earlier in this chapter we considered the important distinctions between formative consultancy, meta-supervision, and supervision-of-supervision. To recap, when supervision-of-supervision is arranged within an organization, it differs in being an obligatory activity within a hierarchical relationship. This is just like clinical supervision, but the next level up in the educational pyramid. This means that the meta-supervisor has formal authority over that supervisor, having been appointed by their employing organization to do this particular job, including in principle the power to observe and direct the work of the supervisor, in keeping with their role and responsibilities.

Supervision-of-supervision appears to be common among some professions, at least in the UK. A survey of UK counselors by Wheeler and King (2000) indicated that 90% of 81 respondents reported that they had supervision for their supervision. Topics included ethical issues, the competence of supervisees, training, and contracts. On average, these respondents rated supervision of supervision as helpful, important, a necessary part of the code of ethics for supervisors, and a practice that they would adopt even if it were not prescribed. This survey indicated that supervision-of-supervision was perceived as supportive, and had normative aspects, such as answering questions about supervision roles, functions and responsibilities.

One of the rare studies of supervision-of-supervision was reported by Kisthinios and Carlson (2019), who analysed the content of over 100 handwritten records of a sample of three supervision-of-supervision sessions, involving a group of eight supervisors within a university nurse training programme. They met for 90 minutes six times a year, in time allocated by the employer for the participation of the supervisors. The meta-supervisors were a nurse lecturer and an experienced clinical supervisor, who took the participating supervisors through these steps:

"1. Warm up;
2. All group members take turns to describe situations they want/need to reflect on;
3. The group members choose which situation to process;
4. The 'case holder' presents (their) situation based on (their) thoughts, feelings and actions;
5. Questions are asked to the case holder to clarify the situation presented;
6. The participants in turn reflect on the case presented by clarifying what they thought, felt and would have done in the same situation as originally presented;
7. The case holder reflects on what (they) have learned and can perhaps do differently the next time when encountering the same situation;
8. Open reflection to add or change any thoughts on the situation presented;
9. When time allows; all group members reflect on what they have learned" (p403).

Through this procedure, two broad themes were noted from these supervisors' group supervision of the nursing students. The framework for supervision was the focus of 48 of 117 records (the educational process), with 'psychological aspects' the most common (69 records). These aspects included 'challenging group members' (e.g. not participating appropriately; defying the supervisor; reluctant to have supervision). Fifteen of the records concerned the meta-supervisors' emotional reactions to such aspects (e.g. being afraid or worried; self-doubt). In turn, nine of the records concerned group members' feeling reactions, such as being shaken by experiencing difficult clinical situations. Normatively focused records included the meta-supervisors' role, job status and grading in relation to supervision, handling adverse incidents, standards of nursing care, and offering advice. Kisthinios and Carlson (2019, p405) concluded that "...meta-supervision provides clinical supervisors with support and engagement in the clinical supervisor role...", helping supervisors with group relations, deepening their understanding of the supervision role, and guiding them on the educational aspects. Unlike the dubious stance of The Swedish Society of Nursing (2015), Kisthinios and Carlson (2019) drew out implications for training meta-supervisors.

Vignette: Restorative supervision in a problematic work context

My new management position was to oversee training and research and to supervise clinicians who were providing training and consultation to agency staff and staff at partner agencies. After arriving at the agency, I learned that at least three individuals had held my 'new' position. The CEO informed me that he had fired two of these individuals because they were not aligned with his strategic vision and had clearly minimized his description of agency unrest in my initial interviews. I had never experienced such a problematic environment where staff had become paranoid about their jobs and each other and were unable to work together effectively. My immediate concern was: How can I protect my staff and consultants from this toxic environment?

The consultant I was most excited to supervise had been trained in CBT but was still in a learning mode as to how to implement a newly developed training package. I did not want the challenging work environment to negatively impact her learning experience and growth. Most importantly, we had the opportunity to positively impact many client's lives and they needed to be the priority. As the months went on, we continued to build our relationship and I watched her grow into a confident and competent consultant and trainer. Then a critical event occurred when one of the agency training sites balked at evidence-based training and clinicians and site supervisors were highly critical of this trainer. Essentially, they refused to accept evidence-based training and their local manager appeared to either support them or failed to take corrective action. As a result, my supervisee was caught in the middle and blamed herself for the problems, feeling very anxious and demoralized. I painfully watched as her confidence began to fade and knew that I had to take action. Consistent with the history of my predecessors' experiences with the CEO and senior leaders, persistent appeals to leadership for clarification of agency policy and support to resolve this conflict during a critical period were unsuccessful. I judged it wise in the short term to leave that issue for another day.

Staying within a CBT framework, we worked together to continuously challenge her typical way of responding where she tended to take things personally and blame herself. I had joined this supervisee to train two groups of individuals both within the agency and at a partner agency site and had directly observed her and concluded that her teaching style was effective and she received excellent feedback. After working with the supervisee using questioning, feedback and formulation and engaging in meetings with staff, it became apparent that lack of organizational institutional support for evidence-based practices represented the crux of the problem and my supervisee was 'caught in the middle.'

Despite my best efforts as a supervisor, the constant criticism was taxing and created the need to search for additional ways to support my supervisee as she continued to develop expertise. Fortunately, my supervisee had two colleagues who were also providing training and consultation. One supervisee had had a similar experience with this same training site and was able to relate, providing support and empathy. The second colleague was a master trainer who was providing additional supervision to both individuals to assist them in developing competency in the CBT model. The three colleagues were able to encourage each other and provide social support to help normalize and provide buffers against the stressful situation.

I also focused on strengthening my relationship with this supervisee. Overall, she was incredibly sweet and very sensitive, which made it even more difficult for me to observe the impact that the critical site was having on her. I needed to give her space to talk about her feelings. At times, I would challenge thinking errors and clarify feelings, while at other times I would refrain from challenging and offer support and empathy. She learned to challenge thinking errors that had resulted from conflicts within the organization and was able to recognize the positive impact she had on trainees and their work with clients. At the end of our 16-month supervisory relationship when I left the organization, due to fundamental organizational leadership problems that were negatively impacting my work, my supervisee had grown into an independent, confident and competent trainer.

5. Summary

We began this chapter by asking: How can we best support supervisors? As we close, our answer is that training and education represent the primary options, designed to raise supervisory competence and capability. As with staff training in general, consultancy, mentoring and supervision-of-supervision are evidence-based ways of adapting and strengthening supervisors' proficiency, and are vital to the maintenance of improved supervision. And, consistent with a supportive style of supervision, supervisors also benefit from consultancy with a restorative emphasis, alongside management support (e.g. by implementing peer support and peer consultation arrangements). Supervision-of-supervision is a particularly effective option, and appears to be common among some professions, and survey respondents rated it as helpful, important, and necessary (Wheeler & King, 2000). A second rare study of supervision-of-supervision was reported by Kisthinios and Carlson (2019), in which sessions were systematically structured to encourage critical reflection on supervision, and included normative topics (e.g. supervisors' roles, job status and grading). The authors concluded that supervision-of-supervision helped supervisors with group relations, supervision roles, and educational aspects, indicating that a normative focus within supervision-of-supervision can be supportive to supervisors.

The IAPT programme implementation can be taken as a model of a highly successful national effort, which started with the reallocation of central funds. Just as the British government made a financial commitment to IAPT, organizations and clinical leadership internationally must buy into supportive supervision. And, just as a strong financial argument persuaded the British government, others may also be persuaded by the empirical data that make the argument for the cost-effectiveness of supportive supervision (e.g. Bourne *et al*, 2019; Shanafelt & Noseworthy, 2017).

Once committed to investing in supervision, organizations play the key role in supporting its successful implementation through clinical leadership, providing a facilitating environment that removes barriers (logistics, scheduling, performance and productivity demands, etc.) and which strengthens boosters, promoting a culture that values supervision (Lynch & Happel, 2008; White & Winstanley, 2009), encourages staff to make use of supervision, and which develops and rewards supervisors. Creating a culture that values supervision in these ways includes the supportive aspect, addressing practitioners' distress directly, also enabling indirect help by encouraging a culture that values networking, peer support and other types of informal social support. In addition, both formal and informal support can foster individual well-being and restorative improvements in the wider organization.

Chapter 9: Conclusions and Recommendations

1. Introduction

Burnout is a significant and growing problem, with a calamitous and costly cascade of adverse consequences for clinicians, patients, their families, not to mention healthcare organizations. Although prevalence estimates vary considerably (van Mol *et al*, 2015), statistics typically indicate that at least one-third of the healthcare workforce experience some degree of burnout at any one time. This 'alarming' prevalence of workplace burnout appears to be a consistent finding across international studies (Adriaenssens *et al*, 2014, p10; Bourne *et al*, 2019). The problem is even more concerning when one considers the knock-on effects that burnout has all the way through the healthcare system, contributing significantly to sickness/absence among staff, lost organizational productivity, and resulting in accidents that harm patients (Panagioti *et al*, 2018). In turn, the cascade of costs for society of these successive, adverse consequences within healthcare is enormous (Naczenski, 2017). Furthermore, healthcare workers' families and loved ones often suffer the effects of burnout (Thoits, 2010). Therefore, burnout merits urgent attention, as do the related clinical and systemic consequences of distress at work. This conclusion is reinforced by the reaction of The World Health Organization, which has for the first time included burnout in its list of 'factors influencing health status or contact with health services' (WHO, 2019, https://www.who.int/mental_health/evidence/burn-out/en/).

Enhanced practitioner well-being is the perfect counterpoint to these problems, replacing them with a virtuous cycle associated with numerous benefits. Psychological well-being at work concerns emotions associated with expertise, with feelings of choice and control, recognition and reward, support and validation (Begat and Severinsson, 2006). The goal is work 'engagement', the polar opposite of burnout. It refers to social, physical and psychological well-being (e.g. having positive relationships with colleagues; experiencing positive emotions about one's work). Engagement is also correlated with improved work performance (e.g. greater vigour, dedication, and absorption). This positive or virtuous cycle also reduces sickness/absence and accidents, enhancing organizational effectiveness so that staff provide high-quality patient care. In short, adaptive personal coping strategies (and other favourable individual characteristics, such as eliciting social support) contribute to a healthy, adaptive organization.

2. Supportive clinical supervision holds great promise

After an extensive review using an evidence-based approach, what can we now conclude about minimizing burnout, while maximizing the psychological well-being of healthcare workers? Our answer is that supportive clinical supervision is an especially promising approach, based on the distinctive advantages of this leadership role, the straightforward and cost-effective techniques, and the strong links to the organizational determinants of well-being:

■ **Unique leadership role:** Because supervisors combine multiple roles to a unique extent (Knudson *et al*, 2008), they are exceptionally well-placed to address burnout and to foster staff empowerment. Unlike any other individual in the healthcare workplace, the supervisor can consider the organizational context (alleviating depression); raise professional issues to relieve stressors (enhancing well-being); provide training and education (improving personal accomplishment); and to offer social support in ways that a manager cannot. Supervision not only benefits supervisees, it can also enable organizational functioning. Indeed, supervision is possibly the single most valuable organizational support and is a signature leadership method for enhancing personal and professional coping strategies among healthcare staff, in addition to maximizing social support and minimizing stressors (APA, 2015; Department of Health, 2016).

■ **Straightforward techniques:** Although easy to learn and apply, supportive supervision continues to be rare, a minor and under-valued aspect of clinical supervision (e.g. Novoa-Gomez *et al*, 2019). With the right organizational climate, including training and ongoing support for supervisors, the dominant formative and normative functions of supervision can be better balanced up, to make the supportive function a distinctively important aspect of supervision. Figure 9.1 summarizes the techniques and their positive outcomes. The left-hand column of this dendrogram lists seven broad supervision methods, each with the associated techniques and objectives (e.g. 'supporting staff' by offering 'social support' in order to 'buffer them against stressors'). The middle column then lists the associated outcomes, classified as primary (prevention), secondary (stress management) or tertiary prevention (rehabilitation). Supporting staff can lead to reducing their workload and role confusion. These processes contribute towards the purpose of supervision: preventing harm to patients and promoting psychological well-being in staff. More detailed, procedural accounts of these methods can be found in Chapter 3 (Table 3.1) and Chapter 6.

■ **Economical methods:** Supervision needs to be provided regularly, with the minimum frequency and duration as defined by healthcare workers' professional bodies (usually at least an hour per week, at least during initial professional training). In our review of 25 research studies (Chapter 3), we found a range between an hour per week and an hour per month. As many of these 25 studies concerned general clinical supervision, the supportive element of such supervision may only have averaged 15 minutes per fortnight and was often provided within a group format. This makes 'regular' supportive supervision a feasible and highly efficient use of staff time. As noted earlier, such relatively minor resource commitments, together with the huge financial costs of healthcare accidents, contribute to a strong 'business case' for supportive supervision (Shanafelt & Noseworthy, 2017).

- **Effective intervention:** While the evidence-base is weak, research consistently indicates that supportive supervision works, with no indication of harm (e.g. Dugani *et al*, 2018; Edwards *et al*, 2006). We can conclude that supportive supervision helps healthcare staff to feel restored and empowered, helping them to minimize their distress (usually measured as burnout). It helps by developing resilience, encouraging adaptive coping with stressful workplaces, by accessing more social support from peers, and through becoming more competent. In turn, such improvements contribute to better organizational functioning, as indicated by multiple outcomes (improved staff morale and relationships; better peer support; enhanced organizational climate and work satisfaction; staff feeling in control at work; staff retention). Furthermore, studies indicate that the higher the quality of supervision, the better it works. This positive conclusion is entirely consistent with relevant theory, expert consensus, and the findings from neighbouring literatures.

- **Enhancing the organizational foundations of well-being:** As summarized in Figure 9.1 (primary prevention), supervision can contribute to better management of workplace stressors by combining personal and organizational interventions, which tends to be most effective (e.g. Holman *et al*, 2018; West *et al*, 2016). A combined and collaborative approach is incorporated into our definition of supportive supervision in Chapter 2: "... *supportive supervision sometimes attempts to improve the workplace, either directly, through the actions of the supervisor (e.g. liaising with service managers), or indirectly, through guiding and empowering the supervisee (e.g. jointly formulating environmental stressors; discussing and enacting plans to reduce stressors)."* Other examples are reducing interpersonal conflicts; solving system problems through participatory action research; reviewing and adjusting workloads (numbers, tasks, or patient types); matching workplace goals to the supervisee's skills, while maintaining some stimulating challenge; enhancing communication skills; and encouraging peer support (Howard, 2008; Koivu *et al*, 2012).

These characteristics are the essence of what makes supportive clinical supervision an especially promising approach. We next recommend actions that would enable it to flourish.

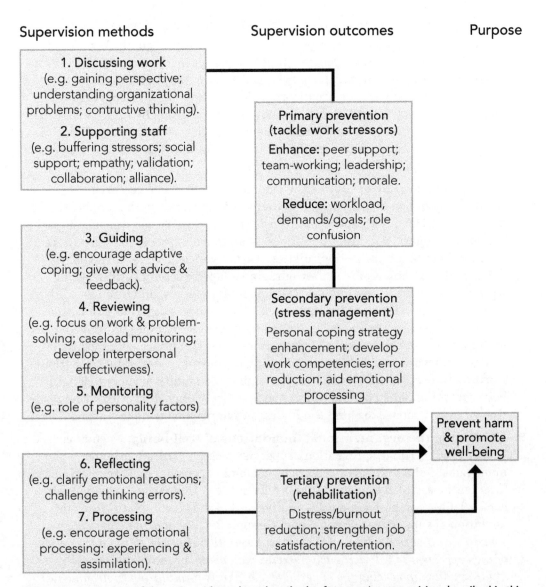

Supervision methods

1. Discussing work
(e.g. gaining perspective;
understanding organizational
problems; contructive thinking).

2. Supporting staff
(e.g. buffering stressors; social
support; empathy; validation;
collaboration; alliance).

3. Guiding
(e.g. encourage adaptive
coping; give work advice &
feedback).

4. Reviewing
(e.g. focus on work & problem-
solving; caseload monitoring;
develop interpersonal
effectiveness).

5. Monitoring
(e.g. role of personality factors)

6. Reflecting
(e.g. clarify emotional reactions;
challenge thinking errors).

7. Processing
(e.g. encourage emotional
processing: experiencing &
assimilation).

Supervision outcomes

Primary prevention
(tackle work stressors)
Enhance: peer support;
team-working; leadership;
communication; morale.

Reduce: workload,
demands/goals; role
confusion

Secondary prevention
(stress management)
Personal coping strategy
enhancement; develop
work competencies; error
reduction; aid emotional
processing

Tertiary prevention
(rehabilitation)
Distress/burnout
reduction; strengthen job
satisfaction/retention.

Purpose

Prevent harm
& promote
well-being

Figure 9.1: A summary of the main evidence-based methods of supportive supervision described in this book, together with their principal restorative outcomes. These outcomes help to prevent personal distress, and to promote well-being among supervisees. In turn, this reduces the likelihood of harm to patients and increases clinical effectiveness. This summary assumes organizational commitment as the context.

3. Recommended actions

What are the most important action implications that arise from these conclusions? The implications for supervisors, supervisees (clinicians and trainees), and clinical managers have been detailed throughout the book, with recommendations for researchers in Chapter 3. We now distil these down to the top three practical recommendations for future action, continuing our emphasis on primary, secondary and tertiary prevention, as set out in Figure 9.1. These steps will hopefully help to guide the next phase of research and training, leading to improved practice and to greater psychological well-being.

Recommendations for supervisors

One priority for primary prevention (i.e. tackling workplace stressors) is to ensure that supervision is provided first to the neediest (triage). This may be prioritizing any supervisee who is experiencing exceptional distress, or more predictably it will be novices who need help most. From our review of research, it seems that younger and less experienced staff tend to have weaker coping strategies (due to immaturity), less social support, less satisfying work, and more unrealistic expectations (Rupert *et al,* 2015; Bourne *et al,* 2019). This increases the correlation between younger staff members and burnout, including an intention to leave the job (Simionato & Simpson, 2017). It follows that younger staff are a priority group for supportive supervision, which should feature a clear structure and lots of practical guidance to reflect the novices' developmental level as young professionals (Stoltenberg *et al,* 2014).

Supervisors should attend to individual personality characteristics that influence how individuals tackle their work, in that some differences between supervisees (e.g. openness to experiencing; resilience) impact on the supervisor and thereby on supervision outcomes (Green *et al,* 2014). Chow *et al* (2015) found that the 'deliberate practice' of clinical skills led to greater effectiveness (i.e. sustained, effortful, and challenging practice, guided by feedback on clinical outcomes). Examples of deliberate practice that these authors cited as especially valuable were supervisees reviewing and reflecting on relevant and cognitively demanding therapy recordings privately and clinical supervision that included review of difficult/non-progressing cases. Therefore, supportive supervision has a role in developing individual differences that support engagement in deliberate practice and other activities that foster clinical effectiveness (e.g. openness to experiential learning).

In terms of secondary prevention (i.e. stress management), a primary supervision goal should be to provide social support, especially emotional support, since support from supervisors is more effective than support from peers (Adriaenssens *et al,* 2014; Stansfield *et al,* 1999). The main engine for this support is the collaborative partnership or working alliance within supervision (see Chapter 8) based on mutual caring, respect, genuineness (openness and honesty), collegial support, empathy, personal warmth, and encouragement (Beinart, 2014). Supervisees are enabled to enter a 'safe base', experiencing trust and security, while feeling valued, enthusiastic and responsive. The alliance is also a practical relationship, similar to the practice of relational leadership (Cummings *et al*, 2010), featuring a shared engagement in the work that can instil confidence and boost coping skills in the supervisee (Mor Barak *et al*, 2009). In turn, this can also empower supervisees to gain and reciprocate essential peer support.

Tertiary prevention (rehabilitation) aims to strengthen job satisfaction and work engagement, improving staff retention. Supervisors should aim to create a non-threatening, supportive setting where the challenges of the workplace environment are considered in conjunction with the personal difficulties of coping at work. In this way, supervisees can be helped to distinguish their responsibilities from those that belong with their managers and service leaders, helping to boost self-esteem, resilience, and empowerment. Just as organizations need to be open to learning and change, so supervisees and supervisors should aim to learn and problem-solve together.

Recommendations for supervisees (clinicians and trainees)

Supervisees can contribute to tackling work stressors by helping their managers and supervisors to ensure that supervision is a regular and useful event. Especially within group supervision, supervisees can analyze the barriers to supervision, and can work on the boosters to supervision (clear communication; participative decision-making; giving constructive feedback to managers). Particularly in situations where the supervisor and the manager are one and the same person, supervisees should be encouraged to play their part by contributing their reflections on their workplace to help everyone to assess and formulate problematic situations (see Table 6.1 in Chapter 6 for more examples). Conversely, where appropriate, supervisees should aim to reframe stressors as workplace challenges, a positive stimulus for personal and professional development. Stressors are not inherently undesirable, and some degree of job challenge is essential for professional development and job satisfaction. There are positive consequences for deploying the right personal coping strategies, as these enable healthcare workers to thrive in relation to manageable stressors, experiencing a sense of well-being and job engagement.

Supervisees can contribute significantly to secondary prevention by playing an active role in their own stress management (e.g. through the accelerated development of their competencies, and the associated job satisfaction). Promising options include encouraging experiential learning opportunities – the closer to 'deliberate practice' the better (Chow *et al*, 2015). Being generally more proactive, prepared and organized, and cultivating resilience are also helpful. Such qualities make supervisees 'supervision ready', leading to better working alliances with supervisors, and better clinical outcomes (Green *et al*, 2014; Rieck *et al*, 2015).

In situations that involve rehabilitation (tertiary prevention), with help supervisees can develop more adaptive personal coping strategies, such as problem-solving, seeking advice, and practical assistance. Adaptive coping strategies enable us to thrive at work, promoting personal effectiveness and well-being (thus contributing to a positive upward spiral, a 'virtuous cycle'). Maladaptive coping strategies revolve around avoidance and escape, leading to a negative downward spiral, the 'vicious cycle' of stress proliferation, culminating in burnout and other forms of personal distress (Adriaenssens *et al*, 2014). Being willing to discuss openly such personal coping efforts and their work-related feelings enables the supervisor to help. For instance, supervisees can guide their supervisors towards the types of support that they most value. In general, the goal is for supervisees to engage fully in the 'experiencing' mode of experiential learning, so that negative emotions can be discussed and resolved in supervision (e.g. comparing their actions with their associated feelings: see Chapter 1 for the definition of 'experiencing'). Enabling supervisees to develop their adaptive coping strategies, resilience, and engagement in supervision lies at the heart of supportive supervision, as indicated by our main summary of evidence-based methods in Table 3.1 (see Chapter 3).

Recommendations for clinical managers

Primary prevention has to start with ensuring that supportive clinical supervision is available, valued, and effective. Supervision needs to be routinely available (weekly or fortnightly, for an hour, in groups or 1:1), although an effective restorative element may only take 10 minutes per fortnight. It also needs to be 'efficacious' (White & Winstanley, 2010, p.18) through including active, experiential methods that conform with evidence-based practice (e.g. Milne & Reiser, 2017). Supervision, when it is done correctly, causes no harm to supervisees or their patients. But supervision that is not done correctly does cause harm (Ellis *et al*, 2014; Mackay *et al*, 2017; Martinko *et al*, 2017). The absence of supervision is associated with maladaptive coping and increased burnout among staff (and other problems, such as high turnover). Practical steps for managers to ensure prevention include organizational policies that clearly endorse supervision and clarify acceptable standards for supervisors and supervisees. Sustainable arrangements should implement these policies, linked to monitoring and joint problem-solving efforts (such as the 'meta-supervision' approach of Gonge & Buus, 2014). Attendance at workshops and policy endorsements of supervision can help to convey the high value placed on supervision within your healthcare organization. To ensure that supervision is effective, managers should require that supervisors attend training workshops (and ideally supervisees too). Clinical supervision is a professional competency and requires specific training and ongoing refinement, like other forms of leadership (Lacerenza *et al*, 2017).

Following training, supervisors require ongoing support and refresher training, both of which could be provided by consultants and which could aid stress management (secondary prevention). For instance, quality control of supervision can be accomplished by monitoring supervisees' perceptions of inadequate or harmful supervision through confidential surveys. This can be supplemented by anonymous links to the organization's HR and OH departments, so that inexperienced or unassertive staff can report unreasonable stressors or unacceptable behaviour (e.g. workplace bullying). These measures can assist in creating a culture in which it is OK to seek support (Pan *et al,* 2017). Other ways that HR can help include confidential coaching, counselling and mentoring services (Mackay, 2017).

In terms of tertiary prevention, managers can help reduce burnout among their staff by increasing the sense of work engagement (Brummelhuis *et al,* 2017). A healthy organizational context also ensures that staff feel supported and valued, which helps with job satisfaction and staff retention (Cutcliffe & McFeely, 2001; Kilcullen, 2007). Not least, managers can use feedback and other indicators to ensure that there is no harmful and unethical supervision, which can start or aggravate supervisees' distress (Tepper, 2000; Ellis *et al,* 2014). We recommend a collaborative style of 'action research' or 'practice-based enquiry' in order to assess, understand and improve workplaces (e.g. audits; force-field analysis; staff surveys). Creating a culture that is educational, self-critical and responsive can greatly boost the healthcare workplace (Shanafelt & Noseworthy, 2017; Tomlinson, 2015). The business case for implementing supportive supervision is compelling (Shanafelt & Noseworthy, 2017), aside from the moral imperative to accord the work environment serious and joined-up attention, alongside the staff. Giving the workplace environment more attention communicates to staff a supportive, collaborative, fair, and understanding approach. It suggests a kind of empathy that can go a long way in raising staff morale.

4. Limitations of our approach

There are several aspects of this book that we recognize as weaknesses, or which we fear that readers will deem limitations. Regrettably, these may reduce the book's value for some readers. Here we pick out our main concerns and explain our thinking, considering some ways forward.

Ignoring well-being

The preceding section emphasised the prevention of burnout through individual and organizational interventions, which is a rather negative or pathological perspective that gave less attention to the role of psychological well-being. This attentional bias is actually fairly typical of the whole book, an imbalanced treatment that could be seen as maintaining the status quo. One reason for prioritizing burnout is to address it first because it is the primary concern reported by individuals and organizational leaders (e.g. minimizing adverse events to reduce harm to patients). To ignore or minimize burnout would risk alienating those who are already grappling with it and who are best-placed to intervene. We also sought to pick up from where things stand at present: rather than being too idealistic, we aimed to anchor our recommendations in current practice. From that foundation we could set out a realistic path to improved practice.

Another reason for emphasising burnout is that well-being interacts with it in complex ways, i.e. processes that can obscure important insights and complicate valuable support efforts. Rather than risk confusing matters, we preferred to keep the basis for our recommendations straightforward. Specifically, we used prevention as our organizing principle, when in theory we could have argued that we should be promoting well-being. We hope and trust that readers who have considered the whole book will realize that in fact we regard well-being as vital to the ultimate purpose of supervision (as depicted in Figure 9.1). The methods in that figure are also as relevant to promoting well-being as to preventing burnout (e.g. personal coping strategy enhancement). In essence, burnout and well-being are two sides of the same coin, one featuring a vicious cycle, the other a virtuous cycle of the same fundamental variables in the support model. In this sense, the methods that boost well-being prevent burnout primary, secondary and tertiary. For example, this model (see Chapter 2) encourages the kind of positive engagement with work and general 'organizational citizenship' that can result in primary prevention through collaboration with managers over communication or feedback systems, or redefining roles. In our own experience, this has included addressing long waiting lists through agreeing more systemic and mutually beneficial ways of working (e.g. staff training to broaden the base for psychological help). Hopefully, in future a primary emphasis on well-being will be more appropriate and timely.

Weak research base for supportive supervision

Our conclusions and recommendations should also be tempered by a clear recognition of the weak status of research on supportive supervision. This includes the scarcity of studies and the generally limited rigour of the studies (e.g. most studies are correlational, almost entirely based on self-report questionnaires). Our criticisms of the existing research literature close Chapter 3, alongside our suggestions to researchers. A weak research literature limits the confidence we can place in the findings and means that there are relatively few suggestions for enhancing supportive supervision. It is only thanks to our approach to 'evidence' that we were able to produce a book with an evidence-based emphasis. While this approach enables us to generate practical recommendations and other useful guidance to supervisors, we are aware that academic researchers will be understandably wary of our unconventional strategy.

A broad brush approach to the evidence base

Given the scarcity of high-quality research studies of supportive supervision, our strategy for assembling a broader evidence base has been inclusive and integrative. This is a tried and tested one, developed through our experience of researching 'evidence-based clinical supervision' (Milne, 2018; Milne & Reiser, 2017). However, there are definite limitations to this approach. As described in Chapter 1, our strategy includes searching carefully for the best available research studies, recognizing that all research has weaknesses. We are certainly not blinded by the letters RCT. Some of the 'best' research for our purposes is of limited experimental rigour, but high in other qualities that we value (e.g. studying supervision qualitatively, in relation to the organizational context). An example has been our exclusive focus on effective interventions, rather than all relevant interventions. This is a pragmatic method, the 'best-evidence synthesis' approach, which we used to select and review the key group of research studies in Chapter 3. We are keenly aware that this is a rare approach, and some would question it for not considering the full range of findings. While there is undoubted value in overviewing a whole research field, the danger is that the negative findings cancel out the positive ones, leaving reviewers unable to recommend any best practices. In a pragmatic context where clinical supervision is already being widely provided in healthcare, our stance is that it is better to figure out and encourage best practices whenever possible. Contrast this with traditional approaches to reviewing the literature. For instance, Pollock *et al* (2017) felt unable to draw any firm conclusions from their sample of 19 supervision studies, whereas Alfonsson *et al* (2017) deemed only five of over 4,000 supervision studies that they located to be worthy of scrutiny. In our view, such strict inclusion criteria do not guarantee valid conclusions either, and risk 'throwing the baby out with the bath-water'. Indeed, none of the five studies selected by Alfonsson *et al* (2017) actually assessed what happened in the name of supervision (i.e. no intervention adherence or fidelity information was reported) and all of the studies relied on self-report questionnaires to assess the outcomes. Such fundamental methodological weaknesses confound any firm conclusions, no matter that the research design is an RCT. In addition, much can be gleaned from research that uses a variety of methodologies, provided that the designs are interpretable (e.g. n=1 studies). However, we completely agree that more high-quality studies are needed and that, once these exist, traditional review methods are ideal.

We also sought to arrive at valid conclusions on the best ways to provide supportive supervision by extrapolating from neighbouring literatures, which is an inclusive stance adopted on the basis that there is much to gain from identifying areas of overlap and mutual interest. This we supplemented by considering other parts of our formula for evidence-based practice (see Chapter 1, Figure 1.1), especially the integration of relevant theory and the consideration of expert consensus statements.

Incomplete list of support methods

We are well aware that the interventions we have covered are only a sample of the supportive arrangements for clinicians, and that many supervisors will have benefitted from other established or popular methods, such as Balint groups (Yazdankhahfard *et al,* 2019), focus groups (Reid *et al,* 2003), coaching (Subramaniam *et al,* 2015), 'personal-professional development' PPD) (Gillmer and Markus, 2003), or combinations of similar methods by other names. We do recognize that these are potentially helpful but chose to focus on the interventions that were identified and empirically demonstrated through our review of the most relevant research (e.g. preceptorship: see Chapter 3). In the future, perhaps research studies of supportive supervision will evaluate these methods.

A related problem is that the packages of techniques used within these methods are typically presented only in the most general terms (i.e. they are largely unspecified and unquantified), like much of the clinical supervision field (Roth *et al,* 2010). This meant that we could not bypass the method's label and conduct a detailed content analysis (or 'unpacking') of the specific techniques used. As a result, we could not isolate and assess the evidence for the various techniques used within these various support methods (such as debriefing or coping strategy enhancement). Future research should include detailed support method specification (e.g. manuals and guidelines) and associated measurement, which would make it possible to aggregate the evidence for support techniques across the different methods (e.g. the effectiveness of debriefing in coaching, focus groups, and PPD).

Managers maligned

In striving to redress the prevailing assumption that individual clinicians are to blame for burnout, in this book we have often laid responsibility at the feet of their managers. We must avoid overdoing this and instead give due regard to the valuable role played by managers. In addition, we realize that our recommendations place significant responsibility on managers (and other organizational leaders), without a corresponding restorative emphasis. That is, while we have considered support arrangements for supervisors and supervisees in great detail, we have not matched that concern in the case of their managers. This is inconsistent with our systemic, inclusive approach. But this treatment of managers is not because we deem such support unnecessary, more that we believe that the topic requires another book. Indeed, many of the methods of supportive supervision appear highly relevant to managers, including consultancy and peer support. Both are leadership roles, after all. Therefore, we regard an effective organization as one that supports all of its members, and our seeming neglect of managers is for purely practical purposes. A saving grace may be that many managers are also the supervisors, in which role we hope that they access the support that they need.

5. Final thoughts

In summary, these conclusions and associated recommendations are wide-ranging, indicating how the different stakeholders can all play a valuable part in minimizing burnout, while maximizing well-being. This is consistent with our collaborative and constructive approach, and with the support model that underpins this book (Chapter 2). Considerable effort is entailed in implementing these recommendations, but the outcomes are well worth it. Much has been written about burnout and well-being in the workplace, and the challenges are increasing:

> *"There is an urgent need to develop interventions that address the high*
> *levels of stress, burnout, and dissatisfaction among mental health nurses"*
> (Scottish Executive, 2006, p57).

The necessity of a healthy workforce for a healthy nation is gaining recognition (Hancock, 2018), as underlined with growing urgency by The World Health Organization (2019). The calamitous cascade of adverse consequences that are associated with burnout was captured in Table 9.1. Welcome as these policy statements are, they have not yet been matched by improved organizational or leadership practices (Department of Health, 2016; Novoa-Gomez *et al,* 2019). Among the possible explanations for this are inadequate training in supportive supervision and the lack of a sound evidence base for its practice. We very much hope that this book provides some impetus for developing those overdue interventions by articulating the nature and significance of supportive supervision as an evidence-based, leadership-focused intervention (for a summary, see Figure 9.1). It is clear to us that supportive supervision is a unique and surprisingly powerful intervention, possessing the capability to efficiently boost psychological well-being among all staff members, while facilitating professional practice and the quality of patient care. Other important benefits include improving staff retention, while reducing the accidents and clinical errors that harm patients. This book is the first to provide an evidence-based, psychological explanation of how supportive supervision achieves such significant results. We hope that you will now feel empowered to play your part in implementing supportive supervision.

References

Addo MA, Stephen AI & Kirkpatrick P (2012) Acute mental health/psychiatric nurses' experiences of clinical supervision in promoting their well-being in their workplace: a systematic review. *JBI Library Systematic Review* 10 (56) 1–16.

Adriaenssens J, de Gucht V & Maes S (2014) Determinants and prevalence of burnout in emergency nurses: a systematic review of 25 years of research. *International Journal of Nursing Studies* 52, 649–661. doi: 10.1016/ijnurstu.2014.11.004.

Ahola K, Toppinen-Tanner S & Seppanen J (2017) Interventions to alleviate burnout symptoms and to support return to work among employees with burnout: Systematic review and meta-analysis. *Burnout Research* 4, 1–11.

Alfonsson S, Parling T, Spännargård A, Andersson G & Tobias Lundgren T (2018) The effects of clinical supervision on supervisees and patients in cognitive behavioural therapy: a systematic review. *Cognitive Behaviour Therapy* 47, 206–228. doi: 10.1080/16506073.2017.1369559.

Almeida DM, Davis KD, Lee S, Lawson KM, Walter K & Moen P (2016) Supervisor support buffers daily psychological and physiological reactivity to work-to-family conflict. *Journal of Marriage and Family*, 78, 165–179. doi:10.1111/jomf.12252.

American Psychiatric Association (2013) *Diagnostic and Statistical Manual of Mental Disorders* (5th edition). Washington, DC: American Psychiatric Association Press.

American Psychological Association [APA] (2006) Evidence-based practice in psychology: APA presidential task force on evidence-based practice. *American Psychologist* 61, 271–285. doi:10.1037/0003-066X.61.4.271.

American Psychological Association (2015) Guidelines for clinical supervision in health service psychology. *American Psychologist* 70, 33–46. https://doi.org/10.1037/a0038112.

Arnold KA, Turner N, Barling J, Kelloway EK, & McKee MC (2007) Transformational leadership and psychological well-being: The mediating role of meaningful work. *Journal of Occupational Health Psychology* 12, 193–203.

Aronson KA, Sieveking N, Laurenceau J-P and Bellet W (2003) Job satisfaction of psychiatric hospital employees: A new measure of an old concern. *Administration and Policy in Mental Health*, 30, 47–452.

Aronsson, G., Theorell, T., Grape, T, Hammarström A , Hogstedt C , Marteinsdottir I , Skoog I, Träskman-Bendz L & Hall C (2017) A systematic review including meta-analysis of work environment and burnout symptoms. *Biomed Public Health*, 17, 264, 1-13. https://doi.org/10.1186/s12889-017-4153-7.

Australian Psychological Society (2008) APS peer consultation network guidelines. Melbourne: Australian Psychological Society.

Australian Psychological Society (2011) Guidelines on continuing professional development (CPD) requirements. Melbourne: Australian Psychological Society.

Avortri GS, Nabukalu JB & Nabyonga-Orem J (2019) Supportive supervision to improve service delivery in low-income countries: is there a conceptual problem or a strategy problem? *British Medical Journal Global Health*, 4, 1-6. doi: 10.1136/bmjgh-2018-001151.

Awa WL, Plaumann M & Walter U (2010) Burnout prevention: a review of intervention programmes. *Patient Education & Counselling* 78, 184–190.

Bailey C, Blake C, Schriver M, Cubaka VK, Thomas T & Hilber M (2015) A systematic review of supportive supervision as a strategy to improve primary healthcare services in sub-Saharan Africa. *Gynaecology & Obstetrics*, 132, 117-25. doi: 10.1016/j.ijgo.2015.10.004.

Bailin A, Bearman SK & Sal R (2018) Clinical supervision of mental health professionals serving youth: Format and micro-skills. *Administration and Policy in Mental Health and Mental Health Services Research*, 45, 800-812. https://doi.org/10.1007/s10488-018-0865-y

Balint M (1954) Analytic training and training analysis. *International Journal Psycho-Analysis* 35, 157–162.

Bambling M, King R, Raue P, Schweitzer R & Lambert W (2006) Clinical supervision: Its influence on client-rated working alliance and client symptom reduction in the brief treatment of major depression. *Psychotherapy Research* 16, 317–331.

Barker KK & Hunsley J (2013) The use of theoretical models in psychology supervisor development research from 1994 to 2010: A Systematic Review. *Canadian Psychology* 54, 176–185.

Barnett JE & Cooper N (2009) Creating a culture of self-care. *Clinical Psychology: Science & Practice* 16, 16–20.

Bearman SK, Bailin A & Sale R (2019) Graduate school training in CBT supervision to develop knowledge and competencies. *The Clinical Supervisor,* 39, 66-84. doi: 10.1080/07325223.2019.1663459

Bearman SK, Schneiderman RL, & Zoloth E (2017) Building an evidence base for effective supervision practices: An analogue experiment of supervision to increase EBT fidelity. *Administration and Policy in Mental Health and Mental Health Services Research*, 44, 293-307. https://doi.org/10.1007/s1048 8-016-0723-8.

Beck AT, Davis DD & Freeman A (Eds) (2015) *Cognitive Therapy of Personality Disorders*. New York: Guilford Publications.

Beck JS (1995) *Cognitive Therapy: Basics and Beyond*. New York: Guilford Publications.

Beckman M, Forsberg L, Lindqvist H et al (2017) *The dissemination of motivational interviewing in Swedish county councils: Results of a randomized controlled trial.* PLoS ONE 12(7): e0181715.https://doi.org/10.1371/journal.pone.0181715

Begat I & Severinsson E (2006) Reflection on how clinical nursing supervision enhances nurses' experiences of well-being related to their psychosocial work environment. *Journal of Nursing Management* 14, 610–616.

Beidas RS & Kendall PC (2010) Training therapists in evidence-based practice: A critical review of studies from a systems-contextual perspective. *Clinical Psychology: Science & Practice*, 17, 1–30.

Beinart H (2014) Building and sustaining the supervisory relationship. In: CE Watkins and DL Milne (Eds) *The Wiley International Handbook of Clinical Supervision*. Chichester: Wiley-Blackwell, pp257–281.

Bennett-Levy J (2019) Why therapists should walk the talk: The theoretical and empirical case for personal practice in therapist training and professional development. *Journal of Behaviour Therapy and Experimental Psychiatry* 62, 133–145.

Bennett-Levy J & Thwaites R (2007) Self and self-reflection in the therapeutic relationship; a conceptual map and practical strategies for the training, supervision and self-supervision of interpersonal skills. In: P Gilbert and RL Leahy (Eds) *The Therapeutic Relationship in Cognitive Behavioural Therapy*. London: Routledge, pp 255–281.

Bennett-Levy J, Thwaites R, Haarhoff B & Perry H (2014) *Experiencing CBT from the inside out: A self-practice / self-reflection workbook for therapists*. New York: Guilford Publications.

Bennett-Levy J, Turner F, Beaty T, Smith M, Paterson B & Farmer S (2001) The value of self-practice of cognitive therapy techniques and self-reflection in the training of cognitive therapists. *Behavioural and Cognitive Psychotherapy* 29 (2) 203–220.

Bohart, A. C., & Tallman, K. (2010). Clients: *The neglected common factor in psychotherapy*. In B. L. Duncan, S. D. Miller, B. E. Wampold, & M. A. Hubble (Eds.), *The heart and soul of change: Delivering what works in therapy* (pp. 83–111). American Psychological Association. https://doi.org/10.1037/12075-003

Beidas RS & Kendall PC (2010) Training therapists in evidence-based practice: A critical review of studies from a systems-contextual perspective. *Clinical Psychology: Science & Practice* 17, 1–30.

Ben-Zur, H & Michael, K (2007) Burnout, social support, and coping at work among social workers, psychologists and nurses. *Social Work in Health Care* 45, 63–82. doi: 10.1300/J010v45n04_04

Berg A, & Hallberg IR (1999) Effects of systematic clinical supervision on psychiatric nurses' sense of coherence, creativity, work-related strain, job satisfaction and view of the effects from clinical supervision: a pre-post test design. *Journal of Psychiatric & Mental Health Nursing* 6, 371–381.

Bernard JM & Goodyear RK (2014) *Fundamentals of Clinical Supervision*. Harlow, Essex: Pearson.

Bertsch KN, Bremer-Landau JD, Inman AG, DeBoer-Kreider ER, Price TA & DeCarlo AL (2014) Evaluation of the critical events in supervision model using gender-related events. *Training and Education in Professional Psychology* 8, 174–181.

Beutler LE, Malik M, Alimohamed S, Harwood TM, Talebi H, Noble S et al (2004) Therapist variables. In: MJ Lambert (Ed) *Bergin and Garfield's Handbook of Psychotherapy and Behaviour Change* (5th ed). New York: Wiley, pp227–306.

Bhatt K & Raman R (2016) Job burnout: a literature review. *Indian Journal of Research* 5, 203–205.

Bhui KS, Dinos S, Stansfeld SA & White PD (2012) A synthesis of the evidence for managing stress at work: A review of the reviews reporting on anxiety, depression, and absenteeism. *Journal of Environmental and Public Health*, 2012, 1-21. doi:10.1155/2012/515874

Blau PM (1964) *Exchange and Power in Social Life*. New York: Wiley.

Blomberg K, Isaksson, A-K, Allvin EE, Bisholt B, Ewertsson M, Engstrom E, Ohlsson U, Johansson S & Gustafsson M (2014) Work stress among newly graduated nurses in relation to workplace and clinical group supervision. *Journal of Nursing Management* 24, 80–87.

Bloom, B.S. (2005) Effects of continuing medical education on improving physician clinical care and patient health: a review of systematic reviews. *International Journal of Technology Assessment in Health Care* 21, 380–385.

Bluestone J, Johnson P, Judith Fullerton J, Carr C, Alderman J & BonTempo J (2013) Effective in-service training design and delivery: evidence from an integrative literature review. *Human Resources for Health* 11, 1-26. doi:10.1186/1478-4491-11-51.

Bond FW & Bunce D (2000) Mediators of change in emotion-focused and problem-focussed worksite stress management interventions. *Journal of Occupational Health Psychology* 5, 156–163.

Bond FW, Hayes SC, Baer RA, Carpenter KM, Guenole N et al (2011) Preliminary psychometric properties of the Acceptance and Action Questionnaire-II. *Behaviour Therapy* 42, 676–688.

Boorman S (2009) *The Final Report of the Independent NHS Health and Well-being Review*. London: Department of Health.

Borders D (2012) Dyadic, triadic, and group models of peer supervision/consultation: What are their components, and is there evidence of their effectiveness? *Clinical Psychologist* 46, 59–71.

Bourne T, Shah H, Falconieri N et al (2019) Burnout, well-being and defensive medical practice among obstetricians and gynaecologists in the UK: cross- sectional survey study. *BMJ Open* 9:e030968. doi:10.1136/ bmjopen-2019-030968.

Bowles N & Young C (1999) An evaluative study of clinical supervision based on Proctor's three function interactive model. *Journal of Advanced Nursing* 30, 958–964.

Bransford JD & Schwartz DL (2009) It takes expertise to make expertise: Some thoughts about why and how. In: KA Ericsson (Ed) *Development of Professional Expertise*. Cambridge University Press, pp432–448.

Browning M & Pront L (2015) Supportive nursing student supervision: an assessment of an innovative approach to student support. *Nurse Education Today* 35, 740–745.

Brown KW & Ryan RM (2003) The benefits of being present: Mindfulness and its role in psychological well-being. *Journal of Personality and Social Psychology* 84, 822–848.

Brummelhuis LLT, Rothbard NP & Uhrich B (2017) Beyond working nine to five: Is working to excess bad for health? *Academy of Management Discoveries* 3, 262–283.

Butler AC, Chapman JE, Forman EM & Beck AT (2006) The empirical status of cognitive-behavioural therapy: a review of meta-analyses. *Clinical Psychology Review* 26, 17–31.

Butterworth T, Carson J, White E, Jeacock J, Clements A & Bishop V (1997) *It's Good to Talk: Clinical Supervision and Mentorship*. Manchester: Manchester University Press.

Buus N, Angel S, Traynor M & Gonge H (2011) Psychiatric nursing staff members' reflections on participating in group-based clinical supervision: A semi-structured interview study. International *Journal of Mental Health Nursing* 20, 95–10.

Buus N, Cassedy P & Gonge H (2013) Developing a manual for strengthening mental health nurses' clinical supervision. *Issues in Mental Health Nursing* 34, 344–349.

Buus N, Delgado C, Traynor M, & Gonge H (2017) Resistance to group clinical supervision: A semi-structured interview study of non-participating mental health nursing staff members. *International Journal of Mental Health Nursing* 27, 83–793. doi: 10.1111/inm.12365

Buus N, Lynch L, & Gonge H (2016) Developing and implementing 'meta-supervision' for mental health nursing staff supervisees: opportunities and challenges. *The Cognitive Behaviour Therapist* 9 9, 1-15. doi:10.1017/S1754470X15000434

Buus N & Gonge H (2009) Empirical studies of clinical supervision in psychiatric nursing: A systematic literature review and methodological critique. *International Journal of Mental Health Nursing* 18, 250–264.

Callahan JL, Almstrom CM, Swift JK, Borja SE & Heath CJ (2009) Exploring the contribution of supervisors to intervention outcomes. *Training and Education in Professional Psychology* 3, 72–77.

Calvert I (2014) Support for midwives: a model of professional supervision based on the recertification programme for midwives in New Zealand. *Women & Birth* 27, 145–150.

Care Quality Commission (2010) *Guidance About Compliance: Essential Standards of Quality and Safety*. Outcome 14: Supporting Workers. London: Care Quality Commission.

Carpenter R (2016) A review of instruments on cognitive appraisal of stress. *Archives of Psychiatric Nursing* 30, 271–279.

Carr A (2006) *The Handbook of Child and Adolescent Psychology*. Hove: Routledge.

Carver CS, Scheier MF & Weintraub JK (1989) Assessing coping strategies: a theoretically based approach. *Journal of Personality and Social Psychology* 56, 267.

Castonguay LG & Hill CE (2017) *How and Why Are Some Therapists Better Than Others? Understanding therapist effects*. Washington, D.C: American Psychological Association.

Center C, Davis M, Detre T, Ford DF, Hansbrough W et al (2003) Confronting depression and suicide in physicians. *Journal of the American Medical Association* 289, 3161–3166.

Chand SP, Chibnall JT & Slavin SJ (2018) Cognitive behavioural therapy for maladaptive perfectionism in medical students: A preliminary investigation. *Academic Psychiatry* 42, 58–61. doi 10.1007/s40596-017-0708-2.

Chang, A, Schyve, PM, Croteau, RJ, O'Leary, DS, & Loeb, JM (2005) The JCAHO patient safety event taxonomy: a standardized terminology and classification schema for near misses and adverse events. *International Journal for Quality in Health Care* 17, 95–105. doi: 10.1093/intqhc/mzi021.

Chena Y, Watson R, Hilton A (2018) The structure of mentors' behaviour in clinical nursing education: Confirmatory factor analysis. *Nurse Education Today* 68, 192–197.

Chow DL, Miller SD, Seidel JA, Kane RT & Thornton JA (2015) The role of deliberate practice in the development of highly effective psychotherapists. *Psychotherapy* 52, 337–345.

Clark DM. (2018) Realising the mass public benefit of evidence-based psychological therapies: The IAPT programme. *Annual Review of Clinical Psychology* 14, 159–183. doi:10.1146/annurev-clinpsy-050817-084833.

Cleary M & Freeman A (2006) Fostering a culture of support in mental health settings: Alternatives to traditional models of clinical supervision. *Issues in Mental Health Nursing* 27, 985–1000.

Clipper B, Cherry B (2015) From transition shock to competent practice: developing preceptors to support new nurse transition. *Journal of Continuing Education in Nursing* 46, 448–454.

Cohen S & Wills TA (1985) Stress, social support, and the buffering hypothesis. *Psychological Bulletin* 98, 10–357.

Connor KM & Davidson JR (2003) Development of a new resilience scale: The Connor–Davidson Resilience Scale (CDRISC). *Depression and Anxiety* 18, 76–82.

Costa PT & McCrae RR (1992) *Revised NEO Five-Factor Personality Inventory: Professional manual.* Odessa, Florida: Psychological Assessment Resources.

Cowen EL (1982) Help is where you find it. *American Psychologist* 37, 385–395.

Craik C (1988) Stress in occupational therapy: how to cope. *British Journal of Occupational Therapy* 51, 40.

Cummings GG, MacGregor T, Davey M, Lee H, Wong CA, Lo E, Muise M & Stafford E (2010) Leadership styles and outcome patterns for the nursing workforce and work environment: A systematic review. *International Journal of Nursing Studies* 47, 363–385. doi:10.1016/j.ijnurstu.2009.08.006.

Cutcliffe J & McFeely S (2001) Practice nurses and their 'lived experience' of clinical supervision. *British Journal of Nursing* 10, 312–323.

Dawson JB (1926) The casework supervisor in a family agency. *Family* 6, 293–295.

DeFife JA & Hilsenroth MJ (2011) Starting off on the right foot: Common factor elements in early psychotherapy process. *Journal of Psychotherapy Integration* 21, 172.

Delgado C, Roche M, Fethney J & Foste K (2019) Workplace resilience and emotional labour of Australian mental health nurses: Results of a national survey. *International Journal of Mental Health Nursing*, 29, 35-46. doi: 10.1111/inm.12598.

Delgadillo J, Saxon D & Barkham M (2018) Associations between therapists' occupational burnout and their patients' depression and anxiety treatment outcomes. *Depression & Anxiety* 35, 844–850.

Delvaux N, Razavi D, Marchal S, Bredart A, Farvacques C & Slachmuylde J-L (2004) Effects of a 105 hours psychological training program on attitudes, communication skills and occupational stress in oncology: a randomized study. *British Journal of Cancer* 90, 106–114.

Department of Health (1993) *A Vision for the Future. Report of the Chief Nursing Officer.* HMSO, London: UK.

Department of Health (2004) *National Standards, Local Action.* London: Department of Health.

Department of Health (2016) *Proposals for Changing the System of Midwifery Supervision in the UK.* London: Department of Health.

Department of Veterans Affairs (2014) *Interim Report: Review of patient wait times, scheduling practices, and alleged patient deaths at the Phoenix Health Care System.* Washington, DC: VA Office of Inspector General, Veterans Health Administration, Department of Veterans Affairs.

Dewa CS, Loong D, Bonato S & Trojanowski L (2017) The relationship between physician burnout and quality of healthcare in terms of safety and acceptability: a systematic review. *BMJ Open* 7 (6) e015141.

Dimidjian S, Hollon SD, Dobson KS, Schmaling KB, Kohlenberg RJ, Addis ME & Atkins DC (2006) Randomized trial of behavioural activation, cognitive therapy and antidepressant medication in the acute treatment of adults with major depression. *Journal of Consulting and Clinical Psychology* 74, 658.

Dorsey S, Pullmann MD, Kerns SEU, Jungbluth N, Meza R, Thompson K & Berliner L (2017) *The Juggling Act of Supervision in Community Mental Health: Implications for Supporting Evidence-Based Treatment. Administrative Policy & Mental Health* 44, 838–852. doi 10.1007/s10488-017-0796-z

Dorsey S, Kerns SEU, Lucid L, Pullmann MD, Harrison JP, Berliner L, Thompson K, Deblinger, E (2018) Objective coding of content and techniques in workplace-based supervision of an EBT in public mental health. *Implementation Science*, 13, doi: 10.1186/s 13012-017-1708-3

Dugani S, Afari H, Hirschhorn LR, Ratcliffe H, Veillard J, Martin G & Bitton A (2018) Prevalence and factors associated with burnout among frontline primary health care providers in low-and middle-income countries: A systematic review. *Gates Open Research*, 2.

Donabedian A (1988) The quality of care: How can it be assessed? *Journal of the American Medical Association* 260, 1743–1748.

Dorman C, Fay D, Zapf D & Frese M (2006) A state-trait analysis of job satisfaction: on the effect of core self-evaluations. *Applied Psychology: An International Review* 55, 27–51.

Dreison KC, Luther L, Bonfils KA, Sliter MT, McGrew JH & Salyers MP (2018) Job burnout in mental health providers: A meta-analysis of 35 years of intervention research. *Journal of Occupational Health Psychology* 23, 18–30. https://doi.org/10.1037/ocp0000047.

Dunning D, Johnson K, Ehrlinger J & Kruger J (2003) Why people fail to recognize their own incompetence. *Current Directions in Psychological Science* 12, 83–87. doi:10.1111/1467-8721.01235.

Dyrbye L & Shanafelt T (2015) A narrative review on burnout experienced by medical students and residents. *Medical Education* 50, 132–149.

Edwards D & Burnard P (2003) A systematic review of stress and stress management interventions for mental health nurses. *Journal of Advanced Nursing* 42, 169–200.

Edwards D, Burnard P, Hannigan B, Cooper L, Adams J, Juggessur T, Fothergil A & Coyle D (2006) Clinical Supervision and burnout: The influence of clinical supervision for community mental health nurses. *Journal of Clinical Nursing* 15, 1007–1015.

Edmunds KP, Yeung HN, Onderdonk C, Mitchell W & Thornberry K (2015) Clinical supervision in the palliative care team setting: A concrete approach to team wellness. *Journal of Palliative Care* 18, 74–277.

Elliott, R. (2002) Hermeneutic single-case efficacy designs. *Psychotherapy Research* 12, 1–21.

Ellis MV, Berger L, Hanus AE, Ayala EE, Swords BA & Siembor M (2014) Inadequate and harmful clinical supervision: Testing a revised framework and assessing occurrence. *The Counseling Psychologist* 42, 434–472. doi:10.1177/0011000013508656

Ellis M & Ladany N (1997) Inferences concerning supervisees and clients in clinical supervision. An integrative review. In: CE Watkins (Ed) *Handbook of Psychotherapy Supervision*. New York: Wiley, pp447–507.

Erera IP (2008) Supervisors can burnout too. *The Clinical Supervisor* 9, 131–148.

Ericsson KA (2009) *Development of Professional Expertise*. Cambridge: Cambridge University Press.

Ericsson KA & Towne TJ (2010) Expertise. *Wiley Interdisciplinary Reviews: Cognitive Science* 1, 404–416.

Evans C & Marcroft E (2015) Clinical supervision in a community setting. *Nursing Times* 111, 16–18.

Fagin, L. (1996) Teamwork among professionals involved with disturbed families. In: M Watkins, N Hervey, J Carson and S Ritter (Eds) *Collaborative Community Mental Health Care*. London: Arnold.

Falender C, Cornish JAE, Goodyear R, Hatcher R, Kaslow NJ, Leventhal G, Shafranske E, Sigmon ST, Stoltenberg C & Grus C (2004) Defining competencies in psychology supervision: A consensus statement. *Journal of Clinical Psychology* 60, 771–785.

Falender CA & Shafranske EP (2012) *Getting the Most Out of Clinical Training and Supervision: A guide for practicum students and interns*. Washington, D.C: American Psychological Association.

Farber BA & Hazanov V (2014) Informal sources of supervision in clinical training. *Journal of Clinical Psychology: In session* 70, 1062–1072.

Faugier J (1992) The supervisory relationship. In: T Butterworth and J Faugier (Eds) *Clinical Supervision and Mentorship in Nursing*. London: Chapman & Hall.

Felton BJ, Revenson TA & Hinrichsen GA (1984) Stress and coping in the explanation of psychological adjustment among chronically ill adults. *Social Science & Medicine* 18, 889–898.

Folkman S & Nathan PE (Eds) (2010) *The Oxford Handbook of Stress, Health and Coping*. Oxford: Oxford University Press.

Fraser SW & Greenhalgh T (2001) Complexity science: Coping with complexity: Educating for capability. *British Medical Journal* 323, 799–803.

Funderburk B et al (2015) Comparing client outcomes for two evidence-based treatment consultation strategies. *Journal of Clinical Child & Adolescent Psychology* 44, 730–741. doi: 10.1080/15374416.2014.910790

Gardner MJ, McKinstry C & Perrin B (2018) Effectiveness of allied health clinical supervision. *Journal of Allied Health* 47, 126–132.

Gillieatt S et al (2014) Evaluation of an inter-professional training programme for student clinical supervision in Australia. *Human Resources for Health* 12, 60.

Goldberg DP & Williams P (1988) *A User's Guide to the General Health Questionnaire.* Windsor UK: NFER-Nelson.

Goldstein IL & Ford K (2001) *Training in Organizations: Needs assessment, development and evaluation.* Pacific Grove, CA: Brooks/Cole.

Gomes AR, Faria S & Lopes H (2016) Stress and psychological health: Testing the mediating role of cognitive appraisal. *Western Journal of Nursing Research* 38, 1448–1468. doi: 10.1177/0193945916654666.

Gomes AR & Teixeira P (2016) Stress, cognitive appraisal, and psychological health: Testing instruments for health professionals. *Stress & Health* 32, 167–172. doi:10.1002/smi.258.

Gonge H & Buus N (2010) Individual and workplace factors that influence psychiatric nursing staff's participation in clinical supervision: A survey study and prospective longitudinal registration. *Issues in Mental Health Nursing* 31, 345–354.

Gonge H & Buus N (2011) Model for investigating the benefits of clinical supervision in psychiatric nursing: A survey study. *International Journal of Mental Health Nursing* 20, 102–111.

Gonge H & Buus N (2014) Is it possible to strengthen psychiatric nursing staff's clinical supervision? RCT of a meta-supervision intervention. *Journal of Advanced Nursing* 71, 909-921. doi: 10:1111/jan.12569.

Gonzalez DM (2016) Client variables and psychotherapy outcomes. In: DJ Cain, K Keenan and S Rubin (Eds) Humanistic Psychotherapies: Handbook of Research and Practice. Washington, DC, US: *American Psychological Association,* pp455–482.

Gonsalvez CJ, Hamid G, Savage NM & Livni D (2017) The supervision evaluation and supervisory competence scale: Psychometric validation. *Australian Psychologist* 52, 94–10.

Goodrich J (2012) Supporting hospital staff to provide compassionate care: Do Schwartz Center Rounds work in English hospitals? *Journal of the Royal Society for Medicine* 105, 117–122. doi 10.1258/jrsm.2011.110183

Goodyear RK (2014) Supervision as pedagogy: Attending to its essential instructional and learning processes. *The Clinical Supervisor* 33, 82–99.

Gosselin J, Barker KK, Kogan CS, Pomerleau M & Pitre d'Ioro M-P (2015) Setting the stage for an evidence-based model of psychotherapy supervisor development in clinical psychology. *Canadian Psychology* 56, 379–393.

Grant L & Kinman G (2014) Emotional resilience in the helping professions and how it can be enhanced. *Health and Social Care Education* 3, 23–34.

Grant, J., Schofield, M.J. and Crawford, S. (2012) Managing difficulties in supervision: Supervisors' perspectives. *Journal of Counselling Psychology* 59, 528–541.

Green H, Barkham M, Kellett S & Saxon D (2014) Therapist effects and IAPT Psychological Well-being Practitioners (PWPs): A multi-level modelling and mixed methods analysis. *Behaviour Research & Therapy* 63, 43–54.

Greenberg J (2006) Losing sleep over organizational injustice: Attenuating insomniac reactions to underpayment inequity with supervisor training in interactional justice. *Journal of Applied Psychology* 91, 58–69.

Greenburg LS & Malcolm W (2002) Resolving unfinished business: Relating process to outcome. *Journal of Consulting and Clinical Psychology* 70, 406–416.

Gurková E, Žiaková K, Cibríková S, Magurová D, Hudáková A, Mrosková S (2016) Factors influencing the effectiveness of the clinical learning environment in nursing education. *Central European Journal of Nursing & Midwifery* 7, 470–475. doi: 10.15452/CEJNM.2016.07.0017

Hall DS (2007) The relationship between supervisor support and registered nurse outcomes in nursing care units. *Nursing Administration Quarterly* 31, 68–80.

Hancock M (2018) My priorities for the health and social care system. https://www.gov.uk/government/speeches/matt-hancock-my-priorities-for-the-health-and- social-care-system. Retrieved on 27-7-18.

Harris R (2019) *ACT Made Simple: An Easy-to-read Primer on Acceptance and Commitment Therapy.* New Harbinger Publications.

Hattie J & Timperley H (2007) The power of feedback. *Review of Educational Research* 77, 81–112.

Hayes SC, Strosahl KD & Wilson KG (2009) *Acceptance and Commitment Therapy.* Washington, D.C: American Psychological Association.

Hawkins P & Shohet R (2007) *Supervision in the Helping Professions: An individual, group and organizational approach.* Maidenhead: Open University Press.

Health & Safety Executive (HSE) (2009) *How to Tackle Work-related Stress: A guide for employers on making the Management Standards work.* London: HSE.

Health Workforce Australia (2013) *National Clinical Supervision Competency Resource.* Adelaide:Health Workforce Australia.

Henry R, Nantonga L, Wagner AK, Embrey M & Trap B (2017) Competency in supportive supervision: a study of public sector medicines management supervisors in Uganda. *Journal of Pharmaceutical Policy and Practice* 10, 1–11. doi: 10.1186/s40545-017-0121-y

Heron J (1989) *Six Category Intervention Analysis.* Guildford, University of Surrey: Human Potential Resource Group.

Hill CE & Castonguay LG (2017) *Therapist effects: Integration and conclusions. How and Why Are Some Therapists Better Than Others? Understanding Therapist Effects*, 325-341, edited by L. G. Castonguay and C. E. Hill. Washington, D.C: American Psychological Association.

Hobfoll SE (2011) Conservation of resource caravans and engaged settings. *Journal of Occupational and Organizational Psychology* 84, 116–122.

Hobfoll SE, Halbeleben J, Neveu J-P & Westman M (2018) Conservation of resources in the organizational context: the reality of resources and their consequences. *Annual Review of Organizational Psychology & Organizational Behaviour* 5, 103–1028.

Hoehn-Saric R, Frank JD, Imber SD, Nash EH, Stone AR & Battle CC (1964) Systematic preparation of patients for psychotherapy: I. Effects on therapy behaviour and outcome. *Journal of Psychiatric Research* 2, 267–281.

Hogan BE, Linden W & Najarian B (2002) Social support interventions: Do they work? *Clinical Psychology Review* 22, 381–440.

Holloway EL (2014) Supervisory roles within systems of practice. In: CE Watkins and DL Milne (Eds) *Wiley International Handbook of Clinical Supervision.* Chichester: Wiley, pp598–621.

Holman D, Johnson S & O'Connor E (2018) Stress management interventions: improving subjective well-being in the workplace. In: E Diener, S Oishi and L Tay (Eds) *Handbook of Well-being.* Salt Lake City, UT: DEF Publishers. doi:nobascholar.com

Holmes D (2013) Mid Staffordshire scandal highlights NHS cultural crisis. *The Lancet* 381 (9866), 521–522.

Horowitz M, Wilner M & Alvarez W (1979) Impact of event scale: a measure of subjective stress. *Psychomatic Medicine* 41, 209–18.

Howard F (2008) Managing stress or enhancing well-being? Positive psychology's contributions to clinical supervision. *Australian Psychologist* 43, 105–113.

Hyrkäs K (2005) Clinical supervision, burnout, and job satisfaction among mental health nurses in Finland. *Issues in Mental Health Nursing* 26, 531–556. doi: 10.1080/01612840590931975

Improving Access to Psychological Therapies (IAPT Education and Training Group, 2011) *Guidance for Commissioning IAPT Supervisor Training.* London: Department of Health.

Ivanovic M, Swift JK, Callahan JL & Dunn R (2015) A multisite pre/post study of mindfulness training for therapists: The impact on session presence and effectiveness. *Journal of Cognitive Psychotherapy: An International Quarterly* 29, 331–342.

Iwasaki K, Takahashi M & Nakatai A (2006) Health problems due to long working hours in Japan: Working hours, workers' compensation (Karoshi), and preventive measures. *Industrial Health* 44, 537–540.

James IA, Allen K & Collerton D (2004) A post-hoc analysis of emotions in supervision: a new methodology for examining process features. *Behavioural and Cognitive Psychotherapy* 32 (4) 507–513.

James IA & Morse R (2007) The use of questions in cognitive behaviour therapy: Identification of question type, function and structure. *Behavioural and Cognitive Psychotherapy* 35, 507–511.

Jenkins R & Elliott P (2004) Stressors, burnout and social support: nurses in acute mental health settings. *Journal of Advanced Nursing* 48, 622–631.

Johnson WB (2007) Transformational supervision: when supervisors mentor. *Professional Psychology: Research and Practice* 38, 259–267.

Johnson JV & Hall EM (1988) Job strain, workplace social support, and cardiovascular disease: a cross-sectional study of a random sample of the Swedish working population. *American Journal of Public Health* 78 (10) 1336–1342.

Joint Commission on Accreditation of Healthcare Organizations (2002) *Health Care at the Crossroads: Strategies for addressing the evolving nursing crisis*. Washington, DC.

Kadushin A (1976) *Supervision in Social Work*. NY: Columbia University Press.

Kadushin A & Harkness D (2002) *Supervision in Social Work* (4th Edition). NY: Columbia University Press.

Kaeding A, Sougleris C, Reid C, Vreeswijk, MF, Hayes, C., Dorrian, J & Simpson S (2017) Professional burnout, early maladaptive schemas and physical health in clinical and counselling trainees. *Journal of Clinical Psychology* 73, 1782–1796.

Kagan H & Kagan NI (1997) Interpersonal process recall: Influencing human interaction. In: CE Watkins (Ed) *Handbook of Psychotherapy Supervision*. New York: Wiley, pp296–309.

Kangos KA, Ellis MV, Berger L, Corp DA, Hutman H, Gibson A & Nicolas AI (2018) American Psychological Association guidelines for clinical supervision: Competency-based implications for supervisees. *The Counseling Psychologist*, 1–25, doi: 10.1177/001100001880712

Karasek R & Theorell T (1990) *Healthy Work: Stress, productivity and the reconstruction of working life*. New York: Basic Books Inc.

Kennedy-Moore E & Watson JC (2001) How and when does emotional expression help? *Review of General Psychology* 5, 187–212.

Ke Y-T, Kuo C-C & Hung C-H (2017) The effects of nursing preceptorship on new nurses' competence, professional socialization, job satisfaction & retention: A systematic review. *Journal of Advanced Nursing* 73, 2296–2305.

Kilburg RR & Diedrich RC (2007) *The Wisdom of Coaching: Essential papers in consulting psychology for a world of change*. Washington DC: APA.

Kilcullen N (2007) An analysis of the experiences of clinical supervision on Registered Nurses Msc/graduate diploma in renal and urological nursing and on their clinical supervisors. *Journal of Clinical Nursing* 16, 1029–1038.

Kirkup B (2015) Morecambe Bay Investigation. This publication is available at https://www.gov.uk/government/publications. ISBN 9780108561306.

Kisthinios M & Carlson E (2019) The content of meta-supervision in a nursing educational context. *Nursing Open* 6, 401–407. https://doi.org/10.1002/nop2.220

Kivimaki K, Jakela M, Nyberg ST, Singh-Manoux A, Fransson E, Alfredsson L, Bjorner JB, Borritz M, Burr H, Casini A, Clays E, Bacquer DD, Dragano N, Erbel R, Geuskens GA, Hamer M, Hooftman WE, Houtman IL, Jöckel K-H, Kittel F, Knutsson A, Koskenvuo M, Lunau T, Madsen IEH, Nielsen ML, Nordin M, Oksanen T, Pejtersen JH, Pentti J, Rugulies R, Salo P, Shipley MJ, Siegrist J, Steptoe A, Suominen SB, Theorell T, Vahtera J, Westerholm PJM, Westerlund H, O'Reilly D, Kumari M, Batty GD, Ferrie JE, Virtanen M (2015) Long working hours and risk of coronary heart disease and stroke. *The Lancet* 386, 1739–1746.

Knudsen` HK, Ducharme LJ & Roman PM (2008) Clinical supervision, emotional exhaustion and turnover intention: A study of substance abuse treatment counsellors in the Clinical Trials Network of the National Institute on Drug Abuse. *Journal of Substance Abuse Treatment* 35, 387–395.

Knudsen HK, Roman PM & Abraham AJ (2013) Quality of clinical supervision and counsellor emotional exhaustion. *Journal of Substance Abuse Treatment* 44, 528–533.

Koivu A, Saarinen PI & Hyrkas K (2012) Who benefits from clinical supervision and how? The association between clinical supervision and the work-related well-being of female hospital nurses. *Journal of Clinical Nursing* 21, 2567–2578.

Kolb DA (1984; 2014 second edition) *Experiential Learning: Experience as the source of learning and development*. Englewood Cliffs, NJ: Prentice-Hall.

Krisitofferzon M-L, Martensson G Mamhidir A-G & Lofmark A (2013) Nursing students' perceptions of clinical supervision: The contributions of preceptors, head preceptors and clinical lecturers. *Nurse Education Today* 33, 1252–1257.

Lacerenza CN, Reyes DL, Marlow SL, Joseph DL & Salas E (2017) Leadership training design, delivery, and implementation: A meta-analysis. *Journal of Applied Psychology* 102, 1680–1718.

Ladany N, Friedlander ML & Nelson ML (2005) *Critical Events in Psychotherapy Supervision: An interpersonal approach*. Washington, D.C: American Psychological Association.

Ladany N, Hill CE, Corbett MM & Nutt EA (1996) Nature, extent, and importance of what psychotherapy trainees do not disclose to their supervisors. *Journal of Counseling Psychology* 43, 10.

Lakey B & Orehek E (2011) Relational regulation theory: A new approach to explain the link between perceived social support and mental health. *Psychological Review* 118, 482. doi:10.1037/a0023477.

Lambert MJ, Hansen NB, Umpress V, Lunnen K, Okiishi J & Burlingame GM (1996) *Administration and scoring manual for the OQ-45.2*. Stevenson, MD: American Professional Credentialing Services LLC.

Laschober TC, de Thomas LT & Kinkade K (2013) Mentoring support from clinical supervisors: Mentor motives and associations with counsellor work-to-nonwork conflict. *Journal of Substance Abuse and Treatment* 44, 186–192.

Lattie EG, Duffecy JL, Mohr DC & Kashima K (2017) Development and evaluation of an online mental health programme for medical students. *Academic Psychiatry* 41, 642–645. doi: 10.1007/s40596-017-0726-0.

Lawson G (2007) Counsellor wellness and impairment: A national survey. *Journal of Humanistic Counselling, Education and Development* 46, 20–34.

Lazarus RS (1999) *Stress and Emotion: A new synthesis*. New York: Springer.

Lazarus RS & Folkman S (1984) *Stress, Appraisal and Coping*. New York: Springer.

Lee S, Denniston C, Edourd V, Palermo C, Pope K, Sutton K, Waller S, Ward B, Rees C (2019) Supervision training interventions in the health and human services: Realist synthesis protocol. *BMJ Open*, doi:10.1136/bmjopen-2018-025777.

Lennox S, Skinner J & Foureur M (2008) Mentorship, preceptorship and clinical supervision: Three key processes for supporting midwives. *New Zealand College of Midwives Journal* 39, 7–8.

Levinson DB, Stoll EL, Kindy SD, Merry HL & Davidson RJ (2014) A mind you can count on: validating breath counting as a behavioural measure of mindfulness. *Frontiers in Psychology* 5, 1–10, doi: 10.3389/fpsyg.2014.01202.

Lewin K (1953) *Field Theory in Social Science: Selected theoretical papers*. London: Tavistock.

Livni D, Crowe TP & Gonsalvez CJ (2012) Effects of supervision modality and intensity on alliance and outcomes for the supervisee. *Rehabilitation Psychology* 57, 178–186.

Lizano EK (2015) Examining the impact of job burnout on the health and well-being of human service workers: A systematic review and synthesis. *Human Service Organizations: Management, Leadership & Governance* 39, 167–181.

Lombardo C, Milne D & Proctor R (2009) Getting to the heart of clinical supervision: a theoretical review of the role of emotions in professional development. *Behavioural and Cognitive Psychotherapy* 37 (2), 207–219.

Lucock MP, Hall P & Noble R (2006) A survey of influences on the practice of psychotherapists and clinical psychologists in training in the UK. *Clinical Psychology and Psychotherapy* 13, 123–130.

Lynch L & Happel B (2008) Implementation of clinical supervision in action: Part 2: Implementation and beyond. *International Journal of Mental Health Nursing* 17, 65–72. doi: 10.1111/j.1447-0349.2007.00512.

Lyndon A (2016) *Burnout Among Health Professionals and Its Effect on Patient Safety*. Rockville, MD: Agency for Healthcare Research & Quality.

Mackey JD, Frieder RE, Brees JR & Martinnko MJ (2017) Abusive supervision: a meta-analysis and empirical review. *Journal of Management* 43, 1940–1965.

Marine A, Ruotsalainen JH, Serra C & Verbeek JH (2009) Preventing occupational stress in healthcare workers. *Cochrane Database of Systematic Reviews*, Issue 4. Art. No.: CD002892. doi: 10.1002/14651858. CD002892.pub2.

Marinopoulos, Spyridon S, Dorman T, Ratanawongsa N, Wilson LM, Ashar BH, Magaziner JL, Miller RG et al (2007) Effectiveness of continuing medical education. *Evid Rep Technol Assess* (Full Rep) 149, 1–69.

Martin P, Reiser R & Milne D (2018) Peer supervision: International problems and prospects. *Journal of Advanced Nursing*, 74, 998–999. doi: 10.1111/jan.13413.

Martinko MJ, Harvey P, Brees JR & Mackey J (2013) A review of abusive supervision research. *Journal of Organizational Behaviour* 34, S120–S137, doi: 10.1002/job.1888.

Martino S, Paris M, Añez L, Nich C, Canning-Ball M, Hunkele K et al (2016) The effectiveness and cost of clinical supervision for motivational interviewing: A randomized controlled trial. *Journal of Substance Abuse & Treatment* 68, 11–23.

Maslach C & Jackson SE (1981) The measurement of experienced burnout. *Journal of Occupational Behaviour* 2, 99–113.

Maslach C, Jackson SE & Leiter MP (1996) *Maslach Burnout Inventory Manual*. Mountain View, CA: CPP. Inc., and Davies-Black 3 (3), 219–223.

Maslach C & Leiter MP (1997) *The Truth About Burnout: How Organizations Cause Personal Stress and What To Do About It*. San Francisco, CA Jossey-Bass.

Maslach C, Schaufeli WB & Leiter MP (2001) Job burnout. *Annual Review of Psychology* 52, 397–422. doi:org/10.1146/annurev.psych.52.1.397.

McAllister, M & McKinnon J (2009) The importance of teaching and learning resilience in the health disciplines: A critical review of the literature. *Nurse Education Today* 29, 371–379. http://dx.doi.org/10.1016/j.nedt.2008.10.011.

McAuliffe E, Daly M, Kamwendo F, Masanja H, Sidat M & Helen de Pinho H (2013) The critical role of supervision in retaining staff in obstetric services: A three country study. *PLOS ONE* 8, 1–7. doi:10.1371/journal.pone.0058415.

McCann CM, Beddoe E, McCormick K, Huggard P, Kedge S, Adamson C & Huggard J (2013) Resilience in the health professions: A review of recent literature. *International Journal of Well-being* 3, 60–81. doi:10.5502/ijw.v3i1.4.

McCrae RR & Costa PT (2004) A contemplated revision of the NEO Five-Factor Inventory. *Personality and Individual Differences* 36, 587–596.

McIntosh N, Dircks A, Fitzpatrick J & Shuman C (2006) Games in clinical genetic counselling supervision. *Journal of Genetic Counselling* 15, 225–243.

Medical Research Council (MRC, 2000) *A Framework For Development and Evaluation of RCTs for Complex Interventions to Improve Health*. London: MRC.

Mello MM, Chandra A, Gawande AA et al (2010) National costs of the medical liability system. *Health Affairs* 29, 1569–77.

Michie S & Williams S (2003) Reducing work related psychological ill health and sickness absence: a systematic literature review. *British Medical Journal* 60, 3–9. doi: 10.1136/oem.60.1.3

Milne DL (2007) An empirical definition of clinical supervision. *British Journal of Clinical Psychology* 46, 437–447.

Milne DL (2014) Beyond the 'acid test': A conceptual review and reformulation of outcome evaluation in clinical supervision. *American Journal of Psychotherapy* 68, 213–230.

Milne DL (2010) Can we enhance the training of clinical supervisors? A national pilot study of an evidence-based approach. *Clinical Psychology & Psychotherapy* 17, 321–328.

Milne DL (2009; 2018) *Evidence-based Clinical Supervision* (first and second editions). Chichester: Wiley-Blackwell.

Milne DL, Aylott H, Fitzpatrick H & Ellis MV (2008) How does clinical supervision work? Using a Best Evidence Synthesis approach to construct a basic model of supervision. *The Clinical Supervisor* 27, 170–190.

Milne DL & Dunkerley C (2010). Towards evidence-based clinical supervision: The development and evaluation of four CBT guidelines. *The Cognitive Behaviour Therapist* 3, 43–57.

Milne DL & Gracie J (2001) The role of the supervisee: 20 ways to facilitate clinical supervision. *Clinical Psychology Forum* 5, 13–15.

Milne D & James I (2000) A systematic review of effective cognitive-behavioural supervision. *British Journal of Clinical Psychology* 39, 111–127.

Milne DL & James I (2005) Clinical supervision: 10 tests of the tandem model. *Clinical Psychology Forum* 151, 6–9.

Milne DL, Leck C & Choudhri NZ (2009) Collusion in clinical supervision: Literature review and case study in self-reflection. *The Cognitive Behaviour Therapist* 2, 106–114.

Milne DL & Martin P (2018) Supportive supervision: supported at last. *Journal of Advanced Nursing* 75, 264-265. doi: 10.1111/jan.13816.

Milne DL & Reiser R (2014) SAGE: a scale for measuring competence in CBT supervision. In: CE Watkins & DL Milne (Eds) *The Wiley International Handbook of Clinical Supervision*. Chichester: Wiley-Blackwell, pp402–415.

Milne DL & Reiser R (2016) Supporting our supervisors: sending out an SOS. *The Cognitive Behaviour Therapist*, 9, 1-12. doi:10.1017/S1754470X15000616

Milne DL & Reiser RP (2017) *A Manual for Evidence-based Clinical Supervision*. Chichester: Wiley-Blackwell.

Milne DL, Reiser RP & Cliffe T (2012) An n=1 evaluation of enhanced CBT supervision. *Behavioural & Cognitive Psychotherapy* 41, 210–220.

Milne DL, Reiser RP, Cliffe T, Breese L, Boon A, Raine R & Scarratt P (2011a) A qualitative comparison of cognitive-behavioural and evidence-based clinical supervision. *The Cognitive Behaviour Therapist* 4, 152–166. doi:10.1017/S1754470X11000092.

Milne DL, Reiser RP, Cliffe T, Breese L & Raine R (2011b) SAGE: Preliminary evaluation of an instrument for observing CBT supervision. *The Cognitive Behaviour Therapist* 4, 123–138.

Milne DL, Sheikh AI, Pattison S & Wilkinson A (2011c) Evidence-based training for clinical supervisors: A systematic review of 11 controlled studies. *The Clinical Supervisor* 30, 53–71.

Milne DL & Watkins CE (2014) Defining and understanding clinical supervision: A functional approach. In: CE Watkins and DL Milne (Eds) *The Wiley International Handbook of Clinical Supervision*. Chichester: Wiley-Blackwell, pp3–19.

Milne DL & Westerman C (2001) Evidence-based clinical supervision: rationale and illustration. *Clinical Psychology and Psychotherapy* 8, 444–45.

Mimura C & Griffiths P (2002) The effectiveness of current approaches to workplace stress management in the nursing profession: an evidence-based literature review. *Occupational Environmental Medicine* 60, 10–15.

Moked Z & Drach-Zahavy A (2015) Clinical supervision and nursing students' professional competence: support-seeking behaviour and the attachment styles of students and mentors. *Journal of Advanced Nursing* 72, 316–27. doi: 10.1111/jan.12838

Montgomery A, Panagopoulou E, Kehoe I & Valkanos E (2009) Connecting organizational culture and quality of care in the hospital: is job burnout the missing link? *Journal of Health Organization & Management* 25, 108–123.

Moos RH (1993) *Coping Responses Inventory—Adult Form, Professional Manual*. Odessa, Florida: Psychological Assessment Resources.

Moos R (1994) *Work Environment Scale Manual*. Palo Alto, CA: Consulting Psychologist Press.

Moran AM, Coyle J, Pope R, Boxall D, Nancarrow SA, & Young J. (2014) Supervision, support & mentoring interventions for health practitioners in rural and remote contexts: an integrative review and thematic synthesis of the literature to identify mechanisms for successful outcomes. *Human Resources for Health* 12 (10). http://www.human-resources-health.com/content/12/1/10

Mor Barak ME, Travis DJ, Pyun H & Xi B (2009) The impact of supervision on worker outcomes: A meta-analysis. *Social Service Review* 83, 4–32.

Morrison, T. (2005) *Staff Supervision in Social Care*. Brighton: Pavilion.

Morse G, Salyers MP, Rollins AL, Monroe-DeVita M & Pfahler C (2012) Burnout in mental health services: A review of the problem and its remediation. *Administrative Policy in Mental Health* 39, 341–352.

Muller T, Suetani S, Cutbush J & Parker S (2019) Gaming the system: using transactional analysis to explore dysfunctional processes in clinical supervision. *Australian Psychiatry* 6, 645-650. https://doi.org/10.1177/1039856219848830.

Murphy-Hagan A & Milton L (2019) Towards identifying peer supervision competencies for graduate-level Occupational Therapy students: A scoping review. *Journal of Occupational Therapy* 3 1-28. doi: 10.26681/jte.2019.030104

Naczenski LM, de Vries JD, Madelon LM, Kompier MAJ (2017) Systematic review of the association between physical activity and burnout. *Journal of Occupational Health* 59, 477–494. doi: 10.1539/joh.17-0050-RA

Nelson ML & Friedlander ML (2001) A close look at conflictual supervisory relationships: The trainee's perspective. *Journal of Counseling Psychology* 48, 384–395.

Newman CF (2013) Training cognitive behavioural therapy supervisors: Didactics, simulated practice, and "Meta-Supervision". *Journal of Cognitive Psychotherapy: An International Quarterly* 27, 5–18. http://dx.doi.org/10.1891/0889-8391.27.1.5

Newman CF & Kaplan DA (2016) Supervision Essentials for Cognitive-behavioural Therapy. Washington, DC: American Psychological Society.

Newman-Taylor Gordon K, Grist S & Olding C (2012) Developing supervisory competence: preliminary data on the impact of CBT supervision training. *The Cognitive Behaviour Therapist* 5, 83–92. doi:10.1017/S1754470X13000056

New Savoy Partnership (2016) *Workforce Well-being Survey*, 2014–16. Paper, presented at the Psychological Therapies in the NHS conference, Millenium Centre, 3rd February, London.

NICE (2012) *Developing NICE Guidelines: The Guidelines Manual*. London: National Institute for Health and Care Excellence.

NIOSH (2014) *Stress at Work*. Cincinnati, Ohio: National Institute for Occupational Safety and Health.

Nissen-Lie HA, Havik OE, Høglend PA, Monsen JT & Rønnestad MH (2013) The contribution of the quality of therapists' personal lives to the development of the working alliance. *Journal of Counseling Psychology* 60, 483–495.

Nissen-Lie HA, Monsen JT & Ronnestadt MH (2010) Therapist predictors of early patient-rated working alliance: A multi-level approach. *Psychotherapy Research* 20, 627–646.

Norcross JC & Lambert MJ (2011) *Psychotherapy Relationships That Work II* 48 (1) 4. Educational Publishing Foundation.

Novoa-Gómez M, Córdoba-Salgado O, Rojas N, Sosa L, Cifuentes D & Robayo S (2019) A descriptive analysis of the interactions during clinical supervision. *Frontiers in Psychology* 10, 669. doi: 10.3389/fpsyg.2019.00669

Ochentel O, Humphrey C & Pfeifer K (2018) Efficacy of exercise therapy in persons with burnout: A systematic review and meta-analysis. *Journal of Sports Science and Medicine* 17, 475–484.

O'Connell B, Ockerby CM, Johnson S, Smenda H & Bucknall TK (2011) Team clinical supervision in acute hospital wards: A feasibility study. *Western Journal of Nursing Research* 35, 330 –347.

O'Neill L, Johnson J & Mandela R (2018) Reflective practice groups: Are they useful for liaison psychiatry nurses working within the emergency department? *Archives of Psychiatric Nursing* 33, 85-92. doi: 10.1016/j.apnu.2018.11.003.

Orlinsky DE, Ronnestad MH & Willutzki U (2004) Fifty years of psychotherapy process-outcome research: Continuity and change. In S. L. Garfield & A. E. Bergin (Eds.), Handbook of Psychotherapy and Behaviour Change, Chichester: Wiley (pp. 307-389).

Osman AA, El-Fattah MA & Ragab OHG (2019) Impact of head nurses' supervision   practices on quality of work life as perceived by staff nurses. *Medical Journal of Cairo University* 87, 2531–2537.

Pan T-Y, Fan HS & Owen CA (2016) The work environment of junior doctors: their perspectives and coping strategies. *Postgraduate Medicine* 93, 414–419.

Panagioti M (2017) Controlled interventions to reduce burnout in physicians: A systematic review and meta-analysis. *Journal of the American Medical Association* 177, 195–205. doi:10.1001/jamainternmed.2016.7674

Panagioti M, Geraghty K, Johnson J, Zhou A, Panagopoulou E, Chew-Graham C & Esmail A (2018) Association between physician burnout and patient safety, professionalism, and patient satisfaction: a systematic review and meta-analysis. *JAMA Internal Medicine* 178(10), 1317–1330.

Panagioti M, Geraghty K and Johnson J (2018) How to prevent burnout in cardiologists? A review of the current evidence, gaps and future directions. *Trends in Cardiovascular Medicine* 28, 1–7. ISSN 1050-1738, doi.orcid.org/0000-0003-0431-013X

Parker S, Suetani S & Motamarri B (2017) On being supervised: getting value from a clinical supervisor and making the relationship work when it is not. *Australian Psychiatry* 25, 625–629.

Parry G, Roth A & Fonagy P (1996) Psychotherapy research, funding & evidence-based practice. In: A Roth and P Fonagy (Eds) *What Works for Whom?* New York: Guilford Press, pp37–56.

Pearlin LI (1999) The stress process revisited: Reflections on concepts and their interrelationships. In: CS Aneshensel and JC Phelan (Eds) *Handbook of the Sociology of Mental Health*. New York: Kluwer Academic/Plenum, pp395–415.

Pejtersen JH, Kristensen TS, Borg V & Bjorner JB (2010) The second version of the Copenhagen Psychosocial Questionnaire. *Scandinavian Journal of Public Health* 38 (3 supplement), 8–24.

Pereira J-A & Barkham M (2015) An exceptional, efficient, and resilient therapist: A case study in practice-based evidence. *Pragmatic Case Studies in Psychotherapy* 11, 216–223.

Pereira J-A, Barkham M, Kellett S & Saxon D (2017) The role of practitioner resilience and mindfulness in effective practice: A practice-based feasibility study. *Administration Policy and Mental Health* 44, 691–704.

Pereira S, Fonseca AM & Sofia Carvalho A (2011) Burnout in palliative care: A systematic review. *Nursing Ethics* 18, 317–326.

Petticrew M & Roberts H (2006) *Systematic Reviews in the Social Sciences: A practical guide*. Oxford: Blackwell.

Prince M (2004) Does active learning work? A review of the research. *Journal of Engineering Education* 93 (3) 223–231.

Pollock A, Campbell P, Deery R, Fleming M, Rankin J, Sloan G & Cheyne H (2017) A systematic review of evidence relating to clinical supervision for nurses, midwives and allied health professionals. *Journal of Advanced Nursing* 73, 1825–1837. doi.org/10.1111/jan.13253

Poulsen AD, Sharpley CF, Baumann KC, Henderson J & Poulsen MG (2015) Evaluation of the effect of a 1-day interventional workshop on recovery from job stress for radiation therapists and oncology nurses: A randomized trial. *Journal of Medical Imaging and Radiation Oncology* 59, 491-498. doi: 10.1111/1754-9485.12322

Proctor B (1986) Supervision: a cooperative exercise in accountability. In: M Marken and M Payne (Eds) *Enabling and Ensuring: Supervision in Practice*. National Youth Bureau and Council for Education and Training in Youth and Community Work, Leicester, pp21–34.

Proctor B (2010) Training for the supervision alliance. In: JR Cutcliffe, K Hyrkäs and J Fowler (Eds) *Routledge Handbook of Clinical Supervision, Fundamental International Themes*. London: Routledge. https://www.routledgehandbooks.com/doi/10.4324/9780203843437.ch3

Professional Standards Authority for Health and Social Care (PSA: 2018) *The Nursing and Midwifery Council's handling of concerns about midwives' fitness to practise at the Furness General Hospital*. London: The Professional Standards Authority for Health and Social Care.

Psychology Board of Australia (2010) *Continuing Professional Development Registration Standard*. Available at http:// www.psychologyboard.gov.au/Standards-and-Guidelines/Registration-Standards.aspx

Psychology Board of Australia (2013) *Guidelines for Supervisors and Supervisor Training Providers*. Sydney: Psychology Board of Australia.

Psychology Board of Australia (2015) *Guidelines: Continuing Professional Development*. Sydney: Psychology Board of Australia.

Rakovshik SG & McManus F (2010) Establishing evidence-based training in CBT: A review of current empirical findings and theoretical guidance. *Clinical Psychology Review* 30, 496–516.

Rees CE, Lee SL, Huang E, Denniston C, Edouard V, Pope K, Sutton K, Waller S, Ward B, Palermo C (2019) Supervision training in healthcare: a realist synthesis. *Advances in Health Sciences Education*, 25, 1-39, doi.org/10.1007/s10459-019-09937-x

Reid DH, Rotholz DA, Parsons MB, Morris L, Braswell BA, Green C, Schell SC (2003) Training human service supervisors in aspects of PBS: Evaluation of a state-wide, performance based program. *Journal of Positive Behaviour Interventions* 5, 35–46.

Reiser RP, Cliffe T & Milne DL (2018) An improved competence rating scale for CBT supervision: Short-SAGE. *The Cognitive Behaviour Therapist* 11, e7. doi: 10.1017/S1754470X18000065

Reiser RP & Milne DL (2014) A systematic review and reformulation of outcome evaluation inclinical supervision: Applying the fidelity framework. *Training & Education in Professional Psychology* 8 149-157.

Reiser, R. P., & Milne, D. L. (2017) A CBT formulation of supervisees' narratives about unethical and harmful supervision. *The Clinical Supervisor* 36, 102–115.

Reiser RP & Milne DL (2016) A survey of CBT supervision in the UK: methods, satisfaction and training, as viewed by a selected sample of CBT supervision leaders. *The Cognitive Behaviour Therapist* 9, e20. doi: 10.1017/S1754470X15000689.

Rhodes L, & Eisenberger R (2002) Perceived organizational support: A review of the literature. *Journal of Applied Psychology* 87, 698–714.

Rigazio-DiGilio SA, Daniels TG & Ivey AE (1997) Systemic cognitive-developmental supervision: A developmental-integrative approach to psychotherapy supervision. In: CE Watkins (Ed) *Handbook of Psychotherapy Supervision*. New York: Wiley, pp233–248.

Rogers CR (1957) The necessary and sufficient conditions of therapeutic personality change. *Journal of Consulting Psychology* 21, 95–103. doi:10.1037/h0045357

Roth A & Pilling S (2008) A competence framework for the supervision of psychological therapies. Retrieved 10-1-2013 from http:// www.ucl.ac.uk/clinical psychology/CORE/supervision_framework.

Roth A, Pilling S & Turner J (2010) Therapist training and supervision in clinical trials: Implications for clinical practice. *Behavioural and Cognitive Psychotherapy* 38, 291–302. doi:10.1017/S1352465810000068.

Rousmaniere T (2014) Using technology to enhance clinical supervision and training. In CE Watkins and DL Milne (Eds) *The Wiley International Handbook of Clinical Supervision*, pp204–237.

Rieck T, Callahan JL & Watkins CE (2015) Clinical supervision: An exploration of possible mechanisms of action. *Training and Education in Professional Psychology* 9, 187–194.

Rousmaniere T, Goodyear RK, Miller SD & Wampold BE (2017) The Cycle of Excellence: Using Deliberate Practice to Improve Supervision and Training. Chichester: Wiley-Blackwell.

Rowe AK, de Savigny D, Lanata CF & Victora CG (2005) How can we achieve and maintain high-quality performance of health workers in low-resource settings? *The Lancet* 366, 1026–35. doi:10.1016/S0140-6736(05) 67028-6.

Royal Australasian College of Physicians (RACP, 2012) Cultural Competence – supporting Physicians' Professionalism and Performance: A guide for physicians in Australia and New Zealand. Sydney: RACP.

Ruotsalainen J, Serra C, Marine A & Verbeek J (2008) Systematic review of interventions for reducing occupational stress in health care workers. *Scandinavian Journal of Work, Environment & Health* 34, 169–178. doi:10.5271/sjweh.1240.

Rupert PA, Miller AO & Dorociak KE (2015) Preventing burnout: What does the research tell us? *Professional Psychology: Research & Practice* 46, 168–174.

Ryan R & Hill S (2016) How to GRADE the quality of the evidence. Cochrane Consumers and Communication Group, available at http://cccrg.cochrane.org/author-resources. Version 3.0 December 2016.

Rycroft-Malone J, Seers K, Eldh AC, Cox K, Crichton N, Harvey G, Hawkes C, Kitson A, McCormack B, McMullan C, Mockford C, Niessen T, Slater P, Titchen A, Zijpp T & Wallin L (2018) A realist process evaluation within the FIRE cluster controlled international trial: an exemplar. *Implementation Science* 13, doi: 10.1186/s13012-018-0811-0

Safran JD, Muran CJ, Stevens C & Rothman M (2007) A relational approach to supervision: addressing ruptures in the alliance. In: CA Falender and EP Shafranske (Eds) *Casebook for Clinical Supervision: A competency-based approach*. Washington DC: American Psychological Association, pp137–157.

Saarikoski M (2014) The supervision scale. In: CE Watkins and DL Milne (Eds) *The Wiley International Handbook of Clinical Supervision*. Chichester: Wiley-Blackwell, pp416–430.

Salyers MP, Hudson C, Morse G, Rollins AL, Monroe-DeVita M & Wilson C (2011) BREATHE: A pilot study of a one-day retreat to reduce burnout among mental health professionals. *Psychiatric Services* 62, 214–217. doi:10.1176/appi.ps.62.2.214

Santorelli S (Ed) (2014) *Mindfulness-based Stress Reduction (MBSR): Standards of Practice*. University of Massachusetts Medical School: Center for Mindfulness in Medicine, Health Care & Society.

Sarafis P, Rousaki E, Tsounis A, Lahana L, Bamidis P, Niakes D, & Papastavrou E (2016) The impact of occupational stress on nurses' caring behaviours and their health-related quality of life. *BMC Nursing* 15, 1–9, doi: 10.1186/s12912-016-0178-y

Schaufeli WB & Bakker AB (2004) Job demands, job resources, and their relationship with burnout and engagement: a multi-sample study. *Journal of Organizational Behaviour* 25, 293–315.

Schoenwald SK, Sheidow AJ & Chapman JE (2009) Clinical supervision in treatment transport: effects on adherence and outcomes. *Journal of Consulting and Clinical Psychology* 77, 410–421. doi: 10.1037/a0013788

Schoenwald SK (2016) Clinical supervision in a quality assurance/quality improvement system: multisystemic therapy® as an example. *The Cognitive Behaviour Therapist* 9, 1-15. doi:10.1017/S1754470X15000604

Schwalbe CS, Oh HY & Zweben A (2014) Sustaining motivational interviewing: a meta-analysis of training studies. *Addiction* 109, 1287–1294.

Scott K, Beckham SW, Gross M, Pariyo G, Rao KD, Cometto G & Perry HB (2018) What do we know about community-based health worker programs? A systematic review of existing review on community health workers. *Human Resources for Health* 16, 39. https://doi.org/10.1186/s12960-018-0304-x

Scottish Government (2009) *Health Works: A Review of the Scottish Government's Healthy Working Lives Strategy*. Edinburgh: Scottish Government.

Scottish Executive (2006) *Rights, Relationship and Recovery – The Report of the National Review of Mental Health Nursing in Scotland*. Edinburgh: Scottish Government.

Schoen D (1991) *Educating the Reflective Practitioner*. San Francisco: Jossey-Bass.

Shadish WR, Cook TD & Campbell DT (2002) *Experimental and Quasi-Experimental Designs for Generalised Causal Inference*. NY: Houghton Mifflin.

Shanafelt TD, Balch CM, Bechamps G, Russell T, Dyrbye L, Satele D & Freischlag J (2010) Burnout and medical errors among American surgeons. *Annals of Surgery* 251 (6) 995–1000.

Shanafelt TD, Hasan O, Dyrbye LN, Sinsky C, Satele D, Sloan J & West CP (2015, December) Changes in burnout and satisfaction with work-life balance in physicians and the general US working population between 2011 and 2014. *Mayo Clinic Proceedings* 90 (12) 1600–1613.

Shanafelt TD & Noseworthy JH (2017) Executive leadership and physician well-being: Nine organizational strategies to promote engagement and reduce burnout. *Mayo Clinic Proceedings* 92, 129–46.

Shanafelt TD, Gorringe G, Menaker R, Storz KA, Reeves D, Buskirk SJ, Sloan JA, & Swensen SJ (2015) Impact of organizational leadership on physician burnout and satisfaction. *Mayo Clinic Proceedings* 90, 432–440.

Shapiro SL, Brown K & Biegel GM (2007) Teaching self-care to caregivers: Effects of mindfulness-based stress reduction on the mental health of therapists in training. *Training and Education in Professional Psychology* 1, 105–11.

Shapiro SL, Brown KW, Biegel GM, Wong SM, Simko NW, Oritz-Torres PA (1989) Promoting the well-being of working parents: Coping, social support, and flexible job schedules. *American Journal of Community Psychology* 17, 32–55.

Sheils EA, Loades ME, Medley AR & Marks EM (2016) A fair exchange: The reciprocal relationship between universities and clinical placement supervisors. *International Journal of Practice-based Learning in Health and Social Care* 4, 28–39. doi: 0.18552/ijpblhsc.v4i1.304

Sholomskas DE, Syracuse-Siewert G, Rounsaville BJ, Ball SA, Nuro KF & Carroll KM (2005) We don't train in vain: a dissemination trial of three strategies of training clinicians in cognitive-behavioural therapy. *Journal of Consulting and Clinical Psychology* 73, 106.

Simionato GK & Simpson S (2017) Personal risk factors associated with burnout among psychotherapists: A systematic review of the literature. *Journal of Clinical Psychology* 74, 1431–1456. doi:10.1002/jclp.22615

Simpson-Southward C, Waller G & Hardy GE (2017) How do we know what makes for 'best practice' in clinical supervision for psychological therapists? A content analysis of supervisory models and approaches. *Clinical Psychology & Psychotherapy* 24, 1228–1245.

Singh D, Negin J, Garimoi Orach C & Cumming R (2016) Supportive supervision for volunteers to deliver reproductive health education: a cluster randomized trial. *Reproductive Health* 13, 1-26. doi: 10.1186/s12978-016-0244-7

Skakon J, Nielsen K, Borg V & Guzman J (2010) Are leaders' well-being, behaviours and style associated with the affective well-being of their employees? A systematic review of three decades of research. *Work & Stress* 24, 107–139, doi: 10.1080/02678373.2010.495262

Slavin RE (1995) Best evidence synthesis: an intelligent alternative to meta-analysis. *Journal of Clinical Epidemiology* 48, 9–18.

Smith LB & Thelen E (2003) Development as a dynamic system. *Trends in Cognitive Science* 7, 343–348.

Snowdon DA, Hau R, Leggat SG & Taylor NF (2016) Does clinical supervision of health professionals improve patient safety? A systematic review and meta-analysis. *International Journal for Quality in Health Care* 28, 447–455.

Snowdon DA, Leggat SG & Taylor NF (2017) Does clinical supervision of healthcare professionals improve effectiveness of care and patient experience? A systematic review. BMC Health Services Research 17, 1–11. doi: 10.1186/s12913-017-2739-5

Snowdon DA, Sargent M, Williams CM, Maloney S, Caspers K & Taylor NF (2020) Effective clinical supervision of allied health professionals: a mixed methods study. BMC Health Services Research 20, 1–11. doi:10.1186/s12913-019-4873-8.

Stacey G, Aubeeluck A, Cook G & Dutta S (2017) A case study exploring the experience of resilience-based clinical supervision and its influence on care towards self and others among student nurses. *International Practice Development Journal* 7, 1–16. doi.org/10.19043/ipdj.72.005

Stafford-Brown J & Pakenham KI (2012) The effectiveness of an ACT informed intervention for managing and improving therapist qualities in clinical psychology trainees. *Journal of Clinical Psychology* 68, 592–613.

Stamm BH (2008) The ProQoL. See: www.proqol.org

Stansfeld S & Candy B (2006) Psychosocial work environment and mental health — a meta-analytic review. *Scandinavian Journal of Work, Environment & Health* 32, 443–446.

Steel C, Macdonald J, Schröder T & Mellor-Clark J (2015) Exhausted but not cynical: burnout in therapists working within Improving Access to Psychological Therapy Services. *Journal of Mental Health* 24, 33–37.

Sterner WR (2009) Influence of the supervisory working alliance on supervisee work satisfaction and work-related stress. *Journal of Mental Health Counseling* 31, 249–263.

Stiles WB, Elliott R, Llewelyn SP, Firth-Cozens JA, Margison FA & Shapiro D (1990) Assimilation of problematic experiences by clients in psychotherapy. *Psychotherapy: Theory, Research, Practice and Training* 27, 411–420.

Stoltenberg CD, Bailey KC, Cruzan CB, Hart JT & Ukuku U (2014) The integrative developmental model of supervision. In: CE Watkins and DL Milne (Eds) *The Wiley International Handbook of Clinical Supervision*. Chichester: Wiley, pp576–597.

Subramaniam A, Silong AD, Uli J & Ismail IA (2015) Effects of coaching supervision, mentoring supervision and abusive supervision on talent development among trainee doctors in public hospitals: moderating role of clinical learning environment. *BMC Medical Education* 15, 129. doi:10.1186/s12909-015-0407-1

Swedish Society of Nursing and the Section for Clinical Supervision (2015a) Available from: ttps:// www.swenurse.se/ Sektioner-och-Natverk/Handledning-i-Omvardnad-sektion-inomSvensk-sjukskoterskeforening-HiO/Utbildning/ [last accessed 13 January 2018].

Teasdale K, Brocklehurst N & Thom N (2001) Clinical supervision and support for nurses: an evaluation study. *Journal of Advanced Nursing* 33, 216–224.

Tepper BJ (2000) Consequences of abusive supervision. *Academy of Management Journal* 43, 178–190.

Thoits PA (1986) Social support as coping assistance. *Journal of Consulting and Clinical Psychology* 54, 416–423. doi:10.1037/0022006X.54.4.416.

Thoits PA (1995) Stress, coping and social support processes: Where are we? What next? *Journal of Health & Social Behaviour*, extra issue, 53–79.

Thoits PA (2010) Stress and health: major findings and policy implications. *Journal of Health and Social Behaviour* 51 (S), S41 –S53. doi: 10.1177/0022146510383499

Thomas JT (2007) Informed consent through contracting for supervision: Minimizing risks, enhancing benefits. *Professional Psychology: Research and Practice* 38 (3), 221.

Thomson JS, Anderson KJ, Mara PR & Stevenson AD (2011) Supervision: growing and building a sustainable practice supervisor system. *Medical Journal of Australia* 194, S101–104.

Thomson K, Nguyen M & Leithhead I (2016) Peer mentoring for clinical educators: a case study in physiotherapy. *Focus on Health Professional Education* 17, 30–44.

Tomaka J, Palacios RL, Champion C & Monks S (2018) Development and validation of an instrument that assesses individual differences in threat and challenge appraisal. *Journal of Depression & Anxiety* 7, 313. doi:10.4172/2167-1044.1000313

Tomlinson J (2015) Using clinical supervision to improve the quality and safety of patient care: a response to Berwick and Francis. *BMC Medical Education* 15, 103. doi: 10.1186/s12909-015-0324-3

Townend M, Iannetta L & Freeston MH (2002) Clinical supervision in practice; a survey of UK cognitive behavioural psychotherapists accredited by the BABCP. *Behavioural and Cognitive Psychotherapy* 30, 485–450.

Tracey TJG, Wampold BE, Lichtenberg JW & Goodyear RK (2014) Expertise in psychotherapy: an elusive goal? *American Psychologist* 69, 218–229.

Tsutsumi A (2011) Development of an evidence-based guideline for supervisor training in promoting mental health: Literature review. *Journal of Occupational Therapy* 53, 1–9.

Turner RJ & Avison WR (2003) Status variations in stress exposure: Implications for the interpretation of research on race, socioeconomic status, and gender. *Journal of Health and Social Behaviour* 44, 488–505.

Turpin G & Wheeler S (2011) *Guidance for Commissioning IAPT Supervisor Training*. London: Department of Health.

Tyrell Z (2010) A cognitive-behavioural model for maintaining processes in burnout. *The Cognitive Behaviour Therapist* 3, 18–26. doi:10.1017/S1754470X10000024

van Mol MMC, Kompanje EJO, Benolt DD, bakker J & Nijkamp MD (2015) The prevalence of compassion fatigue and burnout among healthcare professionals in ICU: a systematic review. *PLOS one (Public Library of Science)* 10, 1-22. doi: 10.1371/journal. pone.0136955.

Vec T, Vec TR & Zorga S (2014) Understanding how supervision works and what it can achieve. In: CE Watkins and DL Milne (Eds). *The Wiley International Handbook of Clinical Supervision*. Chichester: Wiley-Blackwell, pp103–128.

von Bertalanffy L (1968) *Organizmic Psychology and Systems Theory*. Massachusetts: Barre.

Vygotsky LS (1978) *Mind in Society: The development of higher psychological processes*. Cambridge, MA: Harvard University Press.

West MA, Wall TD, Bolden RI, Borrill CS, Bolden RI, Borrill CS, Carter AJ, Golya DA Hardy GE, Haynes CA, Rick JE, Shapiro DA (1997) Minor psychiatric disorder in NHS trust staff: occupational and gender differences. *British Journal of Psychiatry* 171, 519–23.

Walklet E & Percy C (2014) Stress and coping in IAPT Staff: A mixed-methods study. *Applied Psychological Research Journal* 2, 15–25.

Wallbank S (2010) Effectiveness of individual clinical supervision for midwives and doctors in stress reduction: findings from a pilot study. *Evidence-based Midwifery* 8, 65–70.

Wallbank S (2012) Health visitors' needs: national perspectives from the restorative clinical supervision programme. *Community Practitioner* 85, 29–32.

Wallbank S (2013) Maintaining professional resilience through group restorative supervision. *Community Practitioner* 86, 23–25.

Wallbank S & Wonnacott J (2016) The integrated model of restorative supervision for use within safeguarding. *Community Practitioner* 88, 41–45.

Wallbank S & Woods G (2012) A healthier health visiting workforce: findings from the restorative supervision programme. *Community Practitioner* 85, 20–23.

Walklet E & Percy C (2014) Stress and Coping in IAPT Staff: A Mixed Methods Study. *Applied Psychological Research Journal* 1 (2) 15–25.

Wampold BE (2010) The research evidence for the common factors models: A historically situated perspective. In: BL Duncan, SD Miller, BE Wampold and MA Hubble (Eds) The Heart and Soul of Change: Delivering what works in therapy. Washington, DC, US: American Psychological Association, pp49–81.

Warden GL, Mazmanian PE & Leach DC (2010) Redesigning Continuing Education in the Health Professions. Washington, DC: National Academies Press.

Watkins CE (2014a) The supervisory alliance: A half century of theory, practice, and research in critical perspective. *American Journal of Psychotherapy* 68, 19–55. http://dx.doi.org/10.1007/s10879-013-9252-x.

Watkins CE (2014b) The supervision alliance as quintessential integrative variable. *Journal of Contemporary Psychotherapy* 44, 151–161.

Watkins CE & Milne DL (2014) (Eds) *The Wiley International Handbook of Clinical Supervision.* Chichester: Wiley-Blackwell.

Watkins CE & Wang CDC (2014) On the education of clinical supervisors. In: CE Watkins and DL Milne (Eds) *The Wiley International Handbook of Clinical Supervision.* Chichester: Wiley-Blackwell, pp177–203.

Weigl M, Stab N, Herms I, Angere P, Hacker W & Glaser J (2016) The associations of supervisor support and work overload with burnout and depression: a cross-sectional study in two nursing settings. *Journal of Advanced Nursing* 72, 1774–1788. doi: 10.1111/jan.12948

Weiss D, Dawis R, England G & Lofquist L (1967) *Manual for the Minnesota Satisfaction Questionnaire.* University of Minnesota. Minneapolis, MN.

West CP, Dyrbye LN, Erwin PJ & Shanafelt TD (2016) Interventions to prevent and reduce physician burnout: A systematic review and meta-analysis. *The Lancet* 388, 2272–2281.

Westwood S, Morison L, Allt J & Holmes N (2017) Predictors of emotional exhaustion, disengagement and burnout among improving access to psychological therapies (IAPT) practitioners. *Journal of Mental Health* 26, 172–179. doi: 10.1080/09638237.2016.1276540

Wheeler S & King D (2000) Do counselling supervisors want or need to have their supervision supervised? An exploratory study. *British Journal of Guidance and Counselling* 28, 279–290.

Wheeler S & Richards K (2007) *The Impact of Clinical Supervision on Counsellors and Therapists, Their Practice and Their Clients: A systematic review of the literature.* Lutterworth: BACP.

White E (2018) Email received on 10-10-18 by Derek Milne: personal communication.

White E & Winstanley J (2009) Implementation of clinical supervision: educational preparation and subsequent diary accounts of the practicalities involved, from an Australian mental health nursing innovation. *Journal of Psychiatric and Mental Health Nursing* 16, 895–903.

White E & Winstanley J (2010) A randomized controlled trial of clinical supervision: selected findings from a novel Australian attempt to establish the evidence base for causal relationships with quality of care and patient outcomes, as an informed contribution to mental health nursing practice development. *Journal of Research in Nursing* 15, 151–167.

White E & Winstanley J (2011) Clinical supervision for mental health professionals: The evidence base. *Social Work & Social Sciences Review* 14, 77–94. doi: 10.1921/095352211X623227

White E & Winstanley J (2014) Clinical supervision and the helping professions: An interpretation of history. *The Clinical Supervisor* 33, 3–25. http://dx.doi.org/10.1080/07325223.2014.905226

Whitehead B, Owen P, Henshaw L, Beddingham E & Simmons M (2016) Supporting newly qualified nurse transition: A case study in a UK hospital. *Nurse Education Today* 36, 58–63.

Wilkins D, Forrester D & Grant L (2017) What happens in child and family social work supervision? *Child & Family Social Work* 22, 942–951. 10.1111/cfs.12314 file

Wilkins D, Khan M, Stabler L, Newlands F & McDonnell J (2018) Evaluating the quality of social work supervision in UK children's services: comparing self-report and independent observation. *Clinical Social Work Journal* 46, 1-11. doi:org/10.1007/s10615-018-0680-7.

Willard-Grace R, Hessler D, Rogers E, Dube K, Bodenheimer KG (2014) Team structure and culture are associated with lower burnout in primary care. *Journal of the American Board of Family Medicine* 27, 229–238.

Windley M, Lawrence C, Guthrie K, Weeks D, Sullo E & Chapa DW (2015) A systematic review on interventions supporting preceptor development. *Journal of Nurses in Professional Development* 31, 312–323.

Winstanley J (2000) Manchester Clinical Supervision Scale. *Nursing Standard* 14, 31–32.

Winstanley J & White E (2014) The Manchester Clinical Supervision Scale. In: CE Watkins and DL Milne (Eds) *The Wiley International Handbook of Clinical Supervision*. Chichester: Wiley-Blackwell, pp386–401.

Wonnacott J (2016) *Developing and Supporting Effective Staff Supervision*. Hove: Pavilion.

Wood DF (2016) Mens sana in corpore sano: student well-being and the development of resilience. *Medical Education* 50, 3–23.

Woodhead EL, Northrop L & Edelstein B (2016) Stress, social support, and burnout among long-term care nursing staff. *Journal of Applied Gerontology* 35, 84 –105. doi: 10.1177/0733464814542465

World Health Organization (2001) World Medical Association Declaration of Helsinki. Geneva, Switzerland: WHO. www.wma.net.

World Health Organization (2008) *Supportive Supervision*. Geneva, Switzerland: WHO.

World Health Organization (2019) https://www.who.int/mental_health/evidence/burn-out/en/).

Yazdankhahfard M, Haghani F & Omid A (2019) The Balint group and its application in medical education: A systematic review. *Journal of Educational Health Promotion* 8, 1–6. doi:10.4103/jehp.jehp_423_1

Yeun E & Kim H (2015) The effects of supervisor support, emotional exhaustion, and sense of personal accomplishment on hospital nurse turnover intentions. *Indian Journal of Science and Technology* 8, 63–68.

Yoon J, Han NC & Seo Y-J (1996) Sense of control among hospital employees: An assessment of choice process, empowerment, and buffering hypotheses. *Journal of Applied Social Psychology* 26, 686–716.

Yu J, Ren X, Wang Q, He L, Wang J, Jin Y, Chen Y, Wang L, Nie Z, Guo D & Yao Y (2014) The role of social support on occupational stress among hospital nurses. *International Journal of Clinical & Experimental Medicine* 7, 3000–3004.

Žorga S (2002) Supervision: the process of life-long learning in social and educational professions. *Journal of Interprofessional Care* 16, 265–276.

Index

coping strategy enhancement 110
culture 37-38
cultural competence 70, 71

D

decision-making 23, 32, 96, 99, 102, 104, 108, 180, 193, 204
    lack of participation 96, 102
    latitude scale 99, 234
definition of supervision
definitions viii, 6, 16, 17, 20, 21, 22, 23, 24, 31, 33, 37, 38, 43, 58, 64, 72, 73, 87, 93, 95, 118, 175, 176, 187, 192, 201, 205, 222
deliberate practice 151, 167, 203, 204, 214
demographic variables 69-71
developmental model 228
distress ('work-related stress'; 'occupational stress' or work 'strain') 86, 1, 2, 4, 5, 6, 7, 9, 15, 16, 20, 22, 26, 32, 35, 38, 39, 43, 48, 49, 58, 62, 65, 68, 72, 73, 76, 77, 78, 83, 84, 85, 87, 88, 89, 95, 101, 105, 114, 124, 126, 127, 143, 144, 145, 149, 154, 156, 157, 163, 168, 169, 194, 198, 199, 201, 202, 203, 205, 206

E

emotional exhaustion 1, 2, 7, 9, 11, 47, 50, 51, 52, 55, 56, 62, 68, 87, 88, 89, 194, 220, 230, 231
emotional processing 14, 28, 35, 67, 90, 121, 145, 146, 150, 154, 160, 163, 178, 179, 202
emotional support 13, 14, 19, 77, 110, 121, 127, 128, 129, 142, 161, 163, 168, 182, 203
emotions in supervision 219
empathy 34, 39, 68, 73, 76, 87, 95, 110, 128, 143, 182, 187, 197, 202, 203, 206
empowerment 42, 90, 98, 120, 142, 200, 204, 231
environment 3, 14, 16, 30, 35, 36, 37, 47, 63, 67, 68, 73, 92, 93, 94, 99, 104, 105, 106, 108, 109, 110, 114, 159, 175, 177, 189, 191, 194, 196, 198, 204, 206, 211, 212, 215, 217, 224, 228
episode analysis 110-114

evidence-based
    definition 12-14
    model 14
experience 4, 6, 15, 16, 22, 24, 38, 43, 61, 62, 68, 69, 70, 72, 73, 74, 75, 89, 92, 97, 111, 112, 113, 119, 123, 124, 129, 131, 132, 134, 143, 151, 155, 158, 235
experiential learning 6, 22, 25, 26, 29, 31, 35, 39, 58, 75, 109, 120, 124, 131, 143, 150, 152, 153, 175, 176, 203, 204, 205
    experiencing 3, 7, 8, 10, 22, 24, 25, 26, 29, 35, 39, 46, 54, 56, 57, 84, 87, 89, 90, 94, 121, 122, 129, 130, 131, 150, 152, 155, 175, 182, 191, 196, 199, 202, 203, 204, 205
    experimenting 35, 122, 131, 132, 135, 138, 152
expert consensus statements 13, 34, 38, 41, 117, 141, 167, 170, 173, 208

F

feedback 2, 3, 12, 22, 23, 28, 31, 35, 38, 39, 46, 47, 53, 56, 57, 67, 70, 73, 74, 75, 80, 81, 85, 92, 94, 95, 96, 97, 107, 109, 115, 119, 120, 121, 127, 132, 133, 134, 135, 137, 138, 142, 150, 158, 163, 165, 166, 170, 171, 172, 173, 174, 175, 177, 179, 181, 182, 183, 184, 186, 188, 192, 194, 197, 202, 203, 204, 206, 207, 218
formative supervision 5, 11, 20, 22, 23, 27, 28, 29, 35, 39, 45, 52, 54, 56, 60, 97, 133, 169, 170, 172, 175, 176, 178, 180, 183, 184, 185, 186, 188, 190, 191, 193, 194, 200
force-field analysis 100
formulation 6, 16, 20, 22, 25, 39, 88, 95, 96, 97, 100, 101, 105, 125, 143, 166, 176, 188, 189, 197, 225

G

General Health Questionnaire 48, 78, 84, 86, 217
group supervision 45, 47, 49, 50, 53, 59, 62, 90, 94, 100, 103, 110, 161, 162, 190, 195, 204, 213

Appendix

The PowerPoint slides in this Appendix are also available for download at
www.pavpub.com/supportive-clinical-supervision-resources/

Supportive clinical supervision

Enhancing Well-being and Reducing Burnout through Restorative Leadership

Derek Milne & Robert Reiser 2021

 LUMINATE

Supportive Clinical Supervision © Pavilion Publishing and Media Ltd and its licensors 2021.

Workshop plan

We will address this question through these topics:
1. Introduction
2. Empirical definition
3. Theoretical review of literature (support model)
4. Empirical review of literature (research studies)
5. Practical examples
6. Conclusions
7. Workshop closure.

Supportive Clinical Supervision © Pavilion Publishing and Media Ltd and its licensors 2021.

By the end of the workshop, you should be able to:

a. Define supportive (or restorative) supervision

b. Provide 3 reasons for restorative supervision

c. Outline the support model

d. Describe 3 evidence-based methods of SS

e. Clarify any remaining queries or issues &

f. Provide feedback on the workshop.

Slide 1

Introductions & educational needs assessment:

What is your name & workplace?

Think of 2 or 3 learning outcomes for improving your supervision, and write them down now.

Slide 2

1. Introduction

This section addresses these learning outcomes:

a. Define supportive (restorative) supervision;

b. Provide 3 reasons for supportive supervision

Slide 3

Normative, formative & restorative supervision

Normative (13%)
(managerial; quality control)
Policies & practices; roles & rules;
logistics; service planning &
quality; outcome monitoring

Supervision

Formative (70%)
(education & training) Problem-
solving; Sharing knowledge;
Reflection Identifying training
needs; Reviewing case work.

Restorative (supportive: 8%)
Improving morale and job satisfaction through protecting the worker
from excessive stress, by boosting personal coping strategies of
staff, and by offering validation and support (Kadushin, 1976).

% data from survey of community mental health supervisors in USA, by Dorsey, et al, (2017).

Supportive Clinical Supervision © Pavilion Publishing and Media Ltd and its licensors 2021

Slide 4

The neglect of supportive supervision

Slide 3 above illustrates the neglect of supportive supervision
(i.e. it was only used 8% of the time by a sample of American
supervisors).

This quote illustrates resistance to supportive supervision:

**"These functions (restorative & normative), while
important, reduce the time available for clinical functions".**

Dorsey, et al, (2017, p.11)

Supportive Clinical Supervision © Pavilion Publishing and Media Ltd and its licensors 2021

Slide 5

Video illustration

The neglect of supportive supervision

(Chapter 7, video clip 8: 'Group supervision- skill development: Agenda-setting', from, 0-2 mins.).

*Clip shows supervisor Sara discussing the agenda with
supervisees Shilpa & Jordan, who start by mentioning how
stressful work has been latterly. They agree to ignore that issue.*

Discussion

In large group, consider if in your experience this is a common
occurrence, and discuss why neglect arises.

Supportive Clinical Supervision © Pavilion Publishing and Media Ltd and its licensors 2021

Slide 5

2. Empirical definition

Slide 6

An empirical definition of supportive supervision (SS)

- **STRUCTURE:** SS addresses supervisees' emotional experiences of work, and their personal functioning in that context. It is a formal, case-focussed, and intensively relational process, conducted regularly by a trained and authorised supervisor.

- **PROCESS:** Specific SS methods include problem formulation, coping strategy enhancement, social support, and empathic debriefing. Some organizational goals too (primary prevention).

- **OUTCOME:** SS mechanisms are experiential learning (esp. 'experiencing'), strengthening the supervision alliance, and social support (acceptance, validation, & belonging; coping strategy enhancement). The main intended outcomes for supervisees are reduced personal distress and increased psychological well-being.

Milne & Reiser (2020)

Slide 7

Main specific techniques of SS:

Coping strategy enhancement: through questioning (to help to formulate issues; to heighten self-awareness), guided reflection, clarification, reconceptualising problems, & changing expectations: revise/rehearse better (more adaptive, approach-based) coping strategies.

Social support: strengthen support in supervision (e.g. greater collaboration; deeper alliance; more emotional support & empowerment); encourage greater informal support-seeking & reciprocation (e.g. peer support).

Empathic debriefing: attend to & clarify emotional aspects of the job; work-through uncomfortable feelings; challenge thinking errors.

Slide 8

Measurement of supportive supervision: questionnaire.

Most used questionnaire: The Manchester Clinical Supervision Scale (summary in Winstanley & White, 2014).

Trust/rapport factor (5 items about discussing sensitive issues)
'I can discuss sensitive issues encountered during my clinical casework with my supervisor'
'My supervisor is very open with me'

Advice/support factor (5 items about feeling supported; getting advice & guidance)
'My supervisor gives me support and encouragement'
'My supervisor provides me with valuable advice'

Supportive Clinical Supervision © Pavilion Publishing and Media Ltd and its licensors 2021

Slide 9

Measurement of supportive supervision: observation.

'Teachers' PETS' (Milne & Westerman, 2001)

Supervisor 'listening': Active listening/ observing, silent attention.

Supervisor 'feedback': specific feedback intended to weaken/ strengthen supervisee's behaviour/ thoughts/ feelings; can be positive or negative

Supervisor 'supporting': Verbal and non-verbal non-specific reassurance, agreeing and encouraging (e.g. 'well done'; empathy, warmth, genuineness)

Supervisor 'self-disclosing': Supervisor reveals something new about self (e.g. 'I would like to improve myself in...', 'I find it very hard to... ')

Supervisee 'experiencing emotion': expressing emotion or attitude (e.g. 'I feel more confident now'; 'I felt uneasy about this').

Supportive Clinical Supervision © Pavilion Publishing and Media Ltd and its licensors 2021

Slide 10

Why should we provide supportive supervision?

SS can reduce depression & burnout in the workforce, and has other practical benefits (including staff retention; raised productivity; fewer safety concerns, accidents, & disasters).

Staff who feel supported provide support to their patients, and feel valued.

Supervision is often perceived to represent & signal the employer's attitude to support.

Supportive Clinical Supervision © Pavilion Publishing and Media Ltd and its licensors 2021

Slide 11

Political impetus to provide SS

"There is an urgent need to develop interventions that address the high
levels of stress, burnout and dissatisfaction among mental health nurses"
(The Scottish Executive, 2006, p.57).

"The first priority is a healthy workforce: the nation's health is determined
by the health of the workforce".
(Health and Social Care Secretary, Matt Hancock, taking up post, 2018).

Staff retention an urgent priority; increase support; workforce development
(improve skills & motivation); promote well-being.
(The National Health Service long-term plan, 2019)

Slide 12

Why now? It's a growing problem

"…the demands on the existing workforce have increased"
(Bhui et al., 2012, p1).

75% of American employees believe that workers have more on-the-job
stress than a generation ago.
The National Institute of Occupational Safety and Health in the US (NIOSH, 2010)

A survey of 1300 psychological staff in the NHS indicated that… the great
majority (70%) were finding their work stressful, an increase of 12% from
the previous year; 28% said that they did not have enough time to
participate in supervision.
(New Savoy Partnership, 2016).

Slide 13

Attending to SS:

Chapter 9: Support and guidance in CBT supervision

Summary of recommendations:
- Clarify the situation: what is challenging about the supervisee's workplace?
- Encourage emotional processing and personal growth.
- Strengthen the supervisee's coping strategies.
- Boost morale, motivation and job satisfaction.
- Encourage the supervisee to use social support (supervisor and peers).

Milne and Reiser (2017). A Manual for Evidence-Based CBT Supervision. Wiley.

Slide 14

Video illustration

'Restorative supervision with a cultural focus'

Chapter 9, video clip 18, CBT supervision manual, 2.20-end (12.20 mins.)
(Milne & Reiser, 2017).

Clip shows supervisee Sean puzzling over his patient's non-compliance.
Supervisor Louise formulates collaboratively, leading to an action plan.

Learning exercise

1. Use the previous slide as a checklist ('Attending to SS');
2. Participants should form small groups;
3. Together, try to identify all the different SS methods on this clip;
4. Discuss & try to agree the strengths & weaknesses of the supervisor's use of these methods;
5. Engage in large group discussion.

Slide 15

3. Theoretical review

Addresses this learning outcome:

c. Outline the 'support' model of SS.

This model is needed to capture the greater scope & the complex nature of supportive supervision.

Slide 16

The support model

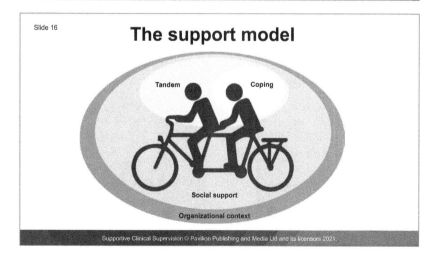

Slide 17

Kolb's experiential learning cycle

Experiencing
**Ability to focus on and
assimilate emotional
experiences of work**

Behaving

Planning

Reflecting

Conceptualising

Slide 18

Learning exercise: experiencing.

1. To attend more deeply to the kinds of emotions that we experience at work, form small groups;

2. Make a shared list of the different feelings experienced in the last week at work:

3. Classify the feelings into the most common positive ones (i.e. linked to your well-being); and the most common negative ones (i.e. linked to personal distress or signs of burnout).

4. Large group: share & discuss

Slide 19

Video illustration:

'Facilitating learning, Part III'

Video clip 12, CBT supervision manual, full 4.20 minutes. (Milne & Reiser, 2017).

Video shows supervisee Louise reflecting on the difference between her approach & that of her supervisor, Valentina. They have just finished an educational role-play in which the supervisor played Louise the therapist.

Learning exercise:

1. Participants should read the 'Alliance' guideline, then form pairs;

2. Together, try to identify how the alliance facilitates the supervisee's experiential learning (especially 'experiencing');

3. Engage in large group discussion.

Slide 20

Experiencing process
for supervisee:

1. Talks about events, ideas, people.
2. Refers to self but without expressing emotions *(problem 'warded off')*.
3. Expresses emotions about external circumstances.
4. Focus directly on emotions and thoughts about self *('clarification')*
5. Engages in exploration of own emotions.
6. Gains awareness of previously implicit feelings *('insight')*
7. In-depth self-understanding; new perspective emerges.
   ('working through' & 'problem solution')

The Experiencing Scale (Klein et al., 1969).
The assimilation process: Stiles, et al., 1990; Psychotherapy, 27, 411-20.

Slide 21

4. Empirical review

Addresses this learning outcome:

d. Describe 3 evidence-based methods of SS.

The review was based on n=25 research studies, published in the last 20 years, & followed the 'best evidence synthesis' method (BES).

Slide 22

Supportive supervision:
the research review findings

Slide 23

Video illustration:

'Providing restorative supervision & support'

Video clip 17, CBT supervision manual, 2.30-6.30 minutes.

(Milne & Reiser, 2017).

Clip shows supervisee Louise explaining why she has again not brought a therapy tape to share; Supervisor Sean explores the issue supportively.

'Rehearsal' learning exercise:

1. Participants should form pairs;
2. Take turns to present a genuine example of a workplace stressor (e.g. excessive caseload; poor communication);
3. Drawing on this video clip, rehearse using a SS method to discuss this stressor (e.g. 'provide social support'. NB: this is not a role-play);
4. Provide feedback to the supervisor, to develop SS skills (use the SS SAGE Scale);
5. Engage in large group discussion.

Slide 24

5. Practical Examples using the model: Support

Survey: n = 113 newly graduated Swedish nurses, working in 3 settings.

Group supervision: addressed stress (uncertainty & fear) by creating a supportive environment, with confidential discussion, questions about incidents, & promoting learning through shared reflection.

Conclusions: "Newly graduated nurses experience great stress and need support, especially those in surgical departments. Nurses participating in clinical group supervision reported significantly less stress… Clinical group supervision should be considered as an option for reducing stress".

(Blomberg, et al., 2016, p.80)

Slide 25

Coping strategies example

- **Logical analysis:** maintain objectivity; case consultation.
- **Positive appraisal:** reflect on positive experiences; sense of control.
- **Seeking support:** clinical supervision; peer support; personal therapy.
- **Problem-solving:** self-awareness; CPD; reflection; read literature.
- **Cognitive avoidance:** put aside thoughts; avoid responsibility.
- **Acceptance/resignation:** vacations; turn to spiritual beliefs.
- **Alternative rewards:** use substances to relax; leisure activities.
- **Emotional discharge:** discuss frustrations with colleagues/friends.

Strategies from the Coping Responses Inventory (Moos)

Examples from Lawson's (2007) survey of 1,000 US counsellors.

Slide 26

Organizational example:
'Meta-supervision'

Group supervision format; supervisees reflect on personal and organizational barriers to their supervision; joint problem-solving; formulate strategies to overcome barriers and strengthen the supervision boosters; follow-up sessions based on action research principles, experiential learning, and coping strategy development.

Results: Experimental group supervisees participate significantly more frequently in supervision; but more frequent participation was not reflected in the perceived formative or restorative benefits of supervision.

(attributed to poorly-established supervision practices).

Gonge & Buus (2014)

Supportive Clinical Supervision © Pavilion Publishing and Media Ltd and its licensors 2021

Slide 27

Tandem example

Restorative group supervision (large-scale implementation)

- **reflection** on practice (organizational problems)
- **discussion** (developing ideas)
- **supportive challenge** ('inappropriate workplace behaviour')
- **modelling** (conflict resolution)
- **behavioural rehearsal**
- **processing emotional experiences**
- **normalising**

Findings: Qualitative: Enhanced resilience, planning & decision-making.
Quantitative: Pre-post questionnaire: significant reductions in burnout).
(Wallbank, 2013)

Supportive Clinical Supervision © Pavilion Publishing and Media Ltd and its licensors 2021

Slide 28

6. Conclusions

What is an evidence-based approach to supportive supervision?

- **Draws on relevant theory**
  (Support model)
- **Clarifies the limited research basis for SS**
  (using BES & extrapolation)
- **Provides sound evidence to justify & guide SS**
  (adding relevant theory & expert consensus to research findings)
- **SS methods are straightforward, familiar, & exceptionally efficient**
  (coping strategy enhancement; empathy & assimilation; social support).

Supportive Clinical Supervision © Pavilion Publishing and Media Ltd and its licensors 2021

Slide 29

7. Workshop closure

This step addresses the final learning outcomes:

e. Clarify any remaining queries or issues &
f. Provide feedback on the workshop.

- Discussion of the workshop experience with participants
- Confidential completion of a workshop evaluation/satisfaction form
- Action plans & farewells

Supportive Clinical Supervision © Pavilion Publishing and Media Ltd and its licensors 2021.

Slide 30

Some key references

(remainder in Milne & Reiser, 2020)

Blomberg et al. (2016). Work stress among newly graduated nurses in relation to workplace and clinical group supervision. *Journal of Nursing Management*, 24: 80-87.

Dorsey, S., et al. (2017). The Juggling Act of Supervision in Community Mental Health: Implications for Supporting Evidence-Based Treatment. *Adm Policy Ment Health* DOI 10.1007/s10488-017-0796-z

Gonge, H., & Buus, N. (2014) Is it possible to strengthen psychiatric nursing staff's clinical supervision? RCT of a meta-supervision intervention. *Journal of Advanced Nursing, doi: 10.1111/jan.12569*

Lawson, G (2007). Counsellor wellness & impairment: A national survey. *Journal of Humanistic Counselling, Education and Development, 46,* 20-34.

Martin, P. , Milne, D.L, & Reiser, R.P. (2018). Peer supervision: International problems and prospects. *Journal of Advanced Nursing* (editorial) DOI: 10.1111/jan.13413.

Milne, D.L. & Martin, P. (2018). Supportive clinical supervision: Supported at last *Journal of Advanced Nursing* (editorial) DOI: 10.1111/jan.13816.

Milne, D.L. & Reiser, R.P. (due out in 2020). *Supportive supervision: An evidence-based approach to restorative supervision.* (provisional title) Brighton: Pavilion books.

Milne DL & Westerman C (2001). Evidence-based clinical supervision: rationale and illustration. *Clinical Psychology & Psychotherapy, 8,* 444-45.

Wallbank S. (2013). Maintaining professional resilience through group restorative supervision. Community Practitioner, 86: 8: 26-28

Winstanley, J., & White, E. (2014). *The Manchester Clinical Supervision Scale©: MCSS-26©.* In: C. E.

Watkins Jr. & D. Milne (Eds). The Wiley International Handbook of Clinical Supervision. Chichester, UK: John Wiley and Sons Ltd.

Supportive Clinical Supervision © Pavilion Publishing and Media Ltd and its licensors 2021.

Slide 31

Appendices

1. The NHS long-term plan (2019): implications for supervision?
(lessons from BABCP, medicine & midwifery, 2017)

- Supervision is now deemed necessary throughout the NHS, to improve quality and promote patient safety (at least an appraisal element, including independent evidence of competence). Employers should ensure that all their staff receive supervision; all staff should seek supervision

- Supervisors should be allocated by their managers, & have sufficient expertise and experience (2 years+) to be both critical and supportive. They should then be trained (for up to 4 days) & guided by a EBP resources (e.g. supervision model; research; guidelines).

- Reflection on practice is the primary 'formative' function, allied to experiential learning (professional development); 'restorative' function also endorsed; 'normative' excluded (regulation separate). The goal is continuous quality improvement, within clinical governance system.

References: Department of Health (2016). *Proposals for changing the system of midwifery supervision in the UK).* GMC (2013). *Revalidation.* NMC (2017). *Changes to midwifery supervision in England.*

Recent overview: Martin, Milne & Reiser (2018).

Supportive Clinical Supervision © Pavilion Publishing and Media Ltd and its licensors 2021.

Slide 32

2. Evidence-based approach
as employed in the SS book:

- **Discriminate:** locate the small seam of affirmative studies, ones that are interpretable (the 'best-evidence synthesis' review).
- **Extrapolate:** from rigorous studies conducted in neighbouring literatures (e.g. harmful clinical supervision: Ellis et al, 2014).
- **Theorise:** draw on relevant theory (e.g. alliance; social support; coping; leadership; stress management; workplace safety).
- **Contextualise:** view research & theory in context of other forms of evidence, within EBP model (Parry, Roth & Fonagy, 1996: supervision guidelines; supervisor training practices; audits, etc.)
- **Moderate:** interpret all studies in the light of experts' opinions.

Supportive Clinical Supervision © Pavilion Publishing and Media Ltd and its licensors 2021

Slide 33

3. Example of a research study which was included in the empirical review

Gardner et al (2018): 100 MDT participants in Australia. Supervision was measured by the MCSS questionnaire.

Between-group comparisons indicated that the 30 respondents from Occupational Therapy (OT) rated their supervision as significantly more effective than their 25 colleagues within Physiotherapy, with higher ratings for the formative & restorative items.

For all respondents, restorative supervision was rated slightly more highly than the normative and formative aspects, at 78%.

The authors attributed these differences to the supervision received, with OT's having trained supervisors, more frequent supervision, and better-structured supervision (e.g. supervision contracts were used).

Only the OT's believed that it improved their skills and the service that they provided (because they were supported to reflect on their practice, and were able to discuss sensitive or confidential issues with their supervisor).

Supportive Clinical Supervision © Pavilion Publishing and Media Ltd and its licensors 2021

Slide 34

4. Learning outcomes list: Experiencing

As a result of your supervision today, what would you like to achieve?

- Be more aware of the current emotions/sensations I experience;
- Recognise/define my own feelings;
- Be more aware of the emotional or sensory accompaniments to my activity;
- Recognise my own attitudes or motivation better (e.g. concerns; barriers; uplifts).
- Better regulate or manage my emotions (positive or negative ones).
- Recognise emotional patterns that arise in my work;
- Draw out the action implications of my patterns/emotions;
- Evaluate how I feel;
- Process some of my affect/sensations.

Supportive Clinical Supervision © Pavilion Publishing and Media Ltd and its licensors 2021

Slide 35

5. Expert consensus statements: examples.

According to the supervision guidelines from The American Psychological Association (APA, 2015, p.37), competent supervision entails creating and maintaining a collaborative relationship, one that includes "responsible caring, honesty, engagement, attentiveness, and professionalism".

A similar emphasis on the supervision alliance exists within the competence framework in the UK (Roth & Pilling, 2008).

Slide 36

REACTS (supportive supervision)

Use this form to give feedback within the 'rehearsal' learning exercise (slide 27).
Please rate the supervision that you have just received with this scale:

1	2	3	4	5	N/A
Strongly disagree	disagree	neither agree nor disagree	agree	strongly agree	not applicable

The supervisor:

1. showed empathy (e.g. understood my reactions)............................ 1 2 3 4 5 N/A
2. boosted my morale (e.g. offered praise or recognition)..................... 1 2 3 4 5 N/A
3. helped to reduce my stress level (e.g. clarified my feelings)............... 1 2 3 4 5 N/A
4. provided emotional support (e.g. validated me)............................. 1 2 3 4 5 N/A
5. offered advice & guidance to aid my coping at work........................ 1 2 3 4 5 N/A
6. boosted my morale/well-being (e.g. praise or recognition)................ 1 2 3 4 5 N/A
7. Which part of supervision do you feel was the most supportive?
8. Any suggested improvements?